Management for Professionals

More information about this series at http://www.springer.com/series/10101

Ezlika M. Ghazali • Dilip S. Mutum •
Mamunur Rashid • Jashim U. Ahmed
Editors

Management of Shari'ah Compliant Businesses

Case Studies on Creation of Sustainable Value

Springer

Editors
Ezlika M. Ghazali
Faculty of Business and Accountancy
University of Malaya
Kuala Lampur, Malaysia

Dilip S. Mutum
University of Nottingham Malaysia Campus
Nottingham University Business School
Semenyih, Malaysia

Mamunur Rashid
School of Business and Economics
Universiti Brunei Darussalam
Gadong, Brunei

Jashim U. Ahmed
School of Business
North South University
Dhaka, Bangladesh

ISSN 2192-8096 ISSN 2192-810X (electronic)
Management for Professionals
ISBN 978-3-030-10906-6 ISBN 978-3-030-10907-3 (eBook)
https://doi.org/10.1007/978-3-030-10907-3

Library of Congress Control Number: 2019934723

This Springer imprint is published by the registered company Springer Nature Switzerland AG.
The registered company address is: Gewerbestrasse 11, 6330 Cham, Switzerland

Contents

Editors and Contributors

About the Editors

Ezlika M. Ghazali is a Senior Lecturer at the Department of Marketing, Faculty of Business and Accountancy, University of Malaya, Kuala Lumpur, Malaysia. Her research interests include switching barriers, augmented-reality marketing, online retailing, sustainable marketing and social entrepreneurship. Ezlika has widely published in journals including *IT and People, Journal of Retailing and Consumer Services, Electronic Markets* and others.

Dilip S. Mutum is Associate Professor of Marketing with Nottingham University Business School, University of Nottingham Malaysia. His research interests include digital consumption and sustainable marketing. Dilip has also advised various organisations on strategic marketing issues. His research work has been published within a range of publications—both in print and online.

Mamunur Rashid received his PhD on Behavioural Finance from National University of Malaysia in 2014. He has awarded the PGCHE from the University of Nottingham in 2018. He is currently a Senior Assistant Professor of Finance in Universiti Brunei Darussalam. Prior to joining UBD, Mamunur taught Finance at Nottingham University Business School, The University of Nottingham (Malaysia Campus) since October 2012 until September 2018, and at East West University, Bangladesh (September 2005–February 2012). His teaching areas include Islamic Finance, International Finance, Corporate Finance and Financial Economics. Dr Mamunur was the founding deputy director of the Centre for Islamic Business and Finance Research at the University of Nottingham Malaysia Campus. Dr Mamunur is also an Associate Editor of International Journal of Islamic and Middle Eastern Finance and Management (Emerald). He is a Fellow of the Higher Education Academy, UK, and a member of Malaysian Finance Association since 2014. His research interest includes a broader investigation into the connection between values and performance in multi-cultural setting.

Jashim Uddin Ahmed is a Professor and Chairman of the Department of Management, School of Business and Economics, North South University, Bangladesh. His principal research interests lie in the field of strategic management and contemporary issues in business. He has published over 90 research articles and case studies in reputed journals. Currently, he is an Advisory Editorial Member of three journals.

Contributors

Balqis Oyindamola Adedokun Independent Research, Abuja, Nigeria

Abu Umar Faruq Ahmad King Abdulaziz University, Jeddah, Kingdom of Saudi Arabia

Sharīʻah Supervisory Board of Islamic Cooperative Finance Australia Limited, Parramatta, NSW, Australia

Sharīʻah Audit, Islamic Bank of Australia Project, Auburn, NSW, Australia

Jashim Uddin Ahmed Department of Management, School of Business & Economics, North South University, Dhaka, Bangladesh

Norhazwani Mohamed Asri International Islamic College, Kuala Lumpur, Malaysia

Azmin Azliza Aziz Faculty of Business and Accountancy, University of Malaya, Kuala Lumpur, Malaysia

Mehmet Bulut Istanbul Sabahattin Zaim University, Istanbul, Turkey

Anita Chakrabarty Nottingham University Business School, University of Nottingham Malaysia, Semenyih, Selangor, Malaysia

Yusuf Dinc Islamic Economics and Finance Department, Faculty of Business Administration and Administrative Sciences, Istanbul Sabahattin Zaim University, Istanbul, Turkey

Ezlika M. Ghazali Faculty of Business and Accountancy, Department of Marketing, University of Malaya, Kuala Lumpur, Malaysia

University of Malaya Halal Research Centre (UMHRC), University of Malaya, Kuala Lumpur, Malaysia

Mohammad Tayeenul Hoque Department of Marketing and International Business, School of Business & Economics, North South University, Dhaka, Bangladesh

Mohan V. Avvari Nottingham University Business School, University of Nottingham Malaysia, Semenyih, Selangor, Malaysia

Aishath Muneeza INCEIF, The Global University of Islamic Finance, Lorong Universiti A, Kuala Lumpur, Malaysia

Dilip S. Mutum Nottingham University Business School, University of Nottingham Malaysia, Semenyih, Selangor, Malaysia

Mardiana Md Radzi Faculty of Business and Accountancy, University of Malaya Graduate Business School, University of Malaya, Kuala Lumpur, Malaysia

Ahmad Rafiki Department of Business Administration, University College of Bahrain, Janabiyah, Bahrain

Nurliana Md Rahin Faculty of Business and Accountancy, University of Malaya, Kuala Lumpur, Malaysia

Mamunur Rashid School of Business and Economics, Universiti Brunei Darussalam, Gadong, Brunei

Buerhan Saiti Department of Islamic Economics and Finance, Istanbul Sabahattin Zaim University, Istanbul, Turkey

Abdiwali Jama Salad Institute of Islamic Banking and Finance, International Islamic University Malaysia, Gombak, Malaysia

William Kong Choon San Nottingham University Business School, University of Nottingham Malaysia, Semenyih, Malaysia

Hafiza Sultana InterResearch, Dhaka, Bangladesh

Meenatharisni Sundramohana Faculty of Business and Accountancy, University of Malaya Graduate School of Business, University of Malaya, Kuala Lumpur, Malaysia

Umar Habibu Umar Department of Accounting, Northwest University, Kano, Nigeria

Priscila Valdivieso Faculty of Business and Accountancy, University of Malaya Graduate School of Business, University of Malaya, Kuala Lumpur, Malaysia

Wei-Pin Woon Faculty of Business and Accountancy, University of Malaya Graduate Business School, University of Malaya, Kuala Lumpur, Malaysia

Managing Shari'ah-Compliant Businesses to Create Sustainable Value

Ezlika M. Ghazali, Dilip S. Mutum, Mamunur Rashid, and Jashim Uddin Ahmed

Abstract

This introduction to the case study book provides a description of the book and explains why it is indeed timely. Brief descriptions of each of the 15 cases are provided. This book is targeted at academics, researchers, practitioners and policymakers, who are interested in Islamic business and finance.

1 Introduction

Muslim consumers spent about US$2 trillion across the lifestyle sectors, $2.2 trillion in Islamic Finance and $1.24 trillion in food and beverage, 25.4 billion on clothing and apparel, $198 billion on media and entertainment, $169 billion on travel, $83 billion on pharmaceuticals and $57.4 billion on cosmetics in 2016 (The State of Global Islamic Economy, 2016/2017). These products include Islamic finance, Halal food, fashion, travel, media and research, pharmaceuticals and cosmetics, among

E. M. Ghazali
Department of Marketing, Faculty of Business and Accountancy, University of Malaya, Kuala Lumpur, Malaysia

D. S. Mutum (✉)
Nottingham University Business School, The University of Nottingham Malaysia Campus, Semenyih, Malaysia
e-mail: dilip.mutum@nottingham.edu.my

M. Rashid
School of Business and Economics, Universiti Brunei Darussalam, Gadong, Brunei

J. U. Ahmed
Department of Management, School of Business & Economics, North South University, Dhaka, Bangladesh

E. M. Ghazali et al. (eds.), *Management of Shari'ah Compliant Businesses*, Management for Professionals, https://doi.org/10.1007/978-3-030-10907-3_1

others. The report brought out by Thomson Reuters in collaboration with DinarStandard shows that the Islamic economy is seeing major growth and has received widespread recognition. It has been highlighted that Muslims remain an untapped and viable market segment (Sandikci, 2011).

The Islamic finance industry has been growing at a double-digit rate over a decade now. The industry has experienced tremendous innovation in product and services, industry structures, regulatory atmosphere and consumer awareness. Even countries which do not have large Muslim populations are showing interest at offering Islamic financial services primarily due to the huge potential for future growth and also because of its resilience during financial crisis and role in promoting a healthy socio-economic ecosystem.

Due to profit and loss sharing mechanism as in an Islamic trade-based environment, Islamic organisations consider their customers as partners. Hence, relevant issues, such as the innovation in Islamic business, sukuk (Islamic bond) to finance large projects, Islamic entrepreneurship, pressures on Islamic banks to reduce the financing gap in society and the need to understand Muslim consumers, require a deeper understanding of the issues and opportunities, which are quite unique. However, despite the importance of Islamic business and finance, there is still a huge lack of understanding and very limited research in this area. This was also highlighted in a previous book coedited by two of the current editors (Mutum, Butt, & Rashid, 2016). Discussions with academics and other users of the book revealed a need for real-life case studies in this area, and this ultimately lead to this current book.

2 Why This Book Is Timely?

This book aims to fill the gaps mentioned above by presenting high-quality and original case studies on Islamic finance, marketing and management that deal with consumer perception, services orientation, new product development, risk management, industry readiness for better customer satisfaction and policy issues coupling strategy and best practices from around the world. It should be pointed out that several of the cases are from Asia. Middle-Eastern countries, ASEAN and the South Asian regions in particular, have been experiencing tremendous growth in Islamic financial and marketing activities, mainly due to the fact that these countries have huge Muslim populations. It should be noted that according to the State of the Global Islamic Economy Report 2017/18, Malaysia leads the Global Islamic Economy Indicator, ahead of UAE and Saudi Arabia. This is one of the reasons why we have several cases looking at Malaysia or Malaysian companies.

The Islamic financial and marketing industries have been growing at double-digit rates for over a decade now. Consumer behaviour has changed in tandem with the economic development, improvements in standards of living as well as increase in disposable income. The governments in several countries have also offered numerous incentives to encourage Islamic industries. These incentives should see a number of changes in the financial, marketing and management landscapes of the Islamic industries. The existing research on Islamic finance is particularly limited to non-Asian global perspectives. Those are limited in focus, and it is hoped that this book would fill the gap by focusing mainly on Asian perspective of Islamic businesses.

3 The Cases

The book is broadly divided into two parts, namely, Part I—cases on Islamic financial management—and Part II, which covers cases on Islamic marketing and management.

The first part has eight cases, covering several areas in Islamic finance and accounting, across several countries, namely, Australia, Bangladesh, Malaysia, Nigeria, Somalia and Turkey.

In the first case study, Abu Umar Faruq Ahmad identifies the key challenges of improving access to Islamic financial services in Australia for its large Muslim minority and also assesses the potential prospects for the emergence of Islamic finance in the country. Some policy recommendations and suggestions for further research are provided.

The second case study critically examines the cash waqf models in Malaysia and Bangladesh. Buerhan and co-authors explores this faith-based endowment could potentially reduce poverty levels in Somalia.

Next, Aishath takes a look at how Malaysian Islamic banks deal in case of default by analysing case law and discussions on guidelines on classification of impaired loans/financing and provisioning for bad and doubtful debts.

In the following case study, Mamunur and William measure the performance of the Malaysian employee provident fund (EPF), which is now Shari'ah compliant.

The next case study focusses on Islami Bank Bangladesh Limited, the pioneer in Shari'ah-based banking in Bangladesh. Jashim Uddin and Hafiza critically analyse the opportunities as well as the challenges faced by the bank.

Balqis and Mamunur then highlight some of the differences among the world's leading Shari'ah equity-screening criteria. They offer insights on how these can be harmonised by analysing the Nigeria Stock Exchange Lotus Islamic Index and listed Shari'ah-compliant companies.

Contemporary musharakah standards have not received much required attention from both practitioners and academics alike. Umar presents a basic comprehensive accounting package for musharakah through consolidation of conventional practices of accounting based on Accounting and Auditing Organization for Islamic Financial Institutions' FAS No.4 and two musharakah standards developed by Bank Negara Malaysia.

The final case in this part analyses the significant role of the Central Union of Agricultural Credit Cooperatives in Turkey. Yusuf Dinc compares it with the conventional banking sector and Islamic banking in the country.

The second part covers various Islamic marketing and management issues in various countries including the Malaysia, Indonesia and the UK. Even though most of these cases are focussed on Malaysia, many of them involve multinational corporations (MNC), which might face similar issues in other countries as well.

In the first case, Avvari and Anita look at the unique case of Malaysian brand, Tanamera, which gained success outside the country and examine the challenges facing the company as it decides the best way to go forward. They also present an interesting overview of the natural and halal personal care industry in Malaysia.

Norhazwani and Azmin take a broad look at the factors influencing the consumption of dietary supplements such as vitamins and minerals and specifically at the rising demand for halal dietary supplements by Muslim consumers in Malaysia.

The next case study shows how Zulaikha, a shop in Medan in Indonesia, had benefited from halal certification. Ahmad also uses the case to highlight several issues related with halal certification in Indonesia.

McDonald's faced a major crisis in Malaysia following calls for boycott of the company in 2014. Ezlika and co-authors examine whether there was a religious motivation for calls of the boycott and also critically examine how the company responded to the crisis.

The next case study goes into detail into one of the most serious crises faced by Cadbury—when porcine DNA was allegedly detected in their chocolate products. This led to an international crisis for the company, when the negative news went viral and lead to investigations of their products in Indonesia and Saudi Arabia.

The following case highlights cultural differences between Muslims and examines whether the telekung, a religious garment for Muslim ladies unique to South-East Asia, can become popular among Muslim women in the UK. The case also briefly examines the role of social media influencers.

Finally, Azmin and co-authors critically analyse the advertising content of a health and beauty products company (Anonymized), on Facebook in order to determine whether they are *Shari'ah* compliant.

4 The Target Audience

As highlighted above, the book addresses several contemporary issues in Islamic finance, marketing and management in various industries. Only original case studies based on primary as well as secondary research that are not published elsewhere were considered for this book. These unique 15 cases should be of interest for both academics and industry practitioners. The issue is expected to be a handbook of reference that covers opportunities and challenges with respect to industry performance, consumer behaviour, business strategy, market structure and pricing, customer relationships, competition, etc., from an Islamic perspective.

For academics, this book can be used in classrooms for fostering discussions on Islamic business and finance and as a guide to learn industry practices. The book would also be useful for practitioners who assist in making *Shari'ah*-centric strategies. Policymakers can also learn from country-, product- and company-specific implications presented in these cases. The book will include a number of country-specific case studies to explore the differences between principles and practices that fulfil the needs of academics and practitioners alike.

References

Mutum, D., Butt, M. M., & Rashid, M. (2016). *Advances in Islamic finance, marketing and management: An Asian perspective.* Bingley: Emerald Group.

Sandikci, Ö. (2011). Researching Islamic marketing: Past and future perspectives. *Journal of Islamic Marketing, 2*(3), 246–258.

State of the Global Islamic Economy 2016/17. (2016). Retrieved March 20, 2018, from https://www.salaamgateway.com/en/story/report_state_of_the_global_islamic_economy_201617-salaam03102016111130/

Ezlika M. Ghazali is a affiliated to the Department of Marketing, Faculty of Business & Accountancy, University of Malaya, Kuala Lumpur, Malaysia. She is also currently attached to the Business and Commercialisation Division of the University of Malaya Halal Research Centre. Her research interests include switching barriers, augmented-reality marketing, online retailing, sustainable marketing and social entrepreneurship. Ezlika has widely published in journals including Information Technology & People, Journal of Retailing and Consumer Services, *Internet Research,* Electronic Markets and others.

Dilip S. Mutum is Associate Professor of Marketing with Nottingham University Business School, University of Nottingham Malaysia. His research interests include digital consumption and sustainable marketing. Dilip has also advised various organisations on strategic marketing issues. His research work has been published within a range of publications—both in print and online.

Mamunur Rashid received his PhD on Behavioural Finance from National University of Malaysia in 2014. He has awarded the PGCHE from the University of Nottingham in 2018. He is currently a Senior Assistant Professor of Finance in Universiti Brunei Darussalam. Prior to joining UBD, Mamunur taught Finance at Nottingham University Business School, The University of Nottingham (Malaysia Campus) since October 2012 until September 2018, and at East West University, Bangladesh (September 2005–February 2012). His teaching areas include Islamic Finance, International Finance, Corporate Finance and Financial Economics. Dr Mamunur was the founding deputy director of the Centre for Islamic Business and Finance Research at the University of Nottingham Malaysia Campus. Dr Mamunur is also an Associate Editor of International Journal of Islamic and Middle Eastern Finance and Management (Emerald). He is a Fellow of the Higher Education Academy, UK, and a member of Malaysian Finance Association since 2014. His research interest includes a broader investigation into the connection between values and performance in multi-cultural setting.

Jashim Uddin Ahmed is a Professor and Chairman of the Department of Management, School of Business & Economics, North South University, Bangladesh. His principal research interests lie in the field of strategic management and contemporary issues in business. He has published over 90 research articles and case studies in reputed journals. Currently, he is an Advisory Editorial Member of three journals.

Part I

Islamic Financial Management

The Challenges and Potential of Improving Access to Islamic Financial Services in Non-Muslim Countries: The Case of Australia

Abu Umar Faruq Ahmad

Abstract

The purpose of this study is twofold: (1) to identify the key challenges of improving access to Islamic financial services (IFS) in Australia for its large Muslim minority and (2) to assess the potential prospects for the emergence of Islamic finance (IF) in the Australian market, parallel with its conventional practice. The method employed is a mixture of direct observation and author's personal experience, curiosity and association with this industry. However, Islamic legal context remains the only theoretical basis of the study. The approach for the study is not supplemented by any empirical work, nor have the attempts been made to evaluate the economic efficiency and profitability or otherwise, of IF in Australia. Through a thorough examination, it seeks to argue that in order to meet the core challenges of IFS in this jurisdiction, a separate legal framework must be established to facilitate its growth and development in the Australian financial market. Besides the direct policy recommendations and suggestions for further research provided for authorities concerned, the study sheds new light on how the relevant challenges are met for improving access to IFS in Australia for its largest minority.

A. U. F. Ahmad (✉)
King Abdulaziz University, Jeddah, Kingdom of Saudi Arabia

Sharī'ah Supervisory Board of Islamic Cooperative Finance Australia Limited, Parramatta, NSW, Australia

Sharī'ah Audit, Islamic Bank of Australia Project, Auburn, NSW, Australia

E. M. Ghazali et al. (eds.), *Management of Shari'ah Compliant Businesses*, Management for Professionals, https://doi.org/10.1007/978-3-030-10907-3_2

1 Introduction

Muslims are considered as the largest religious minority in highly diversified multicultural Australia (Ahmad & Ahmad, 2008). Naturally, the Muslims in Australia are quite keen to conduct their financial activities in accordance with the tenets of their Islamic belief. They feel that the establishment of Islamic banks (IBs) and Islamic financial institutions (IFIs) will enhance competition in the financial market by offering a viable alternative to the interest-based finance, which ultimately would benefit the consumers and contribute to the development of Australian economy and also help expand its existing trade and economic ties with other Muslim countries.

Despite the remarkable growth and development of IBs and IFIs over the last few decades in other comparable developed countries with minority Muslim population, their expansion in Australia is very slow though steady (Al-Salem, 2008). There are some reasons why the IFIs that are functioning in Australia did not bring the expected success. Examination of all these reasons is not quite possible in this current chapter. However, it attempts to focus on the potential problems and huge prospects of IF in Australia. Given the findings of the study, it recommends for making necessary legislative changes to facilitate the growth of IFIs in Australia as demonstrated by the experience of other comparable developed countries in the globe.

The reasons that hinder the growth of IF in Australia are innumerable, the key of which is the lack of regulatory support with specific legal and policy framework continues to hamper the rapid expansion and acceptance of IF in Australia (Ahmad, 2013a, b). The main international regulatory response to the global financial crisis went under the broad banner of 'Basel III'. This has involved a higher minimum quantity of capital and also a better quality of capital, for example, in terms of loss absorbency. While the new Basel III requirements are still being phased in, the Australian prudential regulations administered by the Australian Prudential Regulation Authority (APRA) has moved ahead of the Basel timetable. However, neither of these make provision for Sharī'ah-compliance for IBs and IFIs. Both the accords treat these types of financial arrangements as equity, rather than credit—thus giving them a heavy capital treatment.

Previous studies indicate that due to the unfamiliarity of the relatively new IF system, IFIs in Australia have not been able to play the expected role in the development of Australian economy through mobilising funds and attracting more customers (Ahmad, 2010). Other major flaws in Australian regulatory system lie in its federal structure. All institutions, be they financial or otherwise, are required to follow both State and Federal regulations. These regulations may vary from State to State. The States and Territories may have different regulations. Thus, lack of uniform regulations across all the six States and two Territories are also not conducive for growth of IF in Australia (Ahmad & Hassan, 2009).

The author finds that there is a lack of government support as part of its initiatives to pave the way for a level playing field in Australia, and as such it recommends that the relevant regulations may be developed by the Australian regulatory regime to make IF a viable alternative system of financing for Muslims in Australia. The study also suggests that IFIs would take an intensified awareness programme to familiarise the public and policy makers with the literacy of the Islamic finance as well as the products they use in financing that complies with the tenets of Sharīʻah.

This study is divided into the following sections: Followed by an introduction, Sect. 2 provides key objectives and methodological approach of the study. Section 3 presents an overview of IF practice in Australia. Section 4 discusses the potential problems faced by IFIs in the Australian market. Section 5 delineates the potential prospects of IF in Australia. Section 6 concludes with the summary, concluding remarks, recommendations and need of further research in the relevant field.

2 The Key Objectives and Methodological Approach

2.1 Objectives of the Study

The IF seeks to address the issue by abolishing the concept of *riba* (interest or usury on loaned money) and *gharar* (risk, uncertainty and hazard) from financial transactions. This is achieved through the adoption of a number of financing techniques and structures by IFIs aimed to avoid *riba* and *gharar*. The IF in Australia has been growing slowly though its acceptance is getting momentum since it was first introduced in 1989 with Muslim Community Co-operative (Australia) Limited, better known as MCCA. Since then, another Islamic cooperative financial institution—Islamic Co-operative Finance Australia Limited (ICFAL)—has come into existence in the Australian financial services market during the past two decades (Ahmad & Hassan, 2011).

With the above in mind, this study seeks to:

1. Review the Sharīʻah-compliant issues vis-à-vis the ideals and actual practices of IFIs of Australia under the existing regulatory environment.
2. Provide a comprehensive picture of IF practices in Australia in the context of Australian society.
3. Help expand IF which the Australian vibrant Muslim community can use comfortably as it meets their religious as well as market requirements.

2.2 Methodology and Limitations

The methodology adopted in this study is to critically review the Australian legal framework within which IFIs function in Australia. For this purpose, it:

1. Analyses all accessible data of two selected IFIs, as well as other regulatory compliance sources.
2. Collects primary data to elicit information related to the working of the institutions and the practices followed by them.
3. Accesses all available data on the Internet.

Table 1 Religion: top 20—Australia

2011	2006
Catholic—25.3%	Catholic—25.8%
No religion—22.3%	Anglican—18.7%
Anglican—17.1%	No religion—18.7%
Uniting Church 5.0%	Uniting Church—5.7%
Presbyterian and Reformed—2.8%	Presbyterian and Reformed—3.0%
Eastern Orthodox—2.6%	Eastern Orthodox—2.7%
Buddhism—2.5%	Buddhism—2.1%
Islam 2.2%	Islam—1.7%
Christian, nfd 2.2%	Baptist—1.6%
Baptist—1.6%	Christian, nfd—1.6%
Hinduism 1.3%	Lutheran—1.3%
Lutheran—1.2%	Pentecostal—1.1%
Pentecostal 1.1%	Hinduism—0.7%
Judaism—0.5%	Judaism—0.4%
Jehovah's Witnesses—0.4%	Jehovah's Witnesses—0.4%
Sikhism—0.3%	Salvation Army—0.3%
Seventh-day Adventist—0.3%	Other Protestant—0.3%
Other Protestant—0.3%	Seventh-day Adventist—0.3%
Salvation Army—0.3%	Church of Jesus Christ—0.3%
Latter-day Saints—0.3%	Latter-day Saints—0.3%

Source: www.abs.gov.au

The method employed in this study is a mixture of direct observation from the Sharī'ah perspectives and author's personal experience, curiosity and association with this industry. Also, this study does not attempt to evaluate the economic efficiency and profitability or otherwise of IFIs in Australia.

3 Practice of IF in the Australian Financial Market

Compared to the burgeoning growth of global IF sector which covers products beyond finance, including shares, bonds and insurance, Australia is making small inroads into this fast-growing sector in global finance, and with a growing Muslim population which makes up less than 2% of the population, it has potential to become a major centre for IF (Ahmad, 2011). Also, grappling with a chocking financial meltdown, Australia is eyeing a share of the booming IF market to beat a growing recession and create more jobs. Australia is seeking to take a portion of the booming IF market from Asia since the number of Muslims at home as potential cutomers of IF is increasing (see Table 1).

Interestingly, IF in Australia is not growing rapidly as has been expected since it was first introduced in 1989 with MCCA and developed with another cooperative known as ICFAL in 1998. It has accelerated with the introduction of Iskan Finance Pty Limited back in 2001. Since the introduction of IF in Australia, some international financial institutions are also considering the opening of Islamic banking branches and subsidiaries (Ahmad, Karim, & Osmani, 2010).

Due to the global potential demand for IF and also Sydney's reputation being the world's third busiest financial centre after New York and London, the prospective demand for the IF market in Australia seems to be very high. According to Australian Bureau of Statistics 2006 census, the percentage of Muslims in Australia was 1.7% of the population making Islam the third largest religion after Christianity and Buddhism, while it was 2.2% representing in 2011 census (ABS, 2011). The Australian Muslim community is drawn from more than 70 different countries, is ethnically and linguistically diverse and is geographically scattered (DFAT, 2010). Since the introduction of IF in Australia, local Muslims and non-Muslims have been in a position to invest and borrow in interest-free transactions according to the tenets of the Sharīʻah.

Although insignificant in comparison with the major financial services providers in Australia, the Australian IFIs are now playing an important role, and their customers now include non-Muslims interested in the services provided by these institutions (Saeed, 2001). In the aftermath of the Asian economic trauma, Australia stands out as an investment opportunity as well as a financial centre. Through using IFIs' financial services and investment vehicles, their customers can reinforce the message that they are significant players in the global services economy.

4 Challenges in the Development of IFS in Australian Market

Given that all Australian banks and financial institutions as well as its regulatory system deal in interest, it has proven a significant challenge to develop and deliver noninterest-based IF products and services that will cater to observant Muslims' unique needs. Moreover, since IF is still in a state of infancy in Australia, it has been facing a number of problems and challenges, which can be identified as operational problems. This study highlights some of the issues and challenges that come with introducing IF into Australian financial market. They include but are not restricted to:

4.1 A Wait-and-See Approach

While the major global players in banking sector such as Citibank, HSBC and Standard Chartered in Malaysia; Deutsche Bank in Germany; and HSBC and Lloyds TSB in the UK have embraced Islamic finance, Australian banks appear to have taken a wait-and-see approach (Ahmad & Hassan, 2006). The non-existence of an Australian bank offering IF products could also change once Islamic non-banking financial institutions like the MCCA negotiate the often complex regulatory frameworks that govern both State and Federal financial operations.

4.2 The Size of the Muslim Community

The size and infancy of the Muslim community may be a factor in the growth of IF. With more than 300 thousand members, the Muslim community in Australia makes up less than 2% of the population. As the primary market for IF, the Muslim community's asset base is not strong. The demand for IF products among Australian Muslims is greater than the available supply. This contrasts strongly with the UK, where a Muslim population of 2.4 million is serviced by at least two conventional banks with Islamic windows and several stand-alone IBs (Ahmad, 2013a).

4.3 Doubts Concerning Sharīʻah-Compliant Finance and Investment Products

Scepticism about Sharīʻah-compliant financing and investment products may be a further barrier to the growth of IF. While IF services in Australia have been used by members of the Muslim community and while demand for such services exceeds the supply, not everyone welcomes the growth of IF. Within Australia's Muslim community, there are those who are sceptical about (and in some cases downright hostile to) the first IF products available to Australian Muslims, questioning the validity of the Sharīʻah-compliant label.

4.4 Problem of Operating as a Bank

A major regulatory problem faced by IF in Australia is getting approval from the APRA for IFIs to operate as a full-fledged bank normally would in taking deposits. Like many countries, Australian law generally does not permit taking deposits without having a licence from the appropriate authority. In order to carry on a banking business, a financial institution has to obtain a licence from APRA under section 66 of the *Banking Act 1959*. These licences are not easy to get and have to have detailed examinations by the regulator of the proposed financial institution, with the typical application period taking up to 18 months.

4.5 Regulatory Change

The absence of a regulatory and legal framework to support IBs and IFIs is a major drawback in the proper implementation of IF practices in Australia. For housing loans, there is the double stamp duty problem. Although Sharīʻah-compliant home financing already exists, various legal hurdles make them relatively expensive Ahmad and Shahed (2010). Therefore, regulatory changes would make it easier and cheaper for Muslims in Australia to get financial products that do not conflict with their beliefs. This would in turn help to make homeownership more accessible and affordable for Australia's most significant religious minority.

4.6 The Incompatibility of the Basel Accords

The apparent incompatibility of the current Basel and Basel III accords with IF are also issues in Australian regulation. The Australian prudential regulations that are essentially being administered by the APRA follow the current Basel standards and are in the process of changing over to the Basel III standards. Since neither of these makes provision for Sharī'ah compliance internationally, this has not yet been addressed in Australia. Also, there have been no applications to the regulator to confront the issue yet (APRA, 2010).

4.7 The Burden of Additional Stamp Duty on Islamic Home Financing

One of the simplest of many possible examples of a typical IF arrangement is the finance provided to purchase a home. Here, the IFIs would buy the property and resell it to the customer at a profit on a deferred payment basis over a fixed period. This requires legal title in the property to be transferred twice: once to the financier and subsequently to the customer which means there is double stamp duty to pay. In all States of Australia except for Victoria, the problem of double stamp duty payment on Islamic housing finance exists. Indeed, it is an obstacle in Islamic housing finance, because in Islam, the payment or receipt of interest is strictly forbidden. Islamic housing finance relies on the involvement of a financier who buys the property and then sells it onto the buyer and collects instalment payments (similar to traditional mortgage payments) for the repayment of the capital. Instead of charging interest, the financier often sells the property for the same price but then charges additional profit/rent on it for a specified period of time. Stamp duty is therefore charged twice—as the ownership of the property transfers twice—first to the financier and then to the ultimate buyer. This has necessarily been reflected in the price of the Islamic housing finance. Refinancing also presents a problem because the old lender has to sell the property to the new lender and thus incur another charge of stamp duty.

4.8 Exclusion from Lender of Last Resort Function

A related impediment is that IF in Australia is, by its unique character, excluded from the lender of last resort function. The Reserve Bank of Australia being the central bank of the country by tradition stands behind the conventional banking and financial system to offer liquidity, lending to banks if the system is short of funds. The IF in Australia may not be able to get advantage of this because of the interest payments due on loans which are outlawed by the Sharī'ah.

4.9 Lack of Awareness on IF

The first challenge is that many people—Muslims and non-Muslims alike—do not understand what IF exactly is. The underlying principle that Islamic law does not allow to make money out of money and thus capital should accumulate from buying and selling and possession of real assets is clear to many. However, there does not appear to be a unified definition of an IF product. The key concern is that the respective Sharīʻah Supervisory Boards (SSB) of the IBs or IFIs that in fact define what is and is not an IF product and it interprets transactions differently. This leads to an ambiguity about what is and what is not an Islamic product and a good enough product to conduct business with, which in turn can complicate risk appraisal for both the bank and its customers. This ambiguity so far prevents standardisation and makes it difficult for regulators. Justifiably they would like to know precisely what it is they are authorising (Ainley, Mashayekhi, Hicks, Rahman, & Ravalia, 2007).

4.10 Risk Analysis and Balance Sheet Management

Another problem for IFIs in Australian financial market is the risk analysis and balance sheet management. Like in any other country, the challenge in formulating the risk management infrastructure in IFIs lies in having an accurate assessment of the various risk variants underlying the alternative modes of finance to provide for their effective quantification and management. On the asset side, the IFIs enter into different financing modes that have varying risk characteristics, ranging from the low-risk sales and lease-based modes to the higher-risk equity-based modes of finance. Each of these modes of finance has a distinct intrinsic characteristic dictated by its underlying Sharīʻah principle and thus entail different risk profiles. An equity-based finance may, for example, involve higher risks and therefore attract a higher capital requirement.

5 Opportunities of IF in Australia

There is a lot of potential that the Australian businessmen may leverage on Malaysia's comparative advantage in financial services to penetrate new markets in ASEAN and the West Asia in the areas of IFS. There is a huge potential for IF and Malaysia, which is a Muslim-majority country and is the place to explore these opportunities. Anticipating the increased interest in IF, Malaysia has put into place a comprehensive IF system that includes best practices in legal and regulatory infrastructure, a diversity of market players and a wide range of products and services. Over the next 10 years, Islamic banking in Malaysia is expected to command 20% market share vis-à-vis conventional banking. Therefore, banks in Australia should take these opportunities to use Malaysian banks as a channel to access Islamic banking and financial markets in Asia and other parts of the world especially in West Asia.

Nevertheless, a significant area which has been neglected is the potential for the sale of Australian-sourced financial products overseas. Australia offers well-established and stable political, regulatory and judicial systems. Returns on investments in Australia have, over the long terms favoured by Islamic investors, been very high, and much of the investment in Australia is in *halal* products such as land, mining and agriculture. The first company to issue products to investors globally is likely to encounter some regulatory hurdles, but they are also likely to tap into a deep and growing well of capital.

5.1 Opportunities of Introducing Islamic Banking

There is no full-fledged Islamic bank that exists in Australia. Also, there is not a single conventional bank in Australia which has a separate Islamic banking branch or window or subsidiary like in some Muslim and non-Muslim countries alike that carries out Islamic banking operations. This is due to the existing legal, regulatory and supervisory system of Australia that is exclusively made to control and supervise its conventional banking system, in addition to what the IBs are governed by the supervisory boards of Muslim clerics to ensure compliance with the Sharī'ah.

5.2 Prospects of Islamic Banking and Finance in Academic Level

The brilliant prospects of IF in Australia persist to mark as preparations are ahead by some Australia universities to offer courses in the field of IF. The La Trobe University has announced about the introduction of the first course in Australia dedicated to IF, joining a handful of universities in the West embracing this fast-growing segment of global finance. The university's Master of Islamic Banking and Finance course is believed to be able to provide students with postgraduate training in the technical skills demanded by global Islamic capital markets and institutions. This programme is also expected to appeal to international students from Asia wanting Islamic financial training in English and to local graduates keen to enter the growing sector in Australia. The International Centre of Education in Islamic Finance (INCEIF), a training subsidiary of Bank Negara Malaysia (The Malaysian Central Bank), the equivalent to Australia's Reserve Bank, has assured to provide industry-based certification for graduates of the La Trobe course, opening up employment opportunities throughout the international banking and finance sector.

Besides, the Australian Monash University offers Australian Postgraduate Award Industry (APAI) Scholarships funded by an Australian Research Council (ARC) Linkage Projects grant and worth $25,118 per annum to conduct postgraduate research in the area of over 3-year full-time study for PhD research projects in the general area of IF (Ahmad, 2012). The projects that have to have entail empirical work relating the application of finance theory to some aspect of Islamic banks, insurance companies, fund managers, markets or instruments are considered as a significant development in Australia's IF industry in academic and professional level. The University of Melbourne has also been offering different courses on Islamic banking and finance at undergraduate and postgraduate levels mostly by courses. It has also master's and doctoral research programme on this broad area which offers some scholarships. In addition, National Australia Bank (NAB) is considering to look at introducing IF into its product range to capture an "untapped" market that could be worth millions of dollars.

6 Summary and Concluding Remarks

The findings of this study is summarised as follows. There is no legal and regulatory framework exists in Australia for guiding and supervising the functions of IF to operate in line with the precepts of the Islamic legal system. The IF in Australia was established in an environment where conventional financial service providers are already in the market. The crucial challenge in this regard is that IFIs' customers must enjoy similar, although not necessarily the same, protection as customers of conventional financial institutions. Given that, it is expected that regulatory authorities would ensure there is a level playing field, so that neither IF nor conventional financial institutions are disadvantaged. In Australia where Muslims are minorities and full-fledged IBs are absent, regulators have nevertheless been expected to approve and monitor IF products.

The key philosophies that distinguish conventional from Islamic financial markets may suggest that the regulatory building blocks for regulating Islamic finance need to be different from those used for conventional regulation, but in fact they are not different from a regulatory perspective. Like other regulators, Australian regulatory authorities would like to be satisfied that IF markets have appropriate compliance and enforcement powers and practices; that the conventional and IF are both in good standing with relevant international standard setters; and that they are committed to appropriate levels of information sharing and cooperation. If all of these hurdles can be overcome, obviously they can take comfort that differences of detail in regulatory approach will not prejudice consumers of the Sharīʻah-compliant products.

The IF in Australia is still in its early stages. Because of the character of most of Australian immigrants, lots of incoming Muslims here have naturally been more worried with how to support their families than with developing financial institutions. However, quite a few small financial enterprises have started; with at least three in operation at present. A few of these IFIs, being cooperative in nature, are currently limited to providing facilities for their shareholders and are not allowed to accept normal bank deposits as Australian law normally does not permit taking deposits without an appropriate licence, while others work with a number of other providers and offer mortgage and leasing facilities.

7 Recommendations

The study makes the following recommendations for consideration by regulatory authorities for IF in Australia.

1. There is a strong desire and growing demand among and from Muslims for a full-fledged Islamic bank to function in line with the tenets of the Sharīʻah. Given that, a fully-fledged Islamic bank should be established in Australia. The author believes the Australian government should take necessary steps to enable these growing opportunities to be pursued in this country. Thus, steps should be taken to introduce

legislation in the Australian Parliament for strengthening this country's Islamic financial market system. Such a move to enact legislation by the lawmakers would contribute to the Muslim community in Australia finding a truly viable alternative for banking and finance based on religious and ethical considerations.
2. The regulators in Australia should introduce measures necessary to equalise the revenue duty liabilities of Islamic alternatives for interest-based mortgages with a view to creating a level playing field for financial institutions and customers. Given the differing treatment of similar financial products under the different state regulatory systems, it is recommended that the government consider making changes to facilitate the levying of a single payment of duties/fees on what in effect is a single purchase.
3. Strenuous efforts should be made to educate people given the high level of ignorance of the underlying philosophy and nature of IF among the general populace and those associated with the industry. For example, it is not known to many people that one of the great successes and growth of IF lies in "its value-orientated ethos that enables it to draw finances from both Muslims and non-Muslims alike". Also, since the Sharī'ah contracts that are now used and advertised by IF in Australia appear to be traditional mortgage contracts where the borrower takes the risk and the lender gets a fixed rate of return, it is suggested that Muslim customers should be provided with fully disclosed information about the institutions with whom they enter into business relationships.
4. The IFIs may merge with each other for their future growth and development through attracting more capital and providing investment facilities. This will help expand IF that Australia's vibrant Muslim community could use comfortably as it would meet their religious as well as financial and market requirements.

8 Suggestions for Further Research

The volume of research on IF systems has considerably amplified over the past two decades. However, there are still many significant issues to be critically examined. In relation to the problems and potential of IF in Australia, which is the topic of the present study, there is more work to be done. The author's research was somewhat limited by its focus on theoretical and technical analysis. It should be followed by empirical studies and tests. Within a few years, a sufficient volume of data on the IF of Australia will be available to make such studies practicable.

References

Ahmad, A. (2010). *Theory and practice of modern Islamic finance: The case analysis from Australia*. Florida: BrownWalker.

Ahmad, A. (2011). Current regulation and supervision for Islamic financial market: Evidence from Australia. *International Journal of Excellence in Islamic Banking and Finance, 1*(1), 32–46.

Ahmad, A. (2012). Opportunities of Islamic finance in the Australian market in the aftermath of the global financial crisis. *Journal of Islamic Economics, Banking and Finance, 7*(4), 43–64.

Ahmad, A. (2013a). Islamic finance in Australia: A critical analysis from taxation and prudential standards' perspectives. *Advances in Natural and Applied Sciences, 7*(2), 149–164.

Ahmad, A. (2013b). Regulatory impediments to Islamic finance the UK and Australia compared. *Journal of Islamic Economics, Banking and Finance, 9*(4). https://doi.org/10.12816/0031377

Ahmad, A., & Ahmad, A. (2008). Islamic micro and medium sized enterprises (MMEs) finance: The case study of Australia. In M. Obaidullah & H. S. Abdul Latif (Eds.), *Islamic finance for micro and medium enterprises*. Jeddah: Islamic Research Training Institute.

Ahmad, A., & Hassan, M. K. (2006). The adoption of the UK finance bill proposals on Islamic finance into Islamic banking in Australia. *Review of Islamic Economics, 10*(1).

Ahmad, A., & Hassan, K. (2009). Legal and regulatory issues of Islamic finance in Australia. *International Journal of Islamic and Middle Eastern Finance and Management, 2*(4), 305–322.

Ahmad, A., & Hassan, K. (2011). Developments in Islamic finance practice: The experience of Australia. In M. K. Hassan & H. M. Mahlknecht (Eds.), *Islamic capital markets: Products and strategies*. London: Wiley.

Ahmad, A., Karim, M., & Osmani, N. (2010, January). *Islamic finance in Australia: The potential problems and prospects*. A paper presented at the 7th International Conference, The Tawhidi Epistemology: Zakat and Waqf Economy, in Selangor.

Ahmad, A., & Shahed, A. (2010). Housing finance of Australian Islamic financial services providers (IFSPs): A case analysis from Sharī'ah perspectives. *IIUM Journal of Economics and Management, 18*(1).

Ainley, M., Mashayekhi, A., Hicks, R., Rahman, A., & Ravalia, A. (2007). *Islamic finance in the UK: Regulation and challenges*. London: Financial Services Authority.

Al-Salem, F. (2008, March). The size and scope of the Islamic finance industry: An analysis. *International Journal of Management*. Retrieved October 10, 2018, from http://www.encyclopedia.com/doc/1P3-1460961701.html

Australian Bureau of Statistics. (2011). *Census data – Religious affiliation*. Retrieved October 10, 2018, from http://www.abs.gov.au

Australian Prudential Regulatory Authority. (2010). Islamic banking – A way forward? *Risk Management in Australia*. Retrieved October 10, 2018, from http://ozrisk.net/2006/08/17/islamic-banking-a-way-forward/#more-38

DFAT. (2010). *Australian Government*. Department of Foreign Affairs and Trade. Engaging with Australia's Muslim communities. Retrieved October 10, 2018, from http://www.dfat.gov.au/facts/engaging_with_muslim_community.html

Saeed, A. (2001). The Muslim Community Co-operative of Australia as an Islamic financial service provider. In S. Abdullah & A. Shahram (Eds.), *Muslim communities in Australia*. Sydney: University of New South Wales Press.

Abu Umar Faruq Ahmad is Associate Professor of Islamic Economic Institute, King Abdulaziz University, Kingdom of Saudi Arabia. His research focus is on Islamic law, Islamic Jurisprudence, Islamic Economics, Islamic finance, and Islamic Banking. He has published several books and journal articles on Islamic economics, finance, and banking. He is also the Founding Editor of International Journal of Excellence in Islamic Banking and Finance, and is on the Editorial Advisory Board Member of two Emerald published Scopus indexed journals.

The Role of Cash Waqf in Poverty Reduction: A Multi-country Case Study

Buerhan Saiti, Abdiwali Jama Salad, and Mehmet Bulut

Abstract

Poverty is a severely debilitating problem affecting many countries in the Muslim world. The fight against poverty and alleviating it from the society are imperative. Its reduction and alleviation not only depend on economic and social policies, population size and resource endowments but also on the types of economic undertakings being pursued. This case study explores the potential of faith-based endowments—cash *waqf*—to reduce the level of poverty in Somalia. It analyses critically the cash *waqf* models existing in two selected Muslim countries in relation to the socio-economic situation in Somalia. In line with existing literature, the study adopted the *waqf* shares scheme. This scheme seems to be appropriate to Somalia for several important reasons. It is relatively easy to raise funds from the public via traditional collections of money by cash or mobile payment systems which are widely used in Somalia. It is argued that the funds generated could be used to create employment opportunities, and as a result, many poor Somalis will be empowered financially, socially and educationally.

B. Saiti (✉)
Department of Islamic Economics and Finance, Istanbul Sabahattin Zaim University, Istanbul, Turkey

A. J. Salad
Institute of Islamic Banking and Finance, International Islamic University Malaysia, Gombak, Malaysia

M. Bulut
Istanbul Sabahattin Zaim University, Istanbul, Turkey

E. M. Ghazali et al. (eds.), *Management of Shari'ah Compliant Businesses*, Management for Professionals, https://doi.org/10.1007/978-3-030-10907-3_3

1 Introduction

Poverty is a severely debilitating problem affecting many countries in the Muslim world. The fighting against poverty and alleviating it from the societies are imperative. Its reduction and alleviation not only depend on economic and social policies, population size and resource endowments but also on the types of economic undertakings being pursued. The focus should be on determining which policies contribute effectively to eliminating poverty. Such efforts align with the primary objectives of the *Shariah* to alleviate poverty and establish socio-economic justice and the equitable distribution of wealth.

Poverty is rampant in the Muslim world. Inequality and low productivity have contributed to poor standards of living. A significant number of Muslims in Africa, Asia and the Middle East are living below $2 a day due to their abject and absolute poverty. In fact, the Muslim communities account for a significant number of poor and less privileged globally. This raises numerous questions that need answers to solve the problems threatening the Muslim world (Amuda & Embi, 2013).

The current condition of Muslims is deteriorating because of their financial restrictions and poverty due to unrestrained corruption. The economic challenge affecting numerous Muslims has an undesirable impact on their lives religiously, morally, socially and mentally and requires a solution. Many cannot afford necessities for their immediate families because of financial problems (Ali, 2012).

Given the current financial situation challenging several Muslim countries, there is an urgent need for poverty alleviation through *waqf* properties, *sadaqat,* and public funding. Poverty alleviation requires proper financial systems such as micro-financing, lawful businesses, agriculture, investment, large-scale enterprises and small and medium enterprises. Others include commercialisation, gifts, interest-free loans, partnerships, factories, construction and other lucrative investments (Adebayo, 2008).

Cash *waqf* (CW) is a viable type of Islamic endowment aimed at providing relief to the less fortunate citizens. Several countries such as Malaysia, Indonesia, Bangladesh, Singapore and Nigeria have established cash *waqf* systems and achieved some level of success. However, issues and challenges remain in the current practice of cash *waqf*. This chapter will begin by investigating issues and challenges in the *waqf* system. Secondly, it explores the potential of faith-based endowments to reduce the poverty level in Somalia. Historically, *waqf* in Somalia has not contributed to the development of all sectors. There are no functioning endowment institutions in Somalia that register and care for *waqf* properties. Even though *waqf* in Somalia is as old as the arrival of Islam, the perception of the society towards *waqf* is that it is solely a religious practice.

This study adopts a qualitative research design that draws on information sourced from previous literature, the Quran, Hadith, working papers and Internet sources. It analyses the existing cash *waqf* models in Muslim and Muslim minority countries in relation to the socio-economic situation of Somalia. In line with this, the study adopted the *waqf* shares scheme. This scheme seems to suit Somalia for several important reasons. It is relatively easy to raise funds from the public via traditional approaches to collecting money by cash or by mobile payment systems which is widely used in Somalia. It is argued that the funds generated can be used to create employment opportunities to empower poor Somalis financially, socially and educationally. The result of this study shows that cash *waqf* is viable and can reduce poverty among less privileged Somalis.

1.1 Cash Waqf

Cash *waqf* is not as prevalent as property and land types of *waqf*. It is gradually increasing and getting attention. Among the reasons for the advent of cash *waqf* in recent times is due to its flexibility. The elasticity of cash *waqf* permits for dissemination of *waqf*'s prospective advantages to the poor irrespective of their geographical setting (Ali, 2012).

Cash *waqf* has been recognised for its potential to alleviate poverty. Poverty alleviation programmes require considerable funds, and governments are often unable to provide such financing. In this case, cash endowment can play its part. The cash *waqf* fund trustees or *Mutawalli* will gather the funds from the *waqf* founder or *Waqif* and invest the money in any Islamic-based investment fund or a genuine sector. The profit obtained from this investment can be used to finance enterprises that would assist the ordinary people as a means of poverty alleviation (Beik & Arsyianti, 2013).

Many people have expressed their support for cash *waqf*. Cash *waqf* is perceived to be extra "friendly" to the public, specifically to those who do not own any asset such as a building or land. Table 1 lists the advantages of executing cash *waqf*.

2 Multi-country Case Study on Cash *Waqf*

This section examines the cash *waqf* practices employed by some Muslim countries such as Ottoman Times, Malaysia and Bangladesh. We evaluate the current cash *waqf* models of those countries and identify the problems and suggest possible solutions. However, before presenting the current situation in the mentioned countries, we want to give a general information on the heritage of the cash waqfs from the Ottoman times.

3 Case Study 1: Malaysia

In Malaysia, cash *waqf* is progressively acknowledged and recognised. The implementation of cash *waqf* has increased its acceptance in Malaysia, partially on account of the advertisements prepared by Bank Muamalat Malaysia Berhad (BMMB), which is the pioneer of Islamic banking organisation to manage cash *waqf* alongside Perbadanan Wakaf Selangor (PWS) (Bank Muamalat Malaysia Berhad, 2014).

Table 1 Advantages of cash *waqf*

1	It is easy-going and only needs a trivial amount of wealth which permits the involvement of a larger group of people
2	It has the capability to produce more resources for the benefit of asset development, for instance, *waqf* land that has not been developed
3	It could help educational institutions with the problems of cash flow by forming a temporary fund
4	It has the ability to decrease the reliance of Islamic institutions on the government. It simultaneously empowers them to be more autonomous
5	From the education sector's viewpoint, cash *waqf* has been established to perform an active role in assisting Islamic educational institutions. An outstanding example in the implementation of cash *waqf* in the educational sector is that of Al-Azhar University in Egypt, which was built with cash *waqf* funds
6	It has been active in instituting income-generating undertakings which are appropriate to help the physically challenged people, single mothers, uneducated and inexperienced workers. The income-generating activities will considerably help those persons who might encounter difficulties in getting jobs
7	It can also help in the growth of current *waqf* properties. An important amount of *waqf* properties is left wasting and unused because of a shortage of funds. Cash *waqf* can be restructured with the aim of *waqf* property development financing through *mudharabah and musharakah* methods (Beik & Arsyianti, 2013).

Note: Authors' own table, 2018

With the intention of improving its role as an Islamic bank, in 2012 Bank Muamalat Malaysia Berhad (BMMB) combined with Perbadanan Wakaf Selangor (PWS), a state *waqf* manager served as the major gatherer of cash *waqf*. The bank established a shared deposit account for accumulating cash *waqf*. It is also in charge of providing awareness to the Malaysian Muslims to take part in cash *waqf* collection. Since its incorporation in 2012, many donors began to inquire about the bank's efficiency in handling the fund. This is because of the absence of disclosure on the utilisation of the fund. Since the bank acts as the accumulator of the fund, it should make its cash *waqf* operation more transparent (Bank Muamalat Malaysia Berhad, 2014).

Cash *waqf* has become popular in Malaysia. For instance, the Malaysian National Fatwa Council passed the fatwa that allows cash *waqf* in the year 2007 (Yayasan Wakaf Malaysia, 2014). Furthermore, the massive cash *waqf* fund gathered by the Selangor State Religious Council (SSRC) provides many benefits such as settling of debts such as houses, providing loans for financing small and medium industry business, developing the Islamic economy and investment in property for Muslims (Kahf, 1998).

Cash *waqf* is a donation of a certain amount of money, which is supervised and managed by cash *waqf* trustees (*Mutawalli*) to support a variety of charitable works financially. The pooling of cash in Malaysia will be transformed into a long-lasting property that will be used for the interest and welfare of the community, and it is supported by Yayasan Wakaf Malaysia. A *waqf* fund which is otherwise mentioned as Kumpulan Wang Wakaf is formed to save the donation of money and properties or any other incomes or proceeds obtained from *Mawquf* or *Istibdal*, and it is administered by several statutes (Saad, Kayadibi, & Hamid, 2017).

Cash *waqf* has been presented by the State Islamic Religious Council (MAIN). For example, the State of Selangor Islamic Religious Council (MAIS) announced the formation of a *waqf* scheme called Skim Saham *waqf* (waqf Shares Scheme). The other states in Malaysia that also applied a related *waqf* shares scheme are Malacca Johor, Pahang, Terengganu and Penang. Cash *waqf* is easier to control than fixed assets such as land. Its manageable and distinguishing features allow for varied functions. Moreover, it has been utilised to sponsor development projects and can be capitalised in numerous Islamic investment instruments. The revenues generated from these investments can then be used to fund projects that will assist the Muslim community (Khan, 2010).

Cash *waqf* in Malaysia has numerous benefits because of its suppleness. Many Muslims donate case as *waqf*. Essentially, through cash *waqf* funds, the abandoned assets that lack financial support could be urbanised for the benefit of the Islamic economy. The cash *waqf* fund can also be used to fund institutions of education and Islamic religious schools that are facing financial difficulties in addition to supporting other Islamic assets (Lahsasna, 2010).

The enormous cash *waqf* fund provides many benefits in developing the Islamic economy. It could be utilised as loans for funding small and medium enterprises. It could also assist in relaxing debts comprising of assets such as house foreclosures and bad debts problems encountered by the Islamic community. Furthermore, the cash *waqf* supports the ownership of Muslim assets, as every asset acquired will be *waqf* (Mohammad, 2011).

Likewise, the cash *waqf* in Malaysia has the capability to support the development of the Muslim ummah. It is projected that the collection of cash *waqf* in Malaysia could reach a total of RM4.3 billion a year if every full-grown Malaysian Muslim contributed at least RM1 per day or RM30 per month to the cash *waqf* fund. Moreover, the state of Penang has a great prospect to improve a cash *waqf* fund because of its marketing and planning strategy that is utilised for advertising cash *waqf* funds. Ibrahim et al., (2013) projected that the cash *waqf* fund could extend to RM7 million per year, which could generate numerous opportunities for the Muslim community (Perbadanan Wakaf Selangor, 2014).

3.1 Problems Affecting Cash *Waqf* in Malaysia

1. There are many levels of the decision-making process of *cash waqf* in Malaysia that are time-consuming and do not allow for effective and efficient *cash waqf* accumulation.
2. Cash *waqf* processes are not consistent making coordination and evaluation difficult. Similarly, there are shortages of experienced personnel.
3. The management team of cash *waqf* in Malaysia are new. Instead of concentrating on primary projects, the cash *waqf* managers rely of cash *waqf* funds to execute

secondary projects which they are not supposed to. This situation fails to elicit the confidence of Malaysian population.

4. The lack of *Cash Waqf* Management Committee did not provide room for the development of *waqf* assets which fail to reinforce the Muslim economy.
5. There is lack of a good master plan on the cash *waqf* that is consistent with the Malaysian Vision 2020.
6. There is lack of proper public enlightenment campaigns by the State Islamic Religious Council (MAIN) on the issue of tax rebate provided to donors of *Dana Klinik Wakaf An Nur* by the Malaysian Board of Inland Revenue.
7. The various stakeholders in cash *waqf* affairs such as the State Islamic Religious Council (MAIN), the Department of *Awqar, Zakat* and *Hajj* (JAWHAR) and *Yayasan Wakaf Malaysia* (YWM) failed to provide a wide range of media publicity in order to notify the general community about *waqf* expansion projects.

3.2 Solutions to the Problems of Cash *Waqf*

1. The numerous levels of decision-making of cash *waqf* should be substituted with smaller and fewer time-consuming processes in order to make it well-organised and operational.
2. The cash *waqf* processes should be consistent and standardised. This is essential to produce harmonisation and easy assessment. It will also assist in producing experienced and well-informed staff. The staff should also be provided with training to increase collection and its productivity.
3. The cash *waqf* management is in a developing stage. Therefore, there should be a subordinate project to assist in funding the main project so that the supervisors do not have to rely on cash *waqf* funds. Subordinate projects will also increase the status of the supervisors and promote confidence among the Malaysian public.
4. A Baitul Mal and Cash Waqf Management Committee (CWMC) should be established to make sure that all the *waqf* assets can be promoted consistent with the objective of the contributors in addition to producing income and revenue to the State Islamic Religious Council (MAIN) and reinforce the Muslim economy.
5. Donations should not be limited to buildings or land; the Muslim community should be encouraged to donate cash *waqf* to produce additional revenue and increase the properties and assets of the Muslim community.
6. To make sure that the cash *waqf* development plan is pertinent to the country's transformation policy, a good master plan which corresponds with the Malaysian Vision 2020 should be established. The plan should be the foundation of any future cash *waqf* expansion project to ensure the funds spent on the growth of *waqf* will have robust impacts on the economy of the Muslim community.
7. There should be proper public enlightenment campaigns by the State Islamic Religious Council (MAIN) on the issue of tax rebate provided to donors of *Dana Klinik Wakaf An Nur* by the Malaysian Board of Inland Revenue so that people will be additionally encouraged to donate funds for charitable projects.

8. The State Islamic Religious Council (MAIN), the Department of *Awqaf, Zakat* and *Hajj* (JAWHAR) and *Yayasan Wakaf Malaysia* (YWM) should engage a wide range of channels, for instance, through the print media, publications, seminars and forums, to notify the general community about waqf expansion projects so that they obtain exact information on the role and support of *waqf* in advancing the development and socio-economic status of the nation.

4 Case Study 2: Bangladesh

Cash *waqf* came into existence in Bangladesh in the year 1995 by Social Investment Bank Ltd. (SIBL). The bank introduced the Cash *Waqf* Certificate which was regarded as a fresh product in Bangladesh banking history. This system has been well received by the public for its outstanding features. The Social Investment Bank Ltd. as an inventor of this ground-breaking monetary product of social capital mobilisation received both local and international endorsement. When a person opens a Cash *Waqf* Deposit A/C, he can provide welfare services. People are encouraged to volunteer to gather cash *waqf* deposit with the intention of generating profit, which may be used for the benefit of the people (Thoarlim, Rahman, & Yanya, 2017).

The development of cash *waqf* in Bangladesh is a growing trend, and many people are aware of cash *waqf* in Bangladesh. Cash *waqf* finances many private universities in Bangladesh. The cash *waqf* funds are reserved in the investment fund of an Islamic bank which functions on the foundation of *Mudarabah*. The profits are used for accomplishing stipulated Islamic goals. The cash *waqf* management has a distinctive characteristic that is conceptually dissimilar to the management of charities, donation or foundation funds (Ahmad & Safiullah, 2012).

In Bangladesh, cash *waqf* permits people to provide little contributions to *waqf* institutions. Cash *waqf* pool and management are operated by numerous Islamic banks. The contributors can open the *waqf* cash account by putting a fixed amount or by paying a minimal amount every month which they are not permitted to withdraw (Aziz, Yusof, Johari, & Sabri, 2014).

The banks usually invest those deposits in *Shariah*-compliant investment alternatives and allocate the proceeds to recipients according to their needs or by donors' intentions. The achievement of Social Islamic Bank in distributing and handling the cash *waqf* has led other Islamic banks in Bangladesh to introduce related accounts of cash *waqf* for the benefit of Muslims and non-Muslims. Other banks that have joined include Exim Bank Bangladesh, Prime Bank, Al-Arafah Islami Bank Limited, Shahjalal Islami Bank Limited and Islamic Bank Bangladesh Limited (Abdul Karim, 2010).

It is a common practice in Bangladesh to use banks as agents for collecting cash *waqf*. Consequently, using Islamic banks is viewed as the starting point for collecting cash *waqf* in Bangladesh (Ameen, 2004).

4.1 Problems Affecting Cash Waqf in Bangladesh

There are problems that affect the development of cash *waqf* in Bangladesh. The problems include:

1. Insufficient manpower.
2. Lack of administrative and organisational experience.
3. Unregistered cash *waqf* properties.
4. Lack of provisions in the relevant laws.
5. Lack of social consciousness.
6. Unlawful misappropriation and occupation of cash *waqf*.
7. Possibilities of power exploitation and ineffective supervision. All the decisions for both private and public *waqf* institutions are made by the headquarters which reduces the divisional employees' opportunities to take part in the decision-making.
8. Lack of *Shariah* and advisory board.
9. The aptitudes and qualification of *Mutawallis* in effectively managing cash *waqf* for the continued flow of funds for their sustainable future are questionable.

All these problems bring about serious apprehensions in Bangladesh about the governance structure of the cash *waqf* institutions. They need to resolve the growth and sustainability of such institutions.

4.2 Solutions to Some of the Problems

1. Cash *waqf* administration in Bangladesh should be decentralised to enhance proper communication.
2. The government should employ sufficient experienced staff to monitor the activities of cash *waqf*.
3. Cash *waqf* should be registered.
4. Relevant laws on cash *waqf* must be enacted to guide the management of the funds.
5. A *Shariah* advisory board should be established for cash *waqf* for every institution.
6. The government should employ qualified and experienced *Mutawallis* for effective management of cash *waqf*.

5 Model Building: Cash Waqf Model for Poverty Reduction in Somalia

This *waqf* model proposed for Somalia is developed in a way that makes it possible for *waqf* fund to be managed and invested at the same time so that it will be sustainable. The model is adopted from different cash *waqf* models practised in the Muslim minority and majority countries.

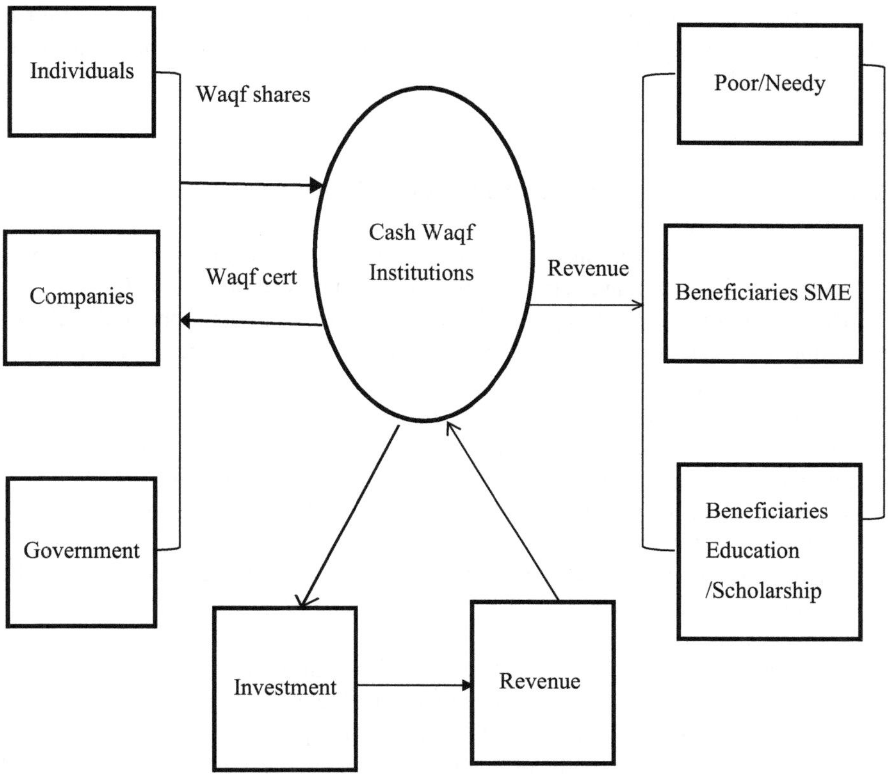

Fig. 1 Conceptual framework of cash *waqf* model in Somalia (Note: Authors' own figure, 2018)

The Somali government has pursued several initiatives to reduce poverty. Besides seeking international help, the government established a national committee as a trustee to collect funds from Somalis in the country as well as in the global Somali diaspora. Although the idea works to some extent and helps the poor who have lost their livelihood, it is worth mentioning that this method of handling problems is not sustainable and calls for researchers and policymakers to come up with models that are reliable and, above all, sustainable. In line with the government objectives, we have proposed a cash *waqf* model as an addition to the existing strategies and policies. The structure of this model is presented in Fig. 1.

The model resembles *waqf* shares schemes. According to Ismail Abdel Mohsin (2013), this scheme is a kind of public participation of *waqf* fundraising. Such a *waqf* scheme is practised by many countries such as Kuwait, Malaysia, Indonesia and the UK. The purpose of this scheme is to raise funds from the public and support the common good of the society. Generated income will finance different lawful activities as per Islamic law. The collected *waqf* fund in this scheme will be invested in businesses that generate good returns, and then the profit generated will be directed to the beneficiaries. Moreover, Ismail Abdel Mohsin (2013) stated that perpetuity as one of the principles of *waqf* could be achieved if only the profit is channelled to poverty alleviation activities, but the collected fund should be intact as much as possible.

5.1 Modus Operandi of the Proposed Model

1. It can be established by any specified institution or company, private or public, and handled by the management of the fund as a trustee or *Mutawalli*.
2. The institution then issues *waqf* shares in various denominations and calls for donors to donate for the specified project. This will make it easier for all, not only for the rich class, to participate.
3. Donors can buy shares according to their ability.
4. Contributors in return will be given a *Cash Waqf* Certificate that shows they purchased shares in a specified project and indicates the amount paid.
5. The amount collected from contributors will be managed and invested by the Cash waqf Institution (CWI) as trustee/*Mutawalli*.
6. Finally, the generated income from the investment will be channelled to the beneficiaries accordingly.

Furthermore, this model is perceived as one of the successful *waqf* institutions for poverty reduction, and it will be suitable to be adopted in Somalia as the first attempt at a *cash waqf* institution. This model is developed to upgrade and help the poor who were affected by the droughts in Somalia. Through the best practices of good governance, the CWI institution will prosper if proper management were to be employed. In Somalia, most of the corporations fail due to the lack of good corporate governance. Also, the publication of detailed annual reports, the appointment of an independent board of directors, external auditors, and the use of an effective information management system can be practised. These are the tools that can guarantee an effective environment for *waqf* institution development that is transparent, accountable and sustainable.

5.2 The Components of the Proposed Cash *Waqf* Model

This proposed model suggests solutions to the current challenges of supporting the internally displaced people in Somalia due to severe droughts and lack of financial support. The model consists of planning a successful *waqf* project, followed by the president's office for the nomination of the committee (*Mutawalli*) to act as a trustee and to manage the collected *cash waqf* fund. This committee, as a board of directors, should appoint a competent CEO to manage the fund in the best interest of the beneficiaries. It must also fulfil the conditions given by the *waqif* (donors) and ensure sustainability of the fund. Finally, there must be checks and balances. Donors and the beneficiaries are also key components of the model.

Government Approval In this proposed model, since there are MPs in the elected committee as discussed earlier in this chapter, they can easily forward a bill to the House of Legislatures to pass a law that will govern the *waqf* institutions in the country.

Donors Donors can be government, businesses and individuals. It is expected from the government to encourage its employees to contribute to the nation-building process by contributing to the *cash waqf* fund. This will help the government's plan to fight poverty and the country's rebuilding process. A properly managed *waqf* will not only improve the life of the society but also reduce the government's expenditure. As of now, the Somali government heavily depends on foreign aid and debts to cover its basic infrastructure. If *waqf* institutions are fully supported, they will have positive impacts on the country.

Businesses and private companies can play essential roles to contribute to the *waqf* fund so that the CWI will have sufficient funds to improve the lives of the vulnerable in the society. Cash *waqf* institutions can cooperate with other financial institutions like Islamic banks and telecommunication companies for greater benefits since engagement of corporate social responsibility (CSR) is required from businesses.

CWI This is the governing body of a cash *waqf* institution. The people who will be appointed should be like-minded because they are the ones who make the decisions. The primary objective of the cash *waqf* institution is raising funds from the donors and issuing cash *waqf* certificates in return. The donors will expect no return from the CWI but reward from Allah since they are helping the needy. The certificate will be useful for recording the transactions and as a transparency tool. The other function of CWI is to invest the collected funds into businesses that will yield a good return. Other operational activities and managerial skills should be done with due diligence.

Sustainability There is a need to ensure sustainability after formation of a successful cash *waqf* institution. Sustainability can only be realised in the form of investment. Investment of the capital can be real estate, transportation or investing in *Shariah*-compliant shares and *sukuk*. It can also be invested in participating financing through lawful transactions like *Murabaha, Istisna'* and *Salam*. Riskier investment can also be engaged through *Musharakah* and *Mudarabah* with a small percentage to minimise the risk.

Beneficiaries The main objective of the cash *waqf* institution is that the profit will be channelled to projects according to the wish of the *Waqif* (donors). It can be for poverty alleviation, needy people, orphanages and poverty alleviation programmes such as microfinance projects and reducing the burden of those who are indebted.

6 Concluding Remarks

The main objective of the study is to examine the impact of cash *waqf* on poverty alleviation. Among the motives of the current advent of cash *waqf* is its flexibility. The research finds that many people appreciate the importance of cash *waqf* as the structures of *cash waqf* are perceived to be extra "friendly" to the community specifically to those who do not have any asset such as a building or land. The advantages of implementing cash *waqf* are as follows:

1. Cash *waqf* is easy-going and only requires a little amount of money which permits participation of a larger group of people.
2. Cash *waqf* can decrease the reliance of Islamic institutions on the government, which simultaneously empowers them to be more autonomous.
3. Cash *waqf* has been known to be conceivably active in introducing income-generating activities which are suitable for the physically challenged people, single mothers and uneducated and inexperienced workers.

These are few points of what cash *waqf* can contribute to humanity to reduce the burden of the less privileged. We have seen the impact of cash *waqf* on poverty alleviation, and the researcher is very optimistic that this method of *waqf* would help Somalia if it is implemented properly.

Finally, another objective of this study is the proposed cash *waqf* model for Somalia for poverty reduction. The study sheds light on how cash *waqf* started and its development in those countries. The researcher modified the above models so that it will be appropriate for Somalia. It is worth mentioning that it is tough to find how the collected funds are invested by these institutions but the projects have great impacts on the society. In line with this, the study adopts the *waqf* shares scheme. This scheme seems to be suitable for Somalia for several important reasons. It is relatively easy to raise funds from the public via the traditional way of collecting money by cash or by mobile payment system, which is widely used in Somalia. The problem with the corporate scheme is that the culture of a corporation is not properly practised as most of the businesses are retail. Cash *waqf* through deposit scheme will also be problematic because most of the people in the country do not use banks. Therefore, this model is believed as one of the fruitful *waqf* institutions for poverty alleviation, and it will be appropriate to be adopted in Somalia as the first attempt at forming a cash *waqf* institution.

The present research offers recommendations for future research. Somalia needs to create awareness about *waqf* to revive the noble culture of helping one another and call for its development and renewal, especially, cash *waqf* societal development. There is the need for coordination between cash *waqf* institutions and other relevant organisations as well as government bodies. For Somalia's *waqf* development, it should cooperate with other cash *waqf* institutions globally to benefit from their successful policies.

Also, there is the need to prepare well-trained human resource to handle cash *waqf* to make it a robust institution. Efforts should be made towards developing managerial skills, advertising *waqf* and making sound investment plans while using knowledgeable persons in all the fields involved. They should take advantage of the flexibility in Islamic law and not be confined to previous opinions. *Fiqh* councils and *waqf* conferences produce many insights that can help *Awqaf* to flourish. Technology should be used for greater participation and more fund collection through crowdfunding platforms and mobile banking. To avoid negligence of the *waqf* fund, the respective authorities should lay down detailed rules and regulations of *waqf*. These rules should include accounting, administration and all necessary information.

To conclude, cash *waqf* is essential to help the poor develop. Having considered the models of cash *waqf* in selected countries, the study indicates that a similar experience could be replicated in Somalia if the above recommendations are implemented properly. Consequently, if the problems faced by the structures of the studied countries can be avoided, greater benefits will be achieved. Lastly, effective cash *waqf* management can improve the standard of living and reduce the poverty level in Somalia.

References

Abdul Karim, S. B. (2010). Contemporary Shari'a compliance structuring for the development and management of waqf assets in Singapore. *Kyoto Bulletin of Islamic Area Studies, 3*(2), 143–164.

Adebayo, M. B. (2008). Zakat: The neglected pillar, *Al-Maslaha. Journal of Law and Religion, 4* (1), 144–156.

Ahmad, M. M., & Safiullah, M. (2012). Management of waqf estates in Bangladesh: Towards a sustainable policy formulation. In *Waqf laws and management (with special reference to Malaysia)* (pp. 229–262). New Delhi: Institute of Objective Studies.

Ali, J. A. (2012). *Islamic revivalism encounters the modern world: A study of the Tabligh Jama'at.* New Delhi: Sterling.

Ameen, M. R. (2004). *Ushr in Islamic economy: A pragmatic analysis in the context of Bangladesh.* Dhaka: Islamic Foundation Bangladesh.

Amuda, Y. J., & Embi, N. A. C. (2013). Alleviation of poverty among OIC countries through sadaqat, cash waqf and public funding. *International Journal of Trade, Economics and Finance, 4*(6), 403–408.

Aziz, M. R. A., Yusof, M. A., Johari, F., & Sabri, H. (2014). Relationship between level of income and method of contribution and appointment of Islamic waqf bank as an agent in collecting waqf fund. *Journal of Emerging Economies and Islamic Research, 2*(2), 1–10.

Bank Muamalat Malaysia Berhad. (2014). *Annual report.* Retrieved April 15, 2018, from https://www.muamalat.com.my/downloads/corporate-overview/audited/Audited-Report-31st-March2014.pdf

Beik, I. S., & Arsyianti, L. D. (2013). *Optimization of Zakat instrument in Indonesias' poverty alleviation programme.* Conference Proceedings presented at Poverty Alleviation - Academic Conference, Jakarta, Indonesia. Retrieved September 27, 2014, from http://www.seadiproject.com/post/povertyAleviation%2D%2D-academicconference-2013

Ibrahim, H., Amir, A., & Masron, T. A. (2013). Cash waqf: An innovative instrument for economic development. *International Review of Social Sciences and Humanities, 6*(1), 1–7.

Ismail Abdel Mohsin, M. (2013). Financing through cash-waqf: A revitalization to finance different needs. *International Journal of Islamic and Middle Eastern Finance and Management, 6*(4), 304–321.

Kahf, M. (1998). *Financing the development of Awqaf property*. Seminar on Development of Awqaf by Islamic Research and Training Institute (IRTI), Kuala Lumpur, Malaysia.
Khan, F. (2010). How 'Islamic'is Islamic banking? *Journal of Economic Behavior & Organization, 76*(3), 805–820.
Lahsasna, A. (2010). *The role of cash waqf in financing micro and medium sized enterprises (MMES), a new Islamic financial approach by using cash waqf model*. In Seventh International Conference – The Tawhidi Epistemology: Zakat and waqf economy. Bangi, Selangor. Malaysia.
Mohammad, M. T. S. H. (2011). Towards an Islamic social (waqf) bank. *International Journal of Trade, Economics and Finance, 2*(5), 381–386.
Perbadanan Wakaf Selangor. (2014). *Saham Wakaf Selangor*. Retrieved May 16, 2018, from http://www.wakafselangor.gov.my/index.php/2012-04-27-03-02-07/2012-05-14-15-44-41/saham-wakaf-selangor
Saad, N. M., Kayadibi, S., & Hamid, Z. (2017). The contribution of waqf institutions in Malaysia and Turkey in improving the socio-economic conditions of the society. *Turkish Journal of Islamic Economics, 4*(1), 1–29.
Thoarlim, A., Rahman, M., & Yanya, A. (2017). Cash waqf in Bangladesh and the need for innovative approach towards Awqaf: Lessons from selected countries. *International Journal of Academic Research in Business and Social Sciences, 7*(4), 151–169.
Yayasan Wakaf Malaysia. (2014). *Cara Berwakaf Tunai*. Online Yayasan Wakaf Malaysia. Retrieved May 16, 2018, from https://www.ywm.gov.my/wakaf/tunai-am/cara

Buerhan Saiti is an Associate Professor at Department of Islamic Finance and Economics in Istanbul Sabahattin Zaim University, Turkey. He specialises in Islamic Banking and Finance.

Abdiwali Jama Salad is a Masters student at the Institute of Islamic Banking and Finance, International Islamic University Malaysia, Kuala Lumpur, Malaysia.

Mehmet Bulut is the rector of Istanbul Sabahattin Zaim University, Turkey and professor at Department of Islamic Finance and Economics. His areas of specialisation include International Political Economy, Ottoman Economics and Civilization, Ottoman-European Economic Relations and waqf among others.

A Case Study on the Default of Islamic Financing Facilities: Malaysian Perspective

Aishath Muneeza

Abstract

Default can occur in Islamic banking. As the law applicable to Islamic banking is derived from Shariah, it is imperative to check whether the current practice of Islamic banks in default aligns with Shariah. The objective of this chapter is to discuss the rules and procedures Islamic banks in Malaysia follow in case of default. This is a qualitative research where data from primary sources such as laws on the matter are extracted to derive conclusions and secondary sources such as case laws and other published materials in the subject matter are explored. It is anticipated that the outcome of this chapter will assist to comprehend the way in which Islamic banks deal in case of default and since Malaysia is considered as the cranium of Islamic banking due to the comprehensive ecosystem it has created for Islamic banking and finance, the rest of the world could learn from this case study to enhance the behaviour of Islamic banks in case of default.

1 Introduction

Default risk of customers is unavoidable in Islamic banking. The expectation of customers of Islamic banking in cases of default differs from the customers of conventional banking in the sense that customers of Islamic banks believe that in case of default, the Islamic banks must relinquish the debt based on the Quranic verse 2:280 where it is stated that 'And if someone is in hardship, then [let there be] postponement until [a time of] ease. But if you give [from your right as] charity, then it is better for you, if you only knew'. Since the *lex loci* applicable to Islamic banking

A. Muneeza (✉)
INCEIF, The Global University of Islamic Finance, Lorong Universiti A, Kuala Lumpur, Malaysia
e-mail: muneeza@inceif.org

E. M. Ghazali et al. (eds.), *Management of Shari'ah Compliant Businesses*, Management for Professionals, https://doi.org/10.1007/978-3-030-10907-3_4

is Shariah, it is believed that in case of default, Islamic banks must follow this verse of Quran without any excuse. Often, Islamic banks are criticised due to the way they act in default cases, and this is one of the area in Islamic banking which is not often explored.

The word *dayn* is the Arabic word for debt that implies submission and humiliation. Loan and sale are similar in nature as both contracts involve exchange of properties (Al-Kasani cited in Al Zuhayli, 2003) and are also a form of prepayment (salaf) as one of the two compensations are paid prior to the other (Ibn Qudamah, cited in Al Zuhayli, 2003). Every loan creates debt but not every sale will create debt. If a spot sale or a *musawamah* sale is made where the price and object of sale are exchanged on the spot, there is no chance of creating a debt. However, if the payment of price is deferred for a future date in a sale transaction, for example, as in Bai' Bithaman Ajil (BBA) or if the object of the sale is to be delivered at a future date as in Salam contract, then in a sale transaction a debt can be created.

Loan is permissible in Islam as a charitable contract to assist people in need. This is based on hadith and consensus of Muslim jurists (Al Zuhayli, 2003). Likewise, sale is permitted too. Islamic banking transactions are created using sale contracts, rather than loan contract. As such, debt in Islamic banking transactions normally arise due to default which occur in payment of deferred price as per the agreement made between the Islamic bank and the customer.

The relationship between Islamic banks and the customers is not definitely debtor-creditor relationship as the contracts created between the customer and the bank do not arise from a loan contract. The Shariah sale contracts made between the Islamic bank and the customer will determine the nature of the relationship between the Islamic bank and the customer. Based on the type of relationship between the Islamic bank and the customer, the duty and obligations of them will differ.

For instance, in Malaysia, in an Islamic bank, a customer can open a deposit account or an investment account to keep the money. The deposits account will be structured using the Shariah contract of Wadiah (safekeeping) or Murabahah (cost plus profit sale) or Qard (benevolent placement). This is equivalent to a current/saving account of a conventional bank. An investment account in Islamic banks will be structured using Musharakah (profit and loss sharing) or Mudarabah (profit sharing and loss bearing) or Wakalah (agency agreement). In these contracts returns are based on performance of underlying assets and maturity and withdrawal conditions agreed at inception of the contract. This is equivalent to a fixed deposit account of a conventional bank. The duty owed to the customer by the Islamic bank in this case is huge as any negligence on the part of the Islamic bank may deplete the money customer has invested. Therefore, the operationalisation of investment accounts is governed by the policy document on investment accounts which is issued by the Central Bank of Malaysia in March 2014. This document sets out the capital adequacy and liquidity requirements for investment accounts that reflect their risk-absorbing characteristics, additional disclosure requirements commensurate with the risks assumed by account holders, and responsibilities of Islamic banks to manage the investments in accordance with sound investment principles.

Furthermore, the Islamic banks will not engage in giving of loan by charging interest to third parties to generate profit. It will enter into a Shariah compliant sale contract with the customer and will deal with the sale of real asset or underlying business activity to generate profit. As such, if the Islamic bank gives an Ijarah (lease) financing facility, the legal relationship between the bank and the customer will be that of lessor and lessee. The rights and duties of the respective parties will be determined based on the Shariah rules governing lease.

The objective of this case study is to discuss the rules and procedures Islamic banks follow in case of default in Malaysia. This is a qualitative research where data from primary sources such as laws on the matter are extracted to derive conclusions and secondary sources such as case laws and other published materials in the subject matter is explored.

2 Out of Court Actions Taken by Islamic Banks in Default Cases: Evidence From Malaysian Case Law

In sale contracts, default may occur due to the deferred component of price. In Malaysia, numerous case laws have been reported on Islamic banking. In order to determine the behaviour of Islamic banks in cases of default, it is imperative to analyse these cases and derive conclusions on the matter. However, in most of the reported case law, the facts are silent about the actions taken by the Islamic banks before the matter is brought to the court. The analysis of the case law shows that negotiation, restructuring and serving of letter of demand to principal debtor and guarantors have been made before the matter is brought to the court. An example of each of these instances is discussed below by showing evidence from case law.

1. **Negotiation**

   In the case of Kamuja Hartamas Sdn Bhd v Bank Kerjasama Rakyat Malaysia Bhd[2017] MLJU 168, the Plaintiff had first filed an action against the First Defendant vide Civil Action No.D22A-743-2010 claiming the sum due and payable in respect of the Tranche1. However, the said action was withdrawn against the defendants with liberty to file afresh, pending settlement negotiations between parties. From this case it is evident that negotiation is given consideration before the matter is taken to the final stage of the court. It must be noted that this case involved a company rather than a natural person.

   Sulh literally means 'to cut off a dispute' or 'to finish a dispute' either directly or with the help of a neutral third party. Arbitration is governed by different regulations; therefore arbitration does not come under sulh. Sulh includes negotiation. Mejelle has formulated 40 articles to deal with sulh (from Articles 1531–1571). This proves that in Islam (not only the sulh), the word exists, but the procedures which are in a codified form exist as well (Muneeza, 2010).
2. **Restructuring**

   In the case of Maybank Islamic Bhd v J and M Power Resources Sdn Bhd and Ors [2017] MLJ 196, the Plaintiff has provided Islamic Banking facilities to the

First Defendant in the sum of RM4 million. The facilities were restructured in 2009 and converted into Bai Bithaman Ajil Facility ('BBA'), and the BBA was secured by a fresh and Joint and Several Guarantee of the Second Defendant and the existing Joint and Several Guarantee of the Third and Fourth Defendants. When the Defendants failed to regularise the BBA Facility Accounts, a Notice of Demand was issued, and the facility was subsequently terminated. The Plaintiff then sued the Defendants, and after hearing the parties, a summary judgement was allowed by the court against the First, Second and Third Defendants on 19 November 2012. From the facts of this case, it is clear that the facility involved in the case was restructured. As such, it shows the willingness and the efforts of the Islamic banks to provide amicable solutions to default before the matter is taken to the court.

Restructuring of indebtedness or debt restructuring is a process that allows debtor who is facing cash flow problems and financial distress to reduce and renegotiate its delinquent debts in order to improve or restore liquidity and rehabilitate its position so that it can continue its operations.

3. **Notice of Demand to the Principal Debtor and Guarantors**

In the case of Bank Muamalat Malaysia Bhd v Ten-Tel Construction Sdn Bhd and Ors [2017] MLJ 398, it is stated that the plaintiff through its solicitors Messrs. Ramli Amar Jit & Tan sent a notice of demand to the defendants to remedy the default, and it is refusal to adhere to notice which led to the plaintiff to take the matter to the court. In the case of Bank Muamalat Malaysia Bhd and Ors v Redha Resources Sdn Bhd and Ors [2017], 2 MLJ 686 notice of demand issued by the solicitor demanding the amount due was not adhered to by the respondents, and a subsequent notice of termination dated 20 January 2014 determined the Islamic syndicated financing and demanded the sum due of RM326,669,571.59 inclusive of ta'widh, as at 30 September 2014 was sent. It is stated in the facts of this case that concurrent to the demand made on the first respondent, a demand on the guarantors on a joint and several liability basis was also issued for the same amount.

It is evident from the above case that serving notice of demand aligns with the principles of Shariah and that adequate time to rectify the matter is given.

There are numerous advantages of these out of court actions taken by the Islamic banks in case of default as these actions taken provides flexibility to parties and assists the defaulted party from going through a bankruptcy proceedings against him in the court. Furthermore, it allows business experts to meet and settle the issues in a less costly and efficient manner without disclosing the critical information making recovery more effective. However, in case out of court actions taken by the Islamic banks, going to the court is necessary to protect the rights of the Islamic banks. In such instances, like conventional banks, Islamic banks also have guidelines to follow which are imposed by the central banks and other regulatory authorities of the financial institutions.

3 3.0 Guidelines on Classification of Impaired Loans/Financing and Provisioning for Bad and Doubtful Debts

It is often said that the biggest challenge facing Islamic banks in cases of debt is to differentiate between the genuine defaulters and intentional defaulters. Genuine defaulters can be defined as those debtors who are unable to pay debt for the reason that they do not have sufficient funds with them to pay it. The genuine defaulters can be further classified into those who are bankrupt and those who are not bankrupt, but due to sudden change of circumstance beyond their control has led to a situation where by the debtor is unable to have sufficient funds to pay back the amount owing to the creditor. On the other hand, the intentional defaulters can be defined as those debtors who default in paying debt even though they have enough funds to pay it. Those debtors who are negligent or reckless in paying can fall under this category.

In this regard it is important to see the guidelines made on the default by the central banks. An example of guidelines made in this regard by a central bank is guideline on classification of impaired loans/financing and provisioning for bad and doubtful debts (BNM/RH/GL 007-17). The guidelines set out the minimum requirements on the classification of impaired loans/financing and provisioning for loan/financing impairment with the adoption of FRS 139—*Financial Instruments: Recognition and Measurement* issued by the Malaysian Accounting Standards Board. It is stated that these guidelines shall be read together with the best practices for the management of credit risk issued by Bank Negara Malaysia that are relevant to classification and provisioning practices. It is also specifically stated there that loans/financing for the purpose of these guidelines includes all facilities provided by the banking institution to a customer which give rise to a credit exposure to the customer. Some of the crucial aspects dealt in these guidelines are credit risk grading, rescheduled and restructured loans/financing, sound loan/financing impairment methodology, use of experienced credit judgement and classification of loans/financing as impaired.

Paragraph 7 of the guidelines deal with credit risk grading where it is stated that banking institutions shall have in place a systematic and consistently applied process to reliably classify loans/financing on the basis of credit risk by supporting the prudent valuation of loans/financing and determination of appropriate impairment provisions for loans/financing.

Paragraph 8 of the guidelines state that banking institutions must have in place policies approved by the board which define the circumstances and conditions under which a loan/financing may be rescheduled or restructured. These policies should address controls to avoid 'ever-greening' of loans/financing, including situations where loans/financing may be rescheduled or restructured more than once, and provisioning policies with respect to such loans/financing; compliance with Shariah rules and principles in rescheduling or restructuring of financing for Islamic banking institutions. This may include administrative policies on the performance of a new agreement ('aqad) and the treatment of charges, i.e. capitalisation of compensation amounts in relation to the restructured financing, and a repayment period (based on the revised and restructured term) to be continuously observed before the rescheduled and restructured facilities can be reclassified as non-impaired.

Paragraph 9 of the guidelines state that banking institutions shall develop and implement a sound loan/financing impairment methodology to identify, monitor, measure and report the quality of the loan/financing portfolio. The methodology should be supported by sound analysis, procedures and information systems and should include criteria for the early identification and reporting of potential problem loans/financing to ensure that they are appropriately monitored, administered and provided for when required.

Paragraph 10 of the guidelines states that credit judgement used to complement historical loss experience or observable data in assessing the loan/financing impairment provisions shall be exercised by an appropriate level of management.

Section C of the guidelines under paragraph 11 deals with the classification of financing as impaired. It is stated that the banking institutions shall, in addition to the disclosure requirements under the applicable IFRS 7 (Financial Instruments: Disclosures) based on repayment conduct, classify a loan/financing as impaired where the principal or interest/profit or both (in the case of credit card facilities, the amount past due refers to the minimum monthly repayments) are past due for more than 90 days or 3 months, and in the case of revolving facilities (e.g. overdraft facilities), the facility shall be classified as impaired where the outstanding amount has remained in excess of the approved limit for a period of more than 90 days or 3 months, or where the amount is past due or the outstanding amount has been in excess of the approved limit for 90 days or 3 months or less, the loan/financing exhibits weaknesses that render a classification appropriate according to the banking institution's credit risk grading framework.

It is also stated that where repayments are scheduled on intervals of 3 months or longer, the loan/financing is classified as impaired as soon as a default (inability to meet the contractual repayment terms) occurs, unless it does not exhibit any weakness that would render it classified according to the banking institution's credit risk grading framework.

Where moratorium on loan/financing repayments is granted in relation to the rescheduling and restructuring exercised, classification of a loan/financing as impaired under as previously stated shall exclude the moratorium period granted; and banking institutions are required to maintain appropriate information on these customers for the Bank's review as and when required.

Rescheduled and restructured facilities can only be reclassified as non-impaired when repayments based on the revised or restructured terms have been observed continuously for a period as determined by the banking institution's policy on rescheduled and restructured facilities. For rescheduling and restructuring of facilities where the amount is past due for 90 days or 3 months or less, these accounts shall be classified as impaired if they exhibit any weaknesses that render such classification as appropriate according to the banking institution's credit risk grading framework.

However, loans/financing rescheduled or restructured by Agensi Kaunseling dan Pengurusan Kredit (AKPK) may be immediately classified as non-impaired once customers and the banking institutions have agreed to the new terms and conditions.

4 AKPK (Credit Counselling and Debt Management Agency, Malaysia) Model to Provide Relief to Debtors of Islamic Banks

There is an existing model in Malaysia introduced in providing relief to the debtors obtaining financing facilities from banks found practically. This model provides a precautionary way of avoiding default, and the other model is to provide relief when the debtor gets defaulted. This is via Credit Counselling and Debt Management Agency.

The Credit Counselling and Debt Management Agency, or commonly known as Agensi Kaunseling dan Pengurusan Kredit (AKPK), is an agency set up by Bank Negara Malaysia, which is the Central Bank of Malaysia in April 2006 to help individuals take control of their financial situation and gain peace of mind that comes from the wise use of credit. The vision of the agency is to make prudent financial management a way of life, and the mission is to create a society that is financially savvy by getting recognition as the trusted provider of financial education to adult consumers and continue to promote financial prudence. For individuals AKPK provides financial counselling, Debt Management Program (DMP) and voluntary arrangement. For corporate AKPK provides financial education, corporate communications and Debt Management Programme (DMP) engagement.

This is an important initiative as before a debtor gets defaulted, he/she can be made aware of the consequences he/she will face. Financial literacy is conducted via this agency, and debt issues can be discussed with the professional counsellors who have the competency to advise on control measures. Furthermore, even if a person is unable to act on the advice given, he/she may opt to apply online to debt management service. The website of the authority provides a calculator function for budgeting, credit card, housing, hire purchase and net worth and is a user-friendly website where lot of information is provided.

DMP is a customised programme, where our credit counsellors will work with customers (person who applies for the programme) to develop a personalised debt repayment plan in consultation and agreement with customer's financial service providers. DMP is available to all individuals who need assistance in managing their personal debts with the participating financial service providers. In providing DMP service, the authority plays a vital role in negotiating with the banks to restructure or reschedule the facilities taken. AKPK's debt management service model is a doable model and which can be adopted in other countries to ensure that burden of debt does not prevent people from enjoying life. In this model, the approach taken is self-help assistance seeking mechanism, and the assistance provided is effective enough to change the situation of the worried debtor. There is no fee for a customer to engage in a counselling session and/or if a customer wish to engage a DMP.

Hashim and Syazana (2017) stated that out of the total number of individuals who had sought financial counselling and advice from AKPK, 29% of them were enrolled into DMP, representing a total debt value of RM21.7 billion. To date, 15,439 borrowers representing 8% of DMP participants have fully settled their debts and graduated from the programme, and about 60% of DMP participants remain active in servicing their debt, while the remaining 32% had either withdrawn from the DMP or had their participation terminated (Hashim & Syazana, 2017). According to Hashim and Syazana (2017), the most common reasons for withdrawal or termination include improved financial circumstances that enable borrowers to fully settle or manage the debt on their own, the death of a participant or the inability to make debt repayments on a consistent basis, and proactive interventions by AKPK play an important role in supporting DMP participants in meeting and sustaining their repayment obligations which include issuing early payment reminders, offering a 'Second Chance' programme to prospective defaulters and active monitoring of payments from all new DMP participants during the first 3 months after being enrolled into DMP under the 'Early Care' initiative to shape good repayment habits. These interventions have contributed towards reducing the numbers of borrowers that are terminated from DMP, from 35% in 2016 to 25% in 2017, and furthermore, the annual debt collected by AKPK under the DMP has increased significantly to RM877 million in 2017 (Hashim & Syazana, 2017).

Furthermore, in the Product Disclosure Sheets of products offered by Islamic banks, there is a clause inserted as below by all banks:

> If you have difficulties in making the monthly installment payments, you should contact us earliest possible to discuss the payment options. Alternatively, you may seek the services of Agensi Kaunseling dan Pengurusan Kredit (AKPK), an agency established by Bank Negara Malaysia to provide free services and money management, credit counseling, financial education and debt restructuring for individuals. You can contact AKPK at. . .

The above statement gives the knowledge of the existence of AKPK to the customers, and they were given a contact number to contact too in case they need assistance in this regard.

5 Conclusion

It is evident that Malaysia has put in place various mechanisms to tackle default cases of Islamic financing facilities including a relief mechanism for customers to deal with default. The analysis of case law and discussion on guidelines on classification of impaired loans/financing and provisioning for bad and doubtful debts proves the existence of procedures for Islamic banks to deal in default cases in Malaysia. Establishment of AKPK shows the humanist approach used in dealing with default case to give relief to those debtors who face hardship in paying debt, and this is indeed an inspiration to the rest of the world. Furthermore, the clause about AKPK inserted to product disclosure sheets provide the information of the role of AKPK to all customers taking Islamic banking facilities is an important document that makes customers of Islamic banks aware about steps they could take if they feel they are having financial hardship. Dealing with default case is not easy task for any financial institution, and this case study of Malaysia shows that it is important to put in place policies to deal with default to provide justice to all parties involved in the transaction.

References

Al Zuhayli, W. (2003). *Financial transactions in Islamic jurisprudence*. Damascus: Dar Al Fikr.

Bank Muamalat Malaysia Bhd & Ors v Redha Resources Sdn Bhd & Ors. (2017). 2 MLJ 686.

Bank Muamalat Malaysia Bhd v Ten-Tel Construction Sdn Bhd & Ors. (2017). MLJ 398.

Bank Negara Malaysia. (N/A). *Guidelines on classification of impaired loans/financing and provisioning for bad and doubtful debts*. Retrieved September 1, 2018, from http://www.bnm.gov.my/guidelines/01_banking/04_prudential_stds/02_gp3_20110613.pdf

Hashim, S., & Syazana, L. (2017). *AKPK – Advancing prudent financial behaviour*. Retrieved September 1, 2018, from http://www.bnm.gov.my/files/publication/fsps/en/2017/cp02_001_box.pdf

Kamuja Hartamas Sdn Bhd v Bank Kerjasama Rakyat Malaysia Bhd. (2017). MLJ 168.

Maybank Islamic Bhd v J & M Power Resources Sdn Bhd & Ors. (2017). MLJ 196.

Muneeza, A. (2010). Is conventional alternative dispute resolution to Islamic law? *Malayan Law Journal, 4*(1), xcvii–xccix.

Aishath Muneeza is an Associate Professor at INCEIF, Malaysia. She is the first female Deputy Minister of Ministry of Islamic Affairs and is the Deputy Minister of Ministry of Finance & Treasury of Republic of Maldives. She is also the chairwoman of Maldives Center for Islamic Finance. She has assisted more than 11 institutions to offer Islamic financial products/services.

Employee Provident Funds' Market Performance: The Case of Malaysia

Mamunur Rashid and William Kong Choon San

Abstract

The ability to time the market and having superior asset selection capabilities indicate violation of efficient market theory. Past studies tested Treynor-Mazuy model to investigate performance of mutual fund managers. This current study has employed similar concepts to measure performance of the Malaysian employee provident fund (EPF). The study has considered Malaysian EPFs over a period 1986–2016 using yearly dividends of EPF, Malaysia market index (KLCI) and Malaysia government bond, as a proxy for the risk-free rate. Treynor and Mazuy model was employed alongside ARDL to get estimates for timing, selectivity and performance indicators. Results indicate that Malaysian pension funds outperform the market index but with a weak market timing ability. The results also indicate that market index does not influence EPF returns. As Malaysian EPF is now *Shari'ah* compliant, the findings will carry significant policy implications for Muslim investors, fund managers in other Islamic markets and regulators of *Shari'ah*-compliant fund markets.

1 Performance of EPF

Retirement planning is important for socio-economic development of a country. Even though financial planning and behavioural attributes mediate the relationship between financial literacy and retirement planning, only 5% of the Malaysians are

M. Rashid (✉)
School of Business and Economics, Universiti Brunei Darussalam, Gadong, Brunei
e-mail: mamunur.rashid@ubd.edu.bn

W. K. C. San
Nottingham University Business School, University of Nottingham Malaysia, Semenyih, Malaysia

E. M. Ghazali et al. (eds.), *Management of Shari'ah Compliant Businesses*, Management for Professionals, https://doi.org/10.1007/978-3-030-10907-3_5

prepared for the retirement (Yoong, See, & Baronovich, 2012). Consequently, governments had to plan a compulsory retirement planning to ensure financial safety of a major portion of the population (Boon, Yee, & Ting, 2011; Folk, Beh, & Baranovich, 2012; Moorthy et al., 2012). Having an average lifespan of 74.7 years in Malaysia, the Malaysian government extended the retirement age from 55 to 60.[1,2] If Malaysian government does not increase the retirement age further, Malaysian employee provident fund (EPF) saving will be insufficient for individuals to spend during their retirement stage.

An Employee Provident Fund (EPF) is a compulsory pension fund where every working adult in Malaysia is to have a saving and retirement plan. EPF in Malaysia is managed by Kumpulan Wang Simpanan Pekerja (KWSP), a federal statutory body under the Ministry of Finance in Malaysia, which is established in 1951 for managing retirement savings and to offer reasonable dividends (minimum of 2.5% annually). Over the years, EPF continues to grow with the size of dividends, offering a relatively secure investment opportunity for Malaysians. Investments in EPF can be compared with other investment opportunities in financial markets or with banks. Since large pension funds can impact the performance and liquidity of financial markets (Allen, 2001), it is important to know whether Malaysian EPFs can significantly earn better return than the overall market return.

Extant literature on Malaysian EPFs discusses the behavioural intention, financial planning and financial literacy issues impacting retirement planning (Ng et al., 2011). EPF in Malaysia is the largest fund and has played vital role in financial development. Moreover, according to KWSP (2017), Simpanan *Shari'ah* has been launched in January 2017. Hence, Muslims will be interested in EPFs more than before. Motivation for this research emerges from two dimensions: firstly, introduction of *Shari'ah* compliant EPF, and secondly, timing and selectivity skills of EPF managers. This study adds to the literature from these two dimensions by measuring performance of Malaysian EPFs over a period from 1986 to 2016 using yearly dividend of EPF, Malaysia market index (KLCI) and Malaysia government bond as a proxy for the risk-free rate. Treynor and Mazuy (1966) model was employed alongside ARDL to get estimates for timing, selectivity and performance indicators. Our results indicate that Malaysian pension funds outperform the market index but show a weak market timing ability. The results also indicate that market index does not influence EPF returns.

There are roughly 15 million (14,806,595 to be exact) EPF members in Malaysia, of which only around half (6,882,983 to be exact) are still actively contributing to the EPF. Total investment is estimated to increase from RM 684 billion in 2015 to RM 731 billion in 2016. In 2016, EPF has paid out 5.7% as dividend, which is equivalent to RM 37 billion, while a total of RM 46 billion has been withdrawn from EPF in

[1]http://www.thestar.com.my/news/nation/2016/05/04/malaysians-not-saving-enough-for-retirement/

[2]http://www.thestar.com.my/news/nation/2017/04/08/govt-studying-viability-of-extending-retirement-age-to-65/

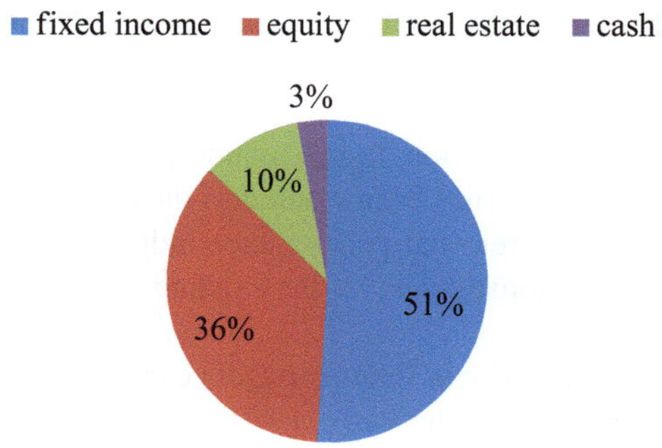

Fig. 1 EPF asset allocation in Malaysia in the year 2016. Source: KWSP (2017)

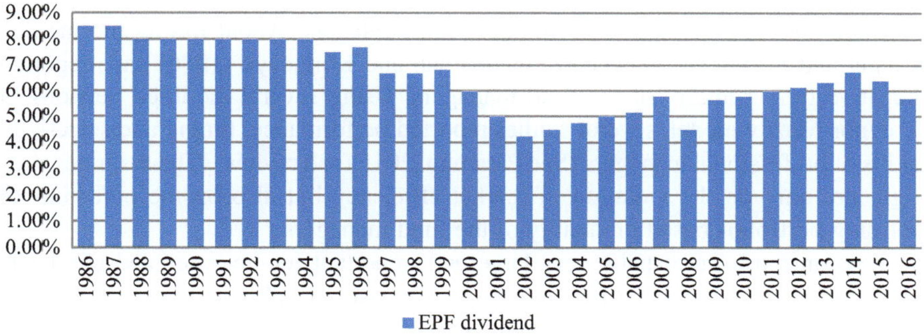

Fig. 2 History of EPF dividend rate in Malaysia. Source: KWSP (2017)

2016. Figure 1 shows allocation of EPF investment in Malaysia for the year 2016. More than half of the assets were allocated in fixed income securities. Figure 2 shows the history of dividend rate of EPF in Malaysia. The dividend rate fell after Asian crisis and started falling again since 2014 until the most recent data shown for the year 2016. The recent fall in dividend rate signifies the need for active management of investment for EPF holders.

Tan Sri Samsudin, the Chairman of KWSP, said that the FTSE Bursa Malaysia KLCI, which was exposed (almost by 33%) by the banking sector, yielded negative return for the third consecutive years (KWSP, 2017). While on the global front, the crude oil price, which tumbled to as low as USD 30 per barrel, had significantly affected the valuation of oil and gas companies. However, EPF still managed to deliver above average performance as EPF investment stood at RM 731.11 billion, indicating a healthy EPF portfolio. According to EPF Chief Executive Officer (CEO) Datuk Shahril Ridza Ridzuan, the initial size of Islamic fund is RM 100 billion, which is equivalent to about 15% of the total asset of EPF (KWSP, 2017). Considering the size of Islamic EPF, further research on Islamic EPF is warranted.

2 Islamic Employee Mutual Fund: Is It Different than Conventional?

Despite the importance of pension funds, major portion of researches on fund management and performance has been catered to the mutual fund industry. In this section, the study discusses relevant performance indicators of both pension funds and mutual funds to get a holistic view of the existing trends in and determinants of performance.

Whether or not the professional fund managers can outperform the market—has been an important question in the early 1970s. To simplify, it will be a gross violation of market efficiency if fund managers can pick efficient combinations of assets or can time the market efficiently on a risk-adjusted basis. Studies done by Jensen (1968), Chang and Lewellen (1984), Elton et al. (1993) have reported average return earned by fund managers. Bello and Janjigian (1997) have reported a positive security selection by mutual fund managers. About timing the market, Chang and Lewellen (1984) and Jagannathan and Korajczyk (1986) have reported negative timing ability of the fund managers. Using several modified versions of Treynor-Mazuy model, several studies reported performance, timing and selectivity skills of professional managers (See Paramita, 2015 for a review). These studies shed light not only on the violation of market efficiency but also on the potentials of forming portfolios based on quality of the fund managers.

Pension funds are usually very large and important for investors and regulators (Lakonishok et al., 1991). Main advantage of pension fund is its long-term liability structure, which enables pension fund to invest in long-term illiquid assets (Novy-Marx & Rauh, 2011). Pension fund faces an environment different from mutual fund as mutual fund manager receives cash inflow based on their mutual fund performances (Sirri & Tufano, 1998). Income of EPF does not depend on the fund performances, but on actuarial and demographic factors (Andonov, 2014).

Earlier evidences suggest that the ability of the pension fund outperform the market (Andonov, 2014). Analysing 774 US and Canadian pension funds from 1990 to 2008, Andonov finds that majority of the pension funds have similar asset allocation, and 55% of the pension fund has allocated asset in equity while 35% in fixed income and the remaining 10% in different alternative asset classes. Moreover, Andonov reports an annual alpha of 17 basis points from changes in asset allocation, 27 basis points from market timing and 45 basis points from security selection.

Due to limited research on EPF, this study will rely on performance of mutual funds, primarily because of two reasons: firstly, there are significant numbers of researches available on performance, timing and selectivity of mutual fund managers, and secondly, research on mutual fund performance is available for both Islamic and conventional funds.

The Islamic mutual fund or *Shari'ah* Fund is one of the fastest growing sectors in the Islamic financial system (Elfakhani, Hassan, & Sidani, 2005). Albaity and Ahmad (2008), Hussein and Omran (2005) and Ahmad and Ibrahim (2002) provide empirical evidence that conventional stock outperform Islamic stock. While Edward and Doug (2010), Mansor and Bhatti (2011), and Lean and Parsva (2012) show a different result where Islamic indices or ethical investments produce more returns than conventional investment.

Often, there is considerable difference between ethical and Islamic funds. Islamic funds are screened using *Shari'ah* screening methodology (Rashid, Hassan, Amin, & Samina, 2017). Taking ethical funds as a benchmark, Atta (2000) reported that the Islamic index outperformed a sample of unscreened ethical benchmark using Sharpe, Treynor and the unconditional Jensen measures. Luther, Matatko and Corner (1992) provided evidence that in the UK, the ethical fund outperformed the conventional fund. Gregory, Matatko and Luther (1997), however, reported no significant difference between the outcomes from an ethical and conventional fund.

Ahmad (2006) compared the performances of Islamic and conventional unit trust funds in Malaysia for a period starting from February 2000 to February 2003 (36 months) and reported a different result that the Islamic fund did not outperform the conventional funds. Particularly due to defensive nature of investment, Islamic funds, however, reported lower volatility than the conventional funds.

Khan et al. (2015) undertook samples from Pakistan for 7 years ranging from 2007 to 2013 and indicated that the portfolio return of the Islamic funds were less volatile than their conventional counterparts. For the overall performance, Islamic funds outperformed the conventional funds. Mansor (2012) found similar results that Islamic fund outperformed the conventional funds during pre-financial crisis and financial crisis periods. Using Malaysian sample, Mansor reported that Islamic fund managers had superior fund selectivity skills, but no evidence of the market timing ability. Confirming similar results in a large sample, Boo, Ee, Li, and Rashid (2017) reported a relatively lower value at risk (VaR) for Islamic mutual funds, which indicated a better risk management by Islamic fund managers. Analysing momentum returns in funds, Li et al. (2016b) reported strong return persistence of *Shari'ah*-compliant funds in Malaysia, which was attributed to underreaction hypothesis. Covering a global sample, Li et al. (2016a, b) reported momentum return for *Shari'ah* complaint portfolios in Pakistan and Malaysia. Small size return reversal was identified as the primary reason behind such trend. These recent analyses on Islamic funds and equities urge more research on performance of other relevant funds in Islamic universe.

3 The Case: Performance of Malaysian EPF

This study conducted two empirical tests. Treynor and Mazuy (1966) model was used in the first stage to examine timing and security selection ability of the EPFs. A second test was conducted to estimate the long-run coefficients of the parameters using ARDL. ARDL offers several benefits, while the approach does not necessitate the variables to be stationary at the same order (Pesaran & Pesaran, 1997; Pesaran, Shin, & Smith, 2001). Similar to Andonov (2014), this study employed yearly EPF dividend rate as the dependent variable, treasure bond's rate as the risk-free rate and Kuala Lumpur Composite Index (KLCI) as the benchmark. Data stream was used to collect data on EPF dividends and treasury rates. This study covered from 1986 to 2016 (31 years), which is relatively larger than other representative studies on fund performance. Before running Treynor and Mazuy model, usual time series data to check the prerequisites (i.e. unit root, etc.) were conducted. Test results for these time series prerequisites are given in Appendix 1. Treynor and Mazuy model is given below in Eq. (1). The difference with the standard CAPM is the additional term c $(r_m - r_f)^2$. If 'c' turns out to be positive and significant, then there is evidence of the timing ability. The idea behind this formula is that manager is able to forecast what will happen in the market and attempt to profit from the forecast.

$$r_i - r_f = \alpha_i + \beta_i(r_m - r_f) + c(r_m - r_f)^2 + \varepsilon_i \tag{1}$$

where:

r_i—return on asset of the selected fund.
r_f—risk-free rate return.
α_i—alpha or selectivity ability.
r_m—return on stock market.
c—the parameter measuring the market timing performance. If $c > 0$, the fund represents better timing ability.

According to Ferson and Schadt (1996), alpha measures the risk-adjusted performance of a security or portfolio in relation to the expected return of the market. A positive alpha indicates that the portfolio return is above the expected return. To simplify alpha, it tells investor whether the portfolio is worth investing. Hence, creating a positive alpha warrants superior asset picking ability of the fund managers. Beta measures how much an asset moves with the benchmark.

Table 1 presents summary of the results on selection and timing ability of EPF and relationship between market return and the EPF return. The alpha represents the selective ability of EPF managers. A positive and significant alpha shows that EPF manager had superior selection ability and was able to outperform the market. The results indicate that EPF has outperformed the market by 2.25% for the last 30 years. Our results show a negative but statistically insignificant beta. This indicates that the movement of the market has no significant impact on EPF performance. The parameter represents the timing ability of EPF managers, which refers to the ability to anticipate the market movement. The result shows a positive timing ability at 10% significance level. This shows that there is relatively weaker evidence on the EPF managers timing the market efficiently.

Table 1 Summary of the results for timing, selection abilities and performance

Variables (measuring)	Coefficient	t	Prob.
Alpha (selection ability)	0.023	3.346	0.004
Beta (market having influence on EPF)	−0.004	−0.422	0.679
Parameter (timing ability)	0.030	1.776	0.095

Note: Adjusted R-squared is 0.434
Source: Authors' own table, 2018

Table 2 ARDL long-run coefficients

Variable	Coefficient	*t*	Prob.
Parameter (timing ability)	−0.064	−1.846	0.083
Beta (market having influence on EPF)	−0.033	−1.131	0.274
Alpha (selection ability)	0.032	6.525	0.000

Source: Authors' own table, 2108

At present, the literature is limited in offering an explanation to such results. Hence, the study offers results from ARDL-based test to unearth long-term estimates. Table 2 can also be considered as a robustness check for the results analysed from Treynor and Mazuy model. The long-run coefficients also show that EPF managers have superior selection ability. However, the coefficient for timing ability is negative in the long-run, even though the variable is significant at 10%. Persistent negative coefficient for timing ability may indicate wrong anticipation of the market performance by EPF managers. Negative but insignificant coefficient of beta, which measures the market performance having an influence on EPF, indicates that the market does not influence the EPF returns even in the long-run.

Overall, results using the Treynor and Mazuy model and ARDL long-run coefficients indicate that EPF managers have better selection ability. The market does not influence EPF. Market timing ability has been inconsistent.

4 Implications for Fund Managers

This study has considered a sample of dividend returns of EPF from Malaysia to investigate the fund's ability to outperform the market. Based on finance theory, on mutual fund management, the presence of market timing ability and selectivity skills results in gross violation of the efficient market theory (Fama, 1972). Extant studies tested these for mutual funds. This study tested the Treynor and Mazuy model in identifying the timing and selection ability of the EPF managers by taking Malaysian EPF as an example. To a greater extent, to support the behaviourism in finance, EPF managers do select better than others and experience superior timing ability, and the market performance does not influence the EPF return. These results indicate violation of efficient market hypothesis and offer significant fund management potentials for managers, EPF savers and relevant stakeholders alike. Since 2017 Malaysian EPF has considered investing in Islamic funds, these performance indicators may lead to significant policy implications for *Shari'ah* scholar and regulators.

Despite measurement and benchmark errors often cited as major issues with Treynor and Mazuy model (Perrina, 1999), this study offers an estimate of the performance of EPF managers in Malaysia. Due to extreme data shortage, the study could not compare the difference between Islamic EPF and conventional EPF in separate models. Future studies may take a lead on this to give significant inputs to *Shari'ah* scholars on financial and retirement planning for Muslims.

Appendix 1

Augmented Dickey Fuller test

Variable	Level	First difference	Test critical value at 1%
rp-rf	1.180761	−4.960818	−3.711457
b(rm-rf)	−6.94959	−8.023655	−3.689194
c(rm-rf)^2	−5.48607	−3.602183	−3.72407

Source: Authors' own

The data series are nonstationary in level but stationary in the first difference for variable rp-rf. The remaining two variables are stationary in level without differencing

Johansen-Juselius Cointegration test

	All period		5% critical value	
Null hypothesis	Trace	Max	Trace	Max
Ho: $r = 0$	52.81716	22.28202	29.79707	21.13162
Ho: $r \leq 1$	30.53514	22.0844	15.49471	14.2646
Ho: $r \leq 2$	8.450732	8.450732	3.841466	3.841466

Source: Authors' own

References

Ahmad, M. (2006). The comparison of performance of Islamic and conventional unit trust funds in Malaysia. *Banker's Journal Malaysia, 1*(1), 1–26.

Ahmad, Z., & Ibrahim, H. (2002). A study of performance of the KLSE Syariah index. *Malaysian Management Journal, 6*(1&2), 25–34.

Albaity, M., & Ahmad, R. (2008). Performance of Syariah and composite indices: Evidence from Bursa Malaysia. *Asian Academy of Management Journal of Accounting and Finance, 4*(1), 23–43.

Allen, F. (2001). Presidential address: Do financial institutions matter. *Journal of Finance, 56*(4), 1165–1175.

Andonov, A. (2014). *Pension fund asset allocation and performance*. PhD. Thesis, Maastricht University School of Business and Economics, Maastricht.

Atta, H. (2000). *Ethical rewards*. University of Durham. Retrieved August 3, 2017, from http://www.djindexes.com/mdsidx/downloads/thesis.pdf

Bello, Z. Y., & Janjigian, V. (1997). A re-examination of the market-timing and security-selection performance of mutual funds. *Financial Analysts Journal, 53*(5), 24–30.

Boo, Y. L., Ee, M. S., Li, B., & Rashid, M. (2017). Islamic or conventional mutual funds: Who has the upper hand? Evidence from Malaysia. *Pacific-Basin Finance Journal, 42*, 183–192.

Boon, T. H., Yee, H. S., & Ting, H. W. (2011). Financial literacy and personal financial planning in Klang Valley. *Malaysia International Journal of Economics and Management, 5*(1), 149–168.

Chang, E. C., & Lewellen, W. G. (1984). Market timing and mutual fund investment performance. *Journal of Business, 57*(1), 57–72.

Edward, C., & Doug, W. (2010). Performance evaluation of U.S. socially responsible mutual funds: Revisiting doing good and doing well. *American Journal of Business, 25*(1), 9–24.

Elfakhani, S., Hassan, M. K., & Sidani, Y. (2005, December). *Comparative performance of Islamic versus secular mutual funds*. In 12th Economic Research Forum Conference in Cairo, Egypt, pp. 19–21.

Elton, E. J., Gruber, M. J., Das, S., & Hlavka, M. (1993). Efficiency with costly information: A reinterpretation of evidence from managed portfolios. *The Review of Financial Studies, 6*(1), 1–22.

Fama, E. (1972). Components of investment performance. *Journal of Finance, 27*(2), 551–567.

Ferson, W. E., & Schadt, R. W. (1996). Measuring fund strategy and performance in changing economic conditions. *The Journal of Finance, 51*(2), 425–461.

Folk, J. Y., Beh, L. S., & Baranovich, D. L. (2012). Financial education: Determinant of retirement planning in Malaysia. *E3 Journal of Business Management & Economics, 3*(2), 69–78.

Gregory, A., Matatko, J., & Luther, R. (1997). Ethical unit trust financial performance: Small company effects and fund size effects. *Journal of Business Finance and Accounting, 24*(5), 705–725.

Hussein, K., & Omran, M. (2005). Ethical investment revisited: Evidence from Dow Jones Islamic indexes. *Journal of Investing, 14*(3), 105–124.

Jagannathan, R., & Korajczyk, R. A. (1986). Assessing the market timing performance of managed portfolios. *Journal of Business, 59*(2), 217–235.

Jensen, M. C. (1968). The performance of mutual funds in the period 1954–1964. *Journal of Finance, 23*(2), 389–416.

Khan, M. M. S., Gillani, S. H. B., & Mansoor, S. (2015). Performance of Islamic mutual funds: A comparison with conventional mutual funds. *Islamic Banking and Finance Review, 2*(1), 29–39.

KWSP. (2017). *Achieving a better future*, Annual Report. Retrieved August 3, 2017, from http://www.kwsp.gov.my/portal/documents/10180/6184569/Facts_at_a_Glance_2016.pdf

Lakonishok, J., Shleifer, A., Thaler, R. & Vishny, R. (1991). *Window dressing by pension fund managers* (Paper no: w3617). National Bureau of Economic Research.

Lean, H. H., & Parsva, P. (2012). Performance of Islamic indices in Malaysia FSTE market: Empirical evidence from CAPM. *Journal of Applied Sciences, 12*(12), 1274–1281.

Li, B., Ee, M. S., Boo, Y. L., & Rashid, M. (2016). The last Alibi: Shari'ah compliant stocks on momentum profitability assessment. In D. S. Mutum, M. M. Butt, & M. Rashid (Eds.), *Advances in Islamic finance, marketing, and management*, pp. 3–26.

Li, B., Ee, M. S., & Rashid, M. (2016). Is momentum trading profitable from Shari'ah compliant stocks? *Review of Financial Economics, 31*, 56–63.

Luther, R., Matatko, J., & Corner, D. (1992). The investment performance of UK "ethical" unit trusts. *Accounting Auditing & Accountability Journal, 5*(4). https://doi.org/10.1108/09513579210019521

Mansor, F. (2012). *Investment performance of Islamic versus conventional mutual funds: Evidence from Malaysia*. Doctoral dissertation, La Trobe University.

Mansor, F., & Bhatti, M. (2011). The Islamic mutual fund performance: New evidence on market timing and stock selectivity. *International Conference on Economics and Finance Research, 4*, 477–484.

Moorthy, M. K., Durai, T., Chelliah, L., Sien, C. S., Leong, L. C., Kai, N. Z., Rhu, W. C., & Teng, W. Y. (2012). A Study on the retirement planning behaviour of working individuals in Malaysia. *International Journal of Academic Research in Economics and Management Sciences, 1*(2), 54–72.

Ng, T. H., Tay, W. Y., Tan, N. L., & Lim, Y. S. (2011). Influence of investment experience and demographic factors on retirement planning intention. *International Journal of Business and Management, 6*(2), 196–203.

Novy-Marx, R., & Rauh, J. (2011). Public pension promises: How big are they and what are they worth? *Journal of Finance, 66*(4), 1211–1249.

Paramita, V. S. (2015). Testing Treynor-Mazuy conditional model in bull and bear market. *Review of Integrative Business and Economics Research, 4*(2), 208–219.

Perrina, V. M. (1999). *The benchmark error problem and international asset pricing: An empirical examination*. Lubbock: Texas Tech University.

Pesaran, H., & Pesaran, B. (1997). *Microfit 4.0 interactive econometric analysis*. Oxford: Oxford University Press.

Pesaran, H. M., Shin, Y., & Smith, R. J. (2001). Bounds testing approaches to the analysis of long-run relationships. *Journal of Applied Econometrics, 16*, 289–326.

Rashid, M., Hassan, M. K., Amin, N., & Samina, Q. S. (2017). Shari'ah compliant companies in Bangladesh. *Journal of Islamic Economics Business and Finance, 13*(2), 129–143.

Sirri, E. R., & Tufano, P. (1998). Costly search and mutual fund flows. *Journal of Finance, 53*(5), 1589–1622.

Treynor, J., & Mazuy, K. (1966). Can mutual funds outguess the market? *Harvard Business Review, 44*, 131–136.

Yoong, F. J., See, B. L., & Baronovich, D. L. (2012). Financial literacy key to retirement planning in Malaysia. *Journal of Management and Sustainability, 2*(1), 75–86.

Mamunur Rashid received his PhD on Behavioural Finance from National University of Malaysia in 2014. He was awarded the PGCHE from the University of Nottingham in 2018. He is currently a Senior Assistant Professor of Finance in Universiti Brunei Darussalam. Prior to joining UBD, Mamunur taught Finance at Nottingham University Business School, The University of Nottingham (Malaysia Campus) since October 2012 until September 2018, and at East West University, Bangladesh (September 2005–February 2012). His teaching areas include Islamic Finance, International Finance, Corporate Finance and Financial Economics. Dr Mamunur was the founding deputy director of the Centre for Islamic Business and Finance Research at the University of Nottingham Malaysia Campus. Dr Mamunur is also an Associate Editor of International Journal of Islamic and Middle Eastern Finance and Management (Emerald). He is a Fellow of the Higher Education Academy, UK, and a member of Malaysian Finance Association since 2014. His research interest includes a broader investigation into the connection between values and performance in multi-cultural setting.

William Kong Choon San is currently working with Phillip Capital, Malaysia. He obtained his MSc in Finance and Investment from University of Nottingham Malaysia Campus. William is interested in capital market research.

Functions, Prospects, and Challenges of *Shari'ah*-Based Banking: Islami Bank Bangladesh Limited

Jashim Uddin Ahmed, Hafiza Sultana, and Mohammad Tayeenul Hoque

Abstract

The case study discusses Islamic banking activities in Bangladesh by focusing on Islami Bank Bangladesh Limited (IBBL), the pioneer in *Shari'ah*-based banking in the country. Although Islamic banking started with limited resources and a few participants, it has shown strong growth potential with a high level of customer acceptance. The introduction of profit and loss sharing banking system proved its worth since IBBL started rendering banking services with goals for social and economic development in 1983. Therefore, there are significant opportunities for the growth of Islamic banking in the country. Several challenges, on the other hand, are needed to be addressed, for example, inadequate diversification of products, lack of regulatory standard, complexity in investment opportunities, wobbly compliance with the Islamic *Shari'ah*, and intense competition from conventional banks with Islamic products and service, in order to improve the efficiency of this sector.

J. U. Ahmed (✉)
Department of Management, School of Business & Economics North South University, Dhaka, Bangladesh
e-mail: jashim.ahmed@northsouth.edu

H. Sultana
InterResearch, Dhaka, Bangladesh

M. T. Hoque
Department of Marketing and International Business, School of Business & Economics, North South University, Dhaka, Bangladesh

E. M. Ghazali et al. (eds.), *Management of Shari'ah Compliant Businesses*,
Management for Professionals, https://doi.org/10.1007/978-3-030-10907-3_6

1 Introduction

The banking sector, by contributing to different industries through disbursement, recovery and growth of credit, plays a vital role to the economy of Bangladesh (Ahmed & Ahmed, 2018). It inherited an interest-based banking system from the British colony (1757–1947) (Siddikee, Parvin, & Hossain, 2013). Bangladesh Bank (BB), as the central bank, supervises the government's monetary policies and all commercial banks. After independence, the Government of Bangladesh initially nationalized the domestic banking system and proceeded to reorganize and rename the banks. Nonetheless, privatization decision of commercial banks has revolutionized the overall banking system in 1980s (Alam, 2000). The present banking sector can be segmented into four major categories: Nationalized Commercial Banks (NCBs), Private Commercial Banks (PCBs), Foreign Commercial Banks (FCBs), and Development Financial Institutions (DFIs) owned by the government (Ahmed, Nisha, & Rifat, 2016). While the overall sector is flourishing, Islamic banking has experienced phenomenal growth in the backdrop of strong local demand and global popularity. Based on the Islamic laws and prohibitions, the key principles for *Shari'ah* (the idea of "spiritual law" (5:48) and "system of divine law; way of belief and practice" (45:18) in the Holy Quran) based banks are profit and loss sharing (PLS) system, predetermined loan repayments, asset-backed financial transactions, and *Shari'ah* approved contracts (Ayub, 2007).

The objective of the case is to analyze the functions, opportunities, and challenges of Islamic banking taking into account the importance of such banking in Bangladesh economy. The study focuses on the leading *Shari'ah* based bank, Islami Bank Bangladesh Limited (IBBL). The rest of the paper has been organized as follows. Section 2 presents the background structure of Islamic banking in the country. Then, Sects. 3 and 4 discuss the activities, products and service, and financial performance of IBBL, and IBBL's major competitor banks, respectively. The next two sections investigate the growth prospects and challenges for Islamic banking. Finally, Sect. 7 concludes the study with policy and managerial implications.

2 Structure of Islamic Banking: The Background

At present, out of 57 commercial banks in Bangladesh, there are eight full-fledged Islamic banks under foreign or private ownership; nine conventional commercial banks offer Islamic banking through Islamic banking windows (New Age, 2018). The services from the Islamic banks are deposit acceptance and mobilization, investment activities that cover short- and long-term, as well as import and export financing. They have multiple Islamic products and service to meet different banking needs of clients. Therefore, the Islamic banks serve as intermediaries between savings surplus and deficit units, whereas the interest is replaced by a number of instruments (Ayub, 2007).

A board, formed according to the regulations and BB guidelines, is responsible for governing the bank, whether it is Islamic or conventional. As a part of *Shari'ah* governance, a Central *Shari'ah* Board for Islamic Banks of Bangladesh (CSBIB) was formed in 2001, with the direction of BB and the objective to offer *Shari'ah* based guidelines to the Islamic banking sector of Bangladesh. However, its activities are mostly limited to organizing training and workshops and publishing books and bulletin for Islamic bankers (Alamgir, 2014). One of the important governance organs in an Islamic bank is the *Shari'ah* Supervisory Committee, though it is not applicable to the conventional counterpart. The committee offers opinion and guidance to implement the *Shari'ah* principles in Islamic banking activities, and, thus, provides clearance for *Shari'ah* compatibility to all products and service. It also confirms that the profit has been derived without violating Islamic regulations. Prime Bank Limited and Dhaka Bank Limited were the pioneer to introduce Islamic banking in addition to conventional banking. In addition, Agrani Bank Limited was the first state-owned commercial bank in Bangladesh to introduce *Shari'ah* based banking in 2010. The main distinct features of Islamic windows are that the banks safeguard the Islamic nature of their operations, ensure separation of their Islamic capital from the main pool, and segregate accounts accordingly. The banks also recruit skilled employees for their Islamic banking functions.

2.1 Modes of Investment

The nature of Islamic banking is based on risk-sharing, owning and handling of physical goods, and involvement in trading, leasing and contracts by using Islamic modes of finance. Different modes that comply with the Islamic *Shari'ah* are partnerships (*Mudaraba/Musharaka*), cost plus sale (*Murabaha*), credit sales (*Bai-Muajjal*), leasing (*Ijarah*), and Islamic forward (*Salam* and *Istisna*). Partnership products like *Musharaka* and *Mudaraba* are ideal instruments of financing, whereas *Murabaha* is the most widely used instrument in Islamic finance worldwide. Nowadays, home finance and Islamic mortgage based on the concept of *Ijarah* has become a very successful tool in Islamic banking (Alamgir, 2014).

Mudaraba, i.e., trust financing, is a mode of Islamic banking that is suitable for "profit and loss sharing." It is a contract between investor/bank/financial institution, which acts as a fiduciary/manager, and entrepreneurs/clients, acting as silent partners to invest in an activity or a predetermined asset class that earns each partner an agreed upon profit portion of the investment. In cost plus sales or *Murabaha* contracts, a financial institution purchases goods according to the request of a client, who makes deferred payments that cover the cost and profit margin for the bank. In such a contract, the Islamic bank must own the item when the customer buys it from the bank with a specified profit margin. Then, *Bai-Muajjal* or credit sale is a deferred payment sales contract between the bank and its client. As per the contract, the bank earns a profit margin on the purchasing price and allows the buyer to pay the price of the commodity at a future date in a lump sum or in installments. In addition, *Ijarah* or leasing is not a sale of the object, but rather a sale of the usufruct (the right to use the object) for a specified period of time. The most important financial difference between the *Shari'ah* permitted leasing and conventional financial leasing is that, the leasing agency must own the leased object during the lease period. *Salam* and *Istisna*, with limited utilization, are contracts in which advance payment is made for goods to be delivered later on. The seller undertakes to supply specific goods to the buyer at a future date in exchange of an advance price fully paid at the time of contract.

2.2 Savings, Investment, and Other Products

The nature of demand deposits in Islamic banks is not different from that of conventional banks. However, the nature of investments and other deposits is significantly different. Funds deposited in Islamic banks with explicit permission from the depositors to utilize and invest the same are called *Al-Wadeeah*. The current accounts are handled on the basis of this *Al-Wadeeah* principle. The banks obtain permission from the depositors to utilize the funds at bank's own responsibility, and, thus, the depositors do not share any profit or loss incurred while using these funds as investment. The banks have to return the deposits as soon as customers want. Generally, no interest is given on current accounts on the ground that such deposits are kept as *Amanah*. Similarly, if the proceed of such accounts are used by the banks in their business, these are treated as investments that are to be returned to respective clients without any increase or decrease.

In addition to *Al-Wadeeah*, Islamic banks receive deposits on the basis of *Mudaraba*, a partnership of labor and capital in which one partner provides full capital and the other manages the business. The deposits received are called *Mudaraba* deposits, which can be classified to *Mudaraba* savings deposits, *Mudaraba* short notice deposits, and *Mudaraba* term deposits. The ratio of profit distribution between the bank and the depositor must be agreed at the time of account opening, subject to the condition of *Shari'ah*. *Bai-Murabaha*, *Bai-Muajjal*, and *Bai-Salam* are particularly suitable for trade, while *Ijarah* and *Istisna* are suitable for industries. Personal finance for consumer durables can be offered through *Murabaha* and leasing, and, in special cases, by means of return-free investments from current accounts, or bank's own funds. The alternatives to auto finance are *Ijarah Muntahia-bi-Tamleek* and *Murabaha*. Housing finance is possible through *Murabaha*, diminishing *Musharaka*, and rent-sharing. Project financing can be provided through various modes of financing, among which *Ijarah* is the most popular. The Islamic banks, as joint investors, are entitled to the remaining percentage after deduction of the amount allocated to the investors. The banks are also entitled to participate in the profit of joint investments in proportion to the amount of its own funds, or the funds it is authorized to risk in joint investments.

The major investment products of the Islamic banks and Islamic banking windows of the conventional banks in Bangladesh are based on the *Bai*-mechanism, or buying and selling as per Islamic *Shari'ah*. Other mechanism includes *Ijarah* and share. Of the *Bai* modes (purchase and sale of goods in cash, or on credit, or in advance at a predetermined profit, which may or may not be disclosed to the client), the common investment products are *Bai-Murabaha*, *Bai-Muajjal*, *Bai-Salam*, *Bai-as-Sarf*, and *Bai-Istisna*. Hire purchase and Hire Purchase under *Shirkatul Meelk* (HPSM) are related to *Ijarah* mechanism, whereas *Mudaraba* and *Musharaka* are linked to share (Alamgir, 2014). The banks also offer trade-related services to their clients, for example, LC, back-to-back LC, foreign bank guarantees, bill purchases, and export bill collections, that are compatible with different *Shari'ah* permissible modes. Inland documentary bills are purchased by the banks under *Musharaka* mechanism. Purchase and negotiation of export bills are done by *Bai-as-Sarf* mode, in which the Islamic bank realizes commission or receives exchange gain (or loss). Last but not least, four types of card are issued by these banks to withdraw cash and to obtain credit, or to pay for goods purchased or service received. These are debit cards, charge cards, credit cards, and ATM cards. The Accounting and Auditing Organization for the Islamic Financial Institutions (AAOIFI) has issued a *Shari'ah* standard for these cards, which provides a useful basis for developing electronic money by Islamic banks.

3 Islami Bank Bangladesh Limited (IBBL): An Overview

The history of Islamic banking can be traced back in 1974, when Bangladesh signed the Charter of Islamic Development Bank and committed itself to reorganize its economic and financial system according to Islamic *Shari'ah.* A delegation of Islamic Development Bank (IDB) showed keen interest to participate in establishing a joint venture Islamic bank in the private sector in 1982. Two professional institutes, Islamic Economics Research Bureau (IERB) and Bangladesh Islamic Bankers' Association (BIBA), made significant contributions towards introduction of Islamic banking in the economy. They came forward to provide training to the top bankers and economists in order to fill up the vacuum of leadership for future Islamic banks. They also held seminars, symposia, and workshops on Islamic economics and banking to mobilize public opinion in favor of the same. At last, the long-drawn effort became a reality when IBBL was established in March, 1983. 19 Bangladeshi national, 4 Bangladeshi institutions, together with 11 banks, financial institutions, and government bodies of the Middle East and Europe, which includes IDB and two eminent personalities from the Kingdom of Saudi Arabia (KSA), joined hands to form IBBL. The subsequent organization is considered as the first interest-free bank in Southeast Asia.

The bank is a joint venture public limited company engaged in commercial banking business based on Islamic *Shari'ah.* It has 63.09% foreign shareholding and the largest branch network (332 branches including 54 authorized dealer branches, and 3 offshore banking units (IBBL, Annual Report, 2017)). Its mission is to establish Islamic banking through the introduction of a welfare-oriented banking system, to ensure equity and justice in all economic activities, as well as to achieve balanced growth and equitable development through diversified investment operations, particularly in the priority sectors and less developed areas of the country. It also encourages socioeconomic growth by offering financial services to

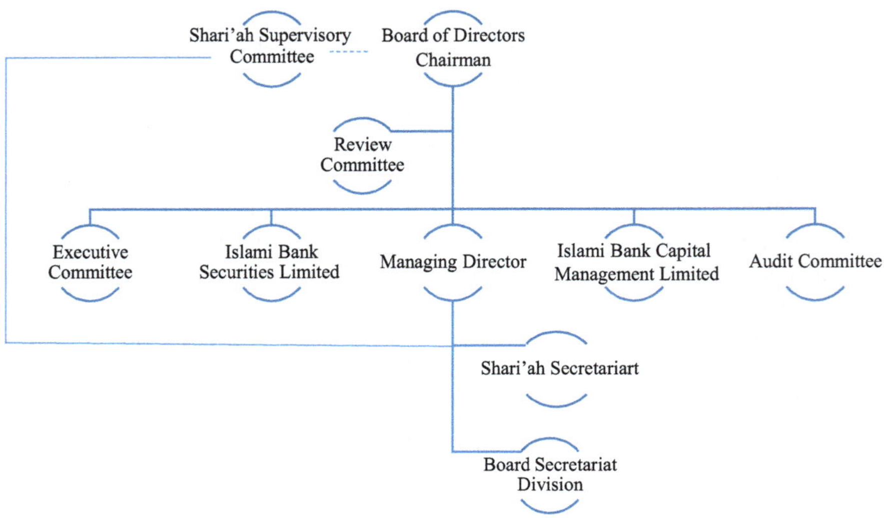

Fig. 1 The Organization Structure of IBBL. Source: IBBL (2018b)

low-income community, particularly in the rural areas (IBBL, 2018a). Its vision is to be engaged in activities that aim to achieve superior financial performance and to develop a market position as the leading Islamic bank by reputation and performance. The current organizational structure of the bank is presented in Fig. 1.

IBBL mobilizes deposits through different types of accounts, namely, *Al-Wadeeah* current account and *Mudaraba* accounts. On behalf of depositors, the bank invests the deposited money through deployment of *Mudaraba* funds. Its deposit products are as follows:

1. Basic *Mudaraba* accounts: savings, short or special notice, and term deposits
2. Specialized *Mudaraba* accounts: monthly profit, *Waqf* cash and foreign currency deposits, savings accounts for Hajj (pilgrimage), pension, student and farmers, along with savings bonds for general clients and Non-Resident Bangladeshis (NRBs)

The bank uses *Bai* modes (*Bai-Murabaha*, *Bai-Istijrar*, *Bai-Muajjal*, *Bai-Salam*, *Istisna*, and *Bai-as-Sarf*) for its investment, while its share modes are *Mudaraba* and *Musharaka*, and *Ijara* mode is HPSM. In consumer financing, the bank meets demand for personal, family and household needs, such as house and car. Its other investment schemes are designed for transport, small business, micro-industry, agriculture, real estate (commercial and working capital) sectors, etc. There are also special investment schemes for doctors, women entrepreneurs, and NRB entrepreneurs. Recent report shows that, IBBL concentrates on the *Bai-Murabaha* mode (55%) for investment, as shown in Fig. 2. In addition, it has invested 22% and 7%, respectively, under HPSM and *Bai-Muajjal*. Conversely, it has the lowest investment in *Bai-Salam*, *Mudaraba*, and *Musharaka* modes, only 1% of each during 2017.

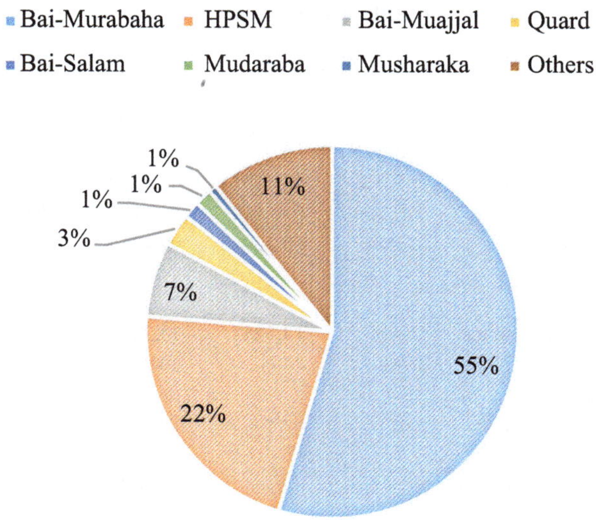

Fig. 2 Mode-wise investment of IBBL as percentage of total investment in 2017. Source: IBBL, Annual Report (2017)

The bank has applied Islamic microfinance model in its rural development scheme with the aim to extend investment facilities to agricultural and other farming and off-farming activities in the rural areas, finance self-employment and income-generating activities of the rural people, particularly the unemployed youths and poor, alleviate rural poverty through integrated rural development, and provide education and medical facilities to the downtrodden people. Initially the customers receive maximum investment of BDT 10,000 (USD145). Then the good performers get additional investment according to their requirement, i.e., BDT 2000 to BDT 5000 in every next term up to the ceiling of a particular sector, namely, crop production, commercial nursery for flowers and fruits, fisheries, livestock, rural transport, rural housing, etc. Through i-banking 0.15 million clients have taken the Internet banking service like fund transfer, online payment, and utility bill payments. In addition, the bank has implemented mCash, a full-scale mobile financial service for cash in and out, fund transfer, mobile recharge, and salary and tuition fee payments. Also, it offers different card service: proprietary card (local), visa debit card (local), Khidmah credit card (local), remittance card (local), Hajj prepaid card (for pilgrimage in the KSA), business prepaid card (local), travelers card (international), etc.

With its strong commitment to the poor and the unbanked people, IBBL has maintained a stable growth (as shown in Table 1). The Islamic banking sector of Bangladesh makes up 35% of the global Islamic banking business, while IBBL is estimated to represent 25% of the global Islamic banking activities (Khaleej Times, 2016). Furthermore, IBBL is a major microfinance institution in Bangladesh and the largest Islamic microfinance provider in the world. It usually increases its balance

Table 1 Financial performance of IBBL in recent years

Particulars	2017	2016	2015	2014	2013
Balance sheet[a]					
Authorized capital	20,000	20,000	20,000	20,000	20,000
Paid-up capital	16,099.91	16,099.91	16,099.91	16,099.91	14,636
Deposits and other accounts	755,022	681,352	615,359	560,696	473,141
Investments[b]	710,729	616,419	530,195	463,475	406,805
Investment (Shares & Securities)	37,944	60,329	99,437	100,857	67,211
Income statement[c]					
Profit before provision and tax	16,805	14,525	14,348	15,323	14,104
Net profit	4693	4465	3029	3999	4973
Market performance					
Earnings per share (EPS) (BDT)	2.91	2.77	1.88	2.48	3.40
Market value per share (BDT) (Highest)	n.a.	n.a.	31.60	36.80	45.00
Financial ratios					
Return on assets (ROA)	0.55%	0.59%	0.44%	0.67%	0.96%
Return on equity (ROE)	8.29%	8.14%	6.28%	8.85%	11.36%
Price-earnings ratio (times)	12.24	10.11	12.54	11.24	12.35

Source: IBBL, Annual Reports (2013–2017)
Notes: [a]Values are truncated to Million BDT
[b]Investments include general investment, bills purchased and discounted, etc., excluding the investment in shares and securities
[c]Values are truncated to Million BDT

sheet by three times in every 4 years. Its deposit, BDT 30 billion in 2000, has crossed BDT 600 billion in 2015 (Khaleej Times, 2016). Nevertheless, the bank is struggling with a liquidity crisis since mid-2018, which was created by a combination of aggressive lending and decline in deposits in the previous year. According to BB, IBBL has crossed the permissible limit of 90% advance-deposit ratio (ADR) (Dhaka Tribune, 2018).

4 Key Competitors of IBBL

Following the footsteps of IBBL, the other seven Islamic banks have started their operations in Bangladesh between 1987 and 2013. Although functions performed by the latter are similar, they differ in range of products and service, scope of operations and financial performance (presented in Table 2).

Table 2 Financial performance in BDT, 2017

Particulars[a]	ICBIBL	AIBL	SIBL	EXIM	FSIBL	SJIBL	UBL
Authorized capital	15,000	15,000	10,000	20,000	10,000	10,000	10,000
Paid-up capital	6647	9943	7383	14,123	6789	7714	5273
Deposits and other accounts	11,294	245,642	228,799	284,026	231,274	145,382	114,050
Investments (general)	8834	232,614	210,046	253,803	187,680	158,668	100,754
Investment (shares and securities)	111	8021	13,083	22,123	13,064	10,526	4985
Profit before provision and tax	(382)	5432	6166	5857	2466	3328	2273
Net profit/loss	(405)	3077	1455	3194	798	1196	890
EPS	(0.61)	3.09	1.97	2.26	1.18	1.55	1.69

Source: Annual Reports (AIBL, 2017; EXIM Bank, 2017; FSIBL, 2017; ICBIBL, 2017; SIBL, 2017; SJIBL, 2017; UBL, 2017)

Note: [a]The data is for the banks only, excluding any subsidiaries; all values are truncated to million, except EPS

4.1 ICB Islamic Bank Limited (ICBIBL)

ICBIBL was incorporated as Al-Baraka Bank Bangladesh Limited in 1987. It is a public limited company to carry out banking, financial and business activities, transactions, and operations in compliance with the principles of Islamic laws. Its investment products are *Manzil* (home) finance, *Rahabar* (auto) finance, *Saahib* (personal) finance, and *Murabaha* under secured guarantee. In addition to these, its deposit products are *Al-Wadeeah* current account, *Mudaraba* deposits, foreign currency account, *Al-Muqafah* executive account, etc. The *Mudaraba* deposits are further classified into savings plans, senior citizen account, corporate term deposit, non-executive account, future leader account, school banking, term deposit, monthly profit, double benefit, etc.

4.2 Al-Arafah Islami Bank Limited (AIBL)

The third Islamic bank of Bangladesh, AIBL, was established as a private limited company in 1995. It offers a diverse array of carefully tailored products and service to satisfy customer needs. Its deposit products are *Al-Wadeeah* current deposit, basic *Mudaraba* deposits, and foreign currency deposit. The bank has developed various special deposits on the basis of *Mudaraba* principle, for instance, monthly profit based term deposit, monthly installment based term deposit, monthly Hajj deposit, termed Hajj deposit, monthly installment based marriage savings investment scheme, savings bond, pension deposit scheme, and cash *Waqf* deposit scheme.

4.3 Social Islami Bank Limited (SIBL)

SIBL started its operations in 1995 as a second-generation Islamic bank. The bank is an example of contemporary three segment banking model in one. In the formal segment, it works as an Islamic participatory commercial bank with human face approach to credit and banking based on PLS. It has a non-formal banking segment, too, with informal finance and investment package, which empowers poor families, creates local income opportunities, and discourages internal migration. Its third segment manages the *Waqf*, or mosque properties. SIBL has introduced cash *Waqf* system for the first time in history of banking in Bangladesh. In addition to cash *Waqf* deposit, the bank offers *Al-Wadeeah* current account, basic *Mudaraba* deposits, and *Mudaraba* scheme deposits, which include schemes for Hajj, Zakat, Mohorana (marriage), education, pension, monthly profit, double growth, etc. It also has three savings schemes designed for lower-income workers and women. Its major investment products are *Bai-Muajjal*, HPSM, HPSM-*Ijara*, *Murabaha*, *Musharaka*, bill purchase and *Quard*. It offers four types of card facilities, namely, credit card, visa Islamic credit card (dual, local and foreign currency), visa Islamic credit card (local), and *Zameel* debit card.

4.4 Export Import (EXIM) Bank of Bangladesh Limited

The Bank was incorporated as Bengal Export Import Bank Limited in 1999, renamed as Export Import Bank of Bangladesh Limited in 1999, and has started Islamic banking from 2004. It was listed in the stock exchanges of the country in the same year. As a third-generation commercial bank operating under Islamic *Shari'ah*, it provides a variety of banking services, which include a wide range of deposit and investment products, foreign exchange, remittance, and other ancillary service, with support of most sophisticated information technology. The investment portfolio of the bank comprises of diversified industry sectors. EXIM Bank offers *Al-Wadeeah* current deposit, *Mudaraba* savings, and *Mudaraba* term deposits. Its *Mudaraba* deposit schemes are classified as monthly savings, monthly income, multi-plus saving, super saving, millionaire, *Kotipoti*, Hajj, *Denmohor* (marriage), education, etc. There are special savings deposit schemes for senior citizens, housewives, entrepreneurs, house buyers, farmers, and women in general. It has three subsidiaries, namely, EXIM Exchange Company (UK) Limited, EXIM Exchange Company (Canada) Limited, and EXIM Islami Investment Limited (a merchant bank).

4.5 First Security Islami Bank Limited (FSIBL)

FSIBL was incorporated as a public limited company in 1999 and has started *Shari'ah* banking since 2009. Its special *Mudaraba* deposit products are designed for monthly deposit, monthly profit, salary saving, pension, education, health care, marriage, Hajj, cash *Waqf*, double benefit, triple benefit, four times, and so on. Its investment schemes are *Bai-Murabaha* and *Bai-Muajjal* (deferred installment or lump sum sale), *Ijara*, *Musharaka* (joint venture and profit sharing), *Mudaraba* (trustee profit sharing), *Bai-Salam*, hire purchase, post-import investment, purchase and negotiation of export bills, purchase of inland bills, *Murabaha* import bills, *Bai-Muajjal* import bills, pre-shipment investment, and *Quard-ul-Hasan* (benevolent investment).

4.6 Shahjalal Islami Bank Limited (SJIBL)

SJIBL commenced its commercial operations as a public limited company in May, 2001, in accordance with principles of Islamic *Shari'ah.* The bank was listed in the stock exchanges of Bangladesh in 2007. Over the years, the bank has diversified its service coverage by opening new branches at different strategically important locations across the country. In addition to *Al-Wadeeah* current account and basic *Mudaraba* deposits, its tailored *Mudaraba* deposit products are monthly income, double money, monthly deposit, millionaire, Hajj, school, cash *Waqf*, and money spinning. It has designed a good number of investment products to facilitate working capital financing, which are *Bai-Murabaha* (for LC and post-import), *Bai-Muajjal* (for commercial, real estate, export bill and term), and *Bai-Salam*. It also has a subsidiary named Shahjalal Islami Bank Securities Limited.

4.7 Union Bank Limited (UBL)

The latest entrant in the Islamic banking sector is UBL. The bank was incorporated in 2013 to carry out *Shari'ah* based commercial banking business. It is a fourth-generation bank and operates with the strategy of diversifying its portfolio. Its products include *Mudaraba* deposit schemes on pension, marriage, Hajj, *Denmohor*, education, monthly, double, triple, millionaire, etc. Besides, its investment products are *Bai-Murabaha*, *Bai-Istisna* (pre-shipment investment), *Bai-Salam*, *Bai-Muajjal*, etc.

5 Growth Prospects for Islamic Banking

Over the past decade the Islamic banking sector in Bangladesh has observed positive growth, specifically in assets and investments. This trend indicates that the activities and customer acceptance of Islamic banks are increasing at an acclaiming rate. Furthermore, the Islamic banks are ahead of conventional banks in profit earning (Miah & Sharmeen, 2015). In addition, the conversion of a few conventional banks to full-fledged Islamic banks and the opening of Islamic banking wings by others specify that the business opportunity is worth pursuing.

Bangladesh has a large population of 157.83 (July 2017 estimate), growing at 1.04% (2017 estimate), with 89.1% Muslim people (2013 estimate) (World Fact Book, 2017). Besides, its Muslim population is predicted to reach 182.36 million by 2050 (Pew Research Center, 2015). Thus, the economy has potentials to become a lucrative market for Islamic banking. Secondly, a significant part of the educated and financially solvent Muslim households are yet to prefer Islamic banking to conventional banking. The Islamic banks should target this untapped segment by introducing a diversified product portfolio and promoting the additional benefits of Islamic banking. Finally, these banks should establish themselves as equally efficient as conventional banks, so they can target clients from other religious belief in addition to Islam.

6 Challenges for Islamic Banking

On the contrary, the Islamic banks in Bangladesh need to address the following challenges for future profit and growth.

6.1 Inadequate Diversification of Products

Currently, the Islamic banks offer products of a limited variety; for instance, they are yet to introduce the Islamic bond known as *Sukuk*, which has been very successful in Saudi Arabia and Malaysia (New Age, 2018). This issue limits options for risk mitigation by the Islamic banks, as well as other banks operating through separate Islamic windows. These banks should design small loans for product diversification, which will ultimately help them hedge risks and compete with other conventional banks, the experts suggested. Besides, the introduction of *Sukuk* bonds can assist in their liquidity management.

6.2 Lack of Regulatory Standards

Bangladesh needs a separate Islamic Banking Act and a unified *Shari'ah* code for its Islamic banks. The establishment of capital adequacy standards by the AAOIFI has helped crystallize the differences between the capital of Islamic and conventional banking. However, the compliance with AAOIFI standards is yet to be fully materialized (Nazim & Bennie, 2012). Absence of a comprehensive standard covering all functions of Islamic banks is creating a number of *Shari'ah* compliance issues. Like most countries, Islamic banks in Bangladesh are under the supervision of the central bank and are given the same treatment as that to commercial banks. So, one major concern of regulators and supervisors of Islamic banks is how to integrate internationally recognized standards with the *Shari'ah*.

6.3 Complexity in Investment Opportunities

Conventional banks can earn interest on their deposits with the central bank. Conversely, the Islamic banks are unable to do the same since they cannot be engaged in any interest-related activities. However, IBBL receives interest against its deposit with BB and credits it to its *Sadaqa* fund since 1993. The interest earning is not considered bank income; it is not added to profit but spent in bank's welfare activities. In addition, the Islamic banks need to be more vigilant in managing their funds because they cannot resort to call money provision at times of fund shortages or similar crisis like the conventional banks. As a result, there may always remain a significant amount of liquidity surplus. Traditional banks can invest their surplus liquid in approved securities and other banks, but Islamic banks cannot take this opportunity due to the existence of interest elements in such transactions. Recently, the introduction of Islami Inter-bank Fund Market (IIFM) by BB has opened a new window of investment for the Islamic banks with excess liquidity.

Although Islamic *Shari'ah* based banks constitute about 22% share of the banking business in Bangladesh (New Age, 2018), they did not have an inter-bank money market (call money market). As a result, the banks had problems in managing excess liquidity. If an Islamic bank needed fund to overcome sudden liquidity shortage, it had no option other than to make an internal arrangement among the *Shari'ah* banks through *Mudaraba* Savings Deposit (MSD) and *Mudaraba* Notice Deposit (MND) account operations. Introduction of IIFM has solved the issue and enabled the Islamic banks to collect funds from inter-bank money market. They transact with each other through a separate fund called IIFM, with BB as the custodian of this fund; the contract is based on *Mudaraba* principle. Conventional banks can invest 30% of their total deposits in shares and securities. Nevertheless, Islamic banks do not purchase shares of companies that undertake interest-based business, shares of companies that take loan from commercial banks on interest, and shares of companies involved in businesses that are not approved by *Shari'ah*. The restrictions curtail the investment opportunities for Islamic banks and, hence, the avenues of lawful earning.

6.4 Intense Competition Among Rivals

Islamic banks have confronted increasing competition when the conventional banks, even international banks, such as City Bank and Standard Chartered Bank (SCB), have offered Islamic products and service. These banks can attract general customers in addition to snatching existing and potential clients from the Islamic banks. However, the Islamic banks may have some advantages with a broader product line from that of the Islamic windows at conventional banks.

6.5 Wobbly Compliance with the Islamic *Shari'ah*

While most Islamic banks in Bangladesh comply with the *Shari'ah* principles, minor violations exist, especially in the investment activities. Prior Research proposed that, the branch management should be more careful about *Shari'ah* compliance to prevent this (Ullah, 2014). Sometimes, there is gap between the standard and actual practice due to lack of awareness among Islamic banking promoters. To improve the current situation, a thorough review of Islamic banking policies is necessary. Until and unless a quick policy change and subsequent clear actions take place, the credibility Islamic banks have achieved could be tarnished away.

7 Moving Forward

Raising awareness and explaining the modes of operations to existing and potential clients can increase profitability and overall competitiveness of Islamic banking (Alamgir, 2014). Islamic banks need to emphasize more on branch level *Shari'ah* inspection and *Shari'ah* compliance. They need to increase *Shari'ah* knowledge of their employees and hold regular review meeting at branch levels to evaluate the Islamic compliance. In addition, IBBL needs to train its people about project appraisal, monitoring, evaluation and performance auditing. Then, the bank should develop an electronic database of its clients so reports on market trend, client demographics, client segmentation, and so on, which are essential for its strategic planning, can be generated.

Although Islamic banking in Bangladesh has observed significant growth in the past few decades, the sector is still at infancy stage compared to the existence of conventional banks. Previous studies argued that, Islamic banking could be the most efficient system if it were allowed to operate as a sole system in an economy. When it starts operations within the conventional banking framework, most of its efficiencies are lost. However, this issue, similar to some challenges discussed in earlier section, is not a weakness of Islamic banking itself. The policy implication suggested is that, conventional banking system needs to be reviewed into PLS framework by considering beneficial impacts of the latter on an economy. Moreover, the Islamic banks fail to receive profit from high-return projects since the owners of these projects prefer borrowing from conventional banks, in which the cost of borrowing might be lower. So, projects with rates of return equal to or below the market interest are handled by the Islamic banks. Therefore, it reduces their capacity to utilize investment opportunities compared to their conventional competitors and hinders the application of PLS modes. As a result, the Islamic banks need to develop appropriate strategies through which they can promote the advantages of *Shari'ah* banking and a positive image of their efficiency to the clients. Pilot schemes can be started in selected urban and rural areas of Bangladesh to test innovative products and service with PLS modes of financing. By doing this, they will achieve real-life experience as well, and, thus, might find a solution to the challenges related to Islamic banking.

References

Ahmed, J. U., & Ahmed, A. (2018). Agrani Doer Banking: Agent banking business in Bangladesh. *Business Perspectives and Research, 6*(2), 154–164.

Ahmed, J. U., Nisha, N., & Rifat, A. (2016). The Dhaka Mercantile Co-operative Bank Limited: A case of Islamic Shari'ah banking in Bangladesh. *International Journal of Financial Innovation in Banking, 1*(1-2), 62–79.

AIBL. (2018). Corporate website. Retrieved July 20, 2018, from https://www.al-arafahbank.com/

Alam, M. N. (2000). Islamic banking in Bangladesh: A case study of IBBL. *International Journal of Islamic Financial Services, 1*(4), 10–29.

Alamgir, M. (2014). Development of Islamic banking in Bangladesh: Issues and challenges. *Thoughts on Banking and Finance, 3*(2), 66–91.

Ayub, M. (2007). *Understanding Islamic finance*. London: Willy-Finance.

(The) Dhaka Tribune. (2018, April 18). *Acute liquidity crisis catalyzed shakeup at Islami Bank*, by Shariful Islam. Retrieved July 20, 2018, from https://www.dhakatribune.com/business/2018/04/18/acute-liquidity-crisis-catalyzed-shakeup-islami-bank/

EXIM Bank. (2017). *Annual Report*. Retrieved July 20, 2018, from http://www.eximbankbd.com/report/ar2017.pdf

Exim Bank. (2018). Corporate website. Accessed July 20, 2018, from http://www.eximbankbd.com/

FSIBL. (2018). Corporate website. Accessed July 20, 2018, from http://www.fsiblbd.com/

IBBL. (2018a). Corporate website. About Us. Accessed July 20, 2018, from http://www.islamibankbd.com/

IBBL. (2018b). Organization structure. Accessed July 20, 2018, from https://www.islamibankbd.com/abtIBBL/abtIBBLORG.php

IBBL Annual Reports, 2013, 2014, 2015, 2016, 2017. IBBL, Dhaka, Bangladesh.

ICBIBL. (2018). Corporate website. Accessed July 20, 2018, from https://www.icbislamic-bd.com/

(The) *Khaleej Times*. (2016, March 20). *Bank aims rural uplift of Bangladesh economy*, by Rizvi, M. Accessed December 28, 2017, from http://www.khaleejtimes.com/business/banking-finance/bank-aims-rural-uplift-of-bangladesh-economy

Miah, M. D., & Sharmeen, K. (2015). Relationship between capital, risk and efficiency: A comparative study between Islamic and conventional banks of Bangladesh. *International Journal of Islamic and Middle Eastern Finance and Management, 8*(2), 203–221.

Nazim, A., & Bennie, G. (2012, December). World Islamic banking competitiveness report 2012–2013. *Ernst & Young*.

(The) *New Age*. (2018, July 5). *Country's Islamic banks lack products to hedge risks, say experts*, by Staff Correspondent. Accessed July 20, 2018, from http://www.newagebd.net/article/45184/countrys-islamic-banks-lack-products-to-hedge-risks-say-experts/

Pew Forum. (2015, April 2). *10 countries with the largest Muslim populations, 2010 and 2050*. Accessed December 28, 2017, from http://www.pewforum.org/2015/04/02/muslims/pf_15-04-02_projectionstables74/

Siddikee, M. A., Parvin, S., & Hossain, M. S. (2013). Banking scenarios in Bangladesh. *Bangladesh Research Publication Journal, 8*(1), 89–95.

SIBL. (2017). *Annual Report*. Retrieved December 8, 2018, from https://www.siblbd.com/annual_report/SIBL%20Annual%20Report%202017.pdf

SJIBL. (2018). Corporate website. Available from http://www.sjiblbd.com/

UBL. (2018). Corporate website. Accessed July 20, 2018, from https://www.unionbank.com.bd/

Ullah, H. (2014). Shari'ah compliance in Islamic banking: An empirical study on selected Islamic banks in Bangladesh. *International Journal of Islamic and Middle Eastern Finance and Management, 7*(2), 182–199.

(The) World Fact Book. (2017). Central Intelligence Agency, Bangladesh Country Profile. Available from https://www.cia.gov/library/publications/the-world-factbook/geos/bg.html

Jashim Uddin Ahmed is a Professor and Chairman of the Department of Management, School of Business & Economics, North South University, Bangladesh. His principal research interests lie in the field of strategic management and contemporary issues in business. He has published over 90 research articles and case studies in reputed journals. Currently, he is an Advisory Editorial Member of three journals.

Hafiza Sultana is a Research Associate in InterResearch, Bangladesh. She has completed MBA as a Marketing major with Distinction from North South University. Her research interest broadly covers International Marketing, Management, International Entrepreneurship, and Sustainability, with special focus on developing economies and emerging markets. Five of her papers have been published in international peer-reviewed journals.

Mohammad Tayeenul Hoque is an Assistant Professor and Chairman of the Department of Marketing & International Business, School of Business & Economics at North South University, Bangladeash. He is an active reviewer of prestigious conferences such as American Marketing Association, European Marketing Academy and Academy of International Business since 2013. His research interest covers dynamic capability, ambidextrous process and sensory marketing within marketing domain.

Harmonisation of Shari'ah Screening in International Markets: The Case of Nigeria

Balqis Oyindamola Adedokun and Mamunur Rashid

Abstract

This study examines the differences among the world's leading Shari'ah equity screening criteria and offers insights on how these differences affect the classification of equities into Shari'ah-compliant and non-Shari'ah-compliant. Financial ratios adopted by DJIM, FTSE and KLSE (used by Shari'ah Advisory Council of Malaysia) were calculated on Nigeria Stock Exchange Lotus Islamic Index (NSELII) and listed Shari'ah-compliant companies. The results indicate that a large percentage of companies in NSELII can be closely categorised using Shari'ah screening criteria used by SAC Malaysia. In a Muslim-dominant environment, Nigeria offers an interesting atmosphere for Islamic companies. It is important to investigate sustainable business performance, while Islamic companies by principle are required to follow Islamic Shari'ah. The findings of this case study are expected to help understand the screening of Islamic firms to enable Muslim investors and Islamic capital market regulators arrive at a more synchronised investment and regulatory decision.

1 Shari'ah Screening and Harmonisation Issue

Several complications associated with the capital market make it difficult to find a fully Shari'ah-compliant investment. As the awareness of Islamic banking increases, the urge by Muslims to invest in Shari'ah-compliant equities also increases, thus

B. O. Adedokun
Independent Research, Abuja, Nigeria

M. Rashid (✉)
School of Business and Economics, Universiti Brunei Darussalam, Gadong, Brunei
e-mail: mamunur.rashid@ubd.edu.bn

E. M. Ghazali et al. (eds.), *Management of Shari'ah Compliant Businesses*, Management for Professionals, https://doi.org/10.1007/978-3-030-10907-3_7

making equity screening a necessity (Htay, Abeedeen, & Salman, 2013). Although Islamic banking transaction is theoretically based on partnership contract, in practice very limited transactions are structured with the profit and loss sharing (PLS) system. Banks usually adopt the cost-plus contract which is argued to be like the conventional interest-based system (Khatkhatay & Nisar, 2007). Therefore, a closer approach that guarantees no returns and satisfies largely the basic principles of Shari'ah is equity investment.

As much as the characteristics of equity investment largely comply with the principles of Shari'ah, it is difficult to get fully Shari'ah-compliant investments due to the exigencies of modern business. The role of the equity index providers is to sort the Shari'ah-compliant investment by allowing a limited percentage of compromise, thereby giving Muslims the opportunity of investing in a less sinful asset (Adam & Abu Bakar, 2014).

The issue encountered with the Shari'ah screening criteria is its dis-uniformity from place to place. Since the major sources of Islamic law which are the Qur'an and Sunnah did not explicitly mention the guidelines for equity investment, the rules for categorising investment therefore rest on the decision of Islamic scholars which may vary due to the complexity of transforming historical sources into formal guidelines. This difference hampers the international acceptability of most Shari'ah-compliant indices which stunts the growth of global Islamic capital market. The principles that Islamic firms follow must comply with sustainable business practices, combining ethical and socially responsible business operation. Nigeria is oil-rich country with a slightly larger proportion of Muslim population than the Christians, the second largest population. Being one of the largest Islamic countries in the world, Nigerian Shari'ah-compliant firms must comply with Islamic business principles.

Consequently, it is important to study different Shari'ah screening guideline and understand how much deviations they have in categorising stocks into Shari'ah-compliant and non-Shari'ah-compliant. This paper represents the first study which compares the acceptability of Nigeria's Shari'ah-compliant companies with other global equity index providers. This study uses the companies that comprise the Nigeria Stock Exchange Lotus Islamic Index (NSELII) as a benchmark in comparing the standards of Dow Jones Islamic Market Index (DJIM), Financial Times Stock Exchange (FTSE) Global Islamic Index and Kuala Lumpur Stock Exchange Islamic Index (KLSEII). Three-year operation and financial information of the companies were collected to understand their business activities and in calculating the appropriate ratios. Also, an out-of-sample study was performed for the three different years to arrive at a more robust finding.

In categorising companies into Shari'ah-compliant and non-Shari'ah-compliant, index providers adopt a two-tier screening approach. A qualitative sector screening is done to ascertain that the business is not involved in prohibited activities. Thereafter companies who qualify will go through the quantitative financial screening to determine if their non-Islamic financial transactions are not above the accepted threshold (Adam & Abu Bakar, 2014).

Table 1 Comparison of qualitative criteria for Shari'ah-compliant screening process

	DJIM	FTSE	KLSEII
Alcohol	Any involvement	Core business	Core business
Broadcasting and entertaining	Any involvement	Core business	Core business
Conventional financial services	Any involvement	Core business	Core business
Gambling	Any involvement	Core business	Core business
Hotels	Any involvement	Core business	Core business
Insurance	Any involvement	Core business	Core business
Media (except newspaper)	Any involvement	Core business	Core business
Pork-related products	Any involvement	Core business	Core business
Restaurant and bars	Any involvement	Core business	Core business
Tobacco	Any involvement	Core business	Core business
Weapon and defence	Any involvement	Core business	Core business

Source: Extracted from Pok (2012)

2 Qualitative Screening: Business of the Company

Shari'ah prohibits Muslims from engaging in certain commercial activities. Hence, investment in a company whose business falls under the prohibited category is unacceptable. However, KLSEII and FTSE categorise such companies as Shari'ah-compliant and justify their action based on *maslaha*, i.e. public interest. A company is considered Shari'ah-compliant provided the prohibited activities are not its core business. Such companies with mixed activities must have a good image, and its income from its non-Shari'ah-compliant transactions must not exceed a certain threshold (Pok, 2012).

On the other hand, DJIM regards a company that has any involvement with such prohibited activities as non-Shari'ah-compliant. Dergis and Marzban (2008) perceive DJIM's criterion regarding the activities of the company to be too stringent. The exclusion of companies with little prohibited activities such as airlines and hotel who serve alcohol reduces the size of Shari'ah-compliant stocks which will deter the growth of Islamic finance. From the above it can be deduced that DJIM is more conservative in screening companies based on their involvement in business activities as compared to KLSEII and FTSE. Table 1 shows the comparison of the equity index providers based on qualitative criteria.

3 Quantitative Screening

Table 2 presents the financial ratios considered by equity index providers with a brief description.

Although the above-mentioned financial ratios are adopted by most Islamic equity screening providers, there are dissimilarities in the threshold levels and also in the application of these ratios. DJIM values the worth of a company based on its market capitalisation and employs this valuation in calculating the relevant ratios. It claims that the real worth of the company is reflected by its market value and it uses moving average

Table 2 Financial ratios and their descriptions

Liquidity ratio	Conventionally, a high level of liquidity is an advantage to a company because it signified its ability to meet its short-term obligations. However, high liquidity from the Shari'ah perspective renders a company impermissible for investment because a company's shares can only be negotiable if it holds a significant proportion of fixed assets (Abdul Rahman, Yahya, & Nasir, 2010)
Debt ratio	From both conventional and Islamic perspective, a high debt ratio is discouraged because it is positively related with bankruptcy risk. This ratio measures the overall financial risk faced by the shareholders (Pok, 2012)
Interest ratio	Usually, companies with excess liquidity channel such funds to banks as deposits which increases their non-compliance due to the interest received from such investments; thus, the income generated from such activities should not exceed certain threshold
Non-permissible income ratio	This measures the ratio of a company's income arising from prohibited activities to its total income. Majority of scholars argue that a company is still Shari'ah-compliant if its non-permissible income is incidental and negligible when compared to the total income (Abdul Rahman et al., 2010)

Source: Summarised from Abdul Rahman et al. (2010) and Pok (2012)

market capitalisation to eliminate seasonal effects (Dergis & Marzban, 2008). However, KLSEII and FTSE use total assets of a company as denominators in calculating financial ratios.

An advantage of using DJIM market capitalisation method over KLSEII and FTSE total assets approach is that companies' market capitalisation values are readily available from time to time. Total assets of companies are usually publicised once in a year and may be a limitation to the screening agencies in carrying out regular review on the companies. Also, the estimation of total value might be inappropriate if the companies adopt different accounting principles. A company which is Shari'ah-compliant might be considered non-Shari'ah-compliant if its revenue recognition strategy undervalues its total assets; this increases its ratios above the threshold as compared to other companies with a different revenue recognition strategy (Dergis & Marzban, 2008).

On the contrary, Khatkhatay and Nisar (2007) criticised the use of market capitalisation and favour total assets as the best measure of a company's worth. They argue that varying conditions which are difficult to predict affects share prices. A company considered Shari'ah-compliant today might not be Shari'ah-compliant tomorrow because of stock price volatility on its market value. This forces Islamic investors to withdraw their investments from the company, leading to a further downside pressure on the share price. They concluded that such market destabilisation which arises as a result of the adoption of market capitalisation in the screening norm is avoidable and unhealthy.

Another notable difference among the different equity indices is the limit of threshold set for classifying companies into Shari'ah-compliant and non-Shari'ah-compliant. Majority of equity screening regulators allow a maximum of 33% for debt and interest ratios. This is justified by the hadith of the prophet (*pbuh*) where he advised Abu Bakr (*ra*) not to donate more than one-third of his wealth.

4 The Case: Nigerian NSELII

The NSELII screening of Shari'ah-compliant stocks is done by an international Shari'ah advisory board which comprises renowned Islamic scholars. The Shari'ah advisory board applies standard criteria in evaluating companies based on the principles of Shari'ah. The screening follows a stage-by-stage process. Phase I which is the qualitative sector screening is presented in Table 3.

After excluding companies with non-compliant business activities, the other companies are screened for the Phase II criteria; companies that meet up with the requirements of this phase are considered Shari'ah-compliant. The process of the quantitative financial screening is presented in Fig. 1.

The population of the study includes 15 companies approved by Lotus capital Shari'ah advisory board. Two companies were excluded from the study due to unavailability of data. Also, five out-of-sample companies were considered to strengthen the validity of the findings. Table 4 shows the industrial categorisation of companies used in this study.

This study employs four financial ratios in comparing the relevance and degree of stringency in the standards set by the most globally recognised Islamic equity index providers. Table 5 shows the different methodologies adopted by various Islamic index providers, in screening equity.

Table 3 Businesses exempted from NSELII

Sector	Business activities
Insurance	All conventional insurance companies
Banking	All financial institutions dealing in conventional finance
Alcohol	Producers, distributors and sellers of liquor
Pork	Companies who derive substantial income from this area
Defence	Manufacture and trade in firearms and ammunitions
Gambling	Casinos, Hotels and other companies involved with gambling
Entertainment	Companies involved with adult entertainment

Source: Summarised based on Pok (2012)

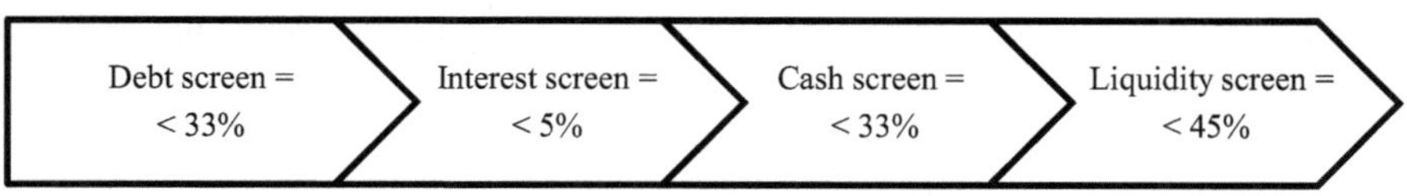

Fig. 1 Quantitative financial screening. Source: Authors' own. Note: Meanings of the terms are provided in Appendix 2

Table 4 Composition of companies according to industry

Type of industries	No of in-sample companies	Percentage	No of out-of-sample companies	Percentage
Food producers	4	30.77	1	20
Oil and gas	2	15.38	2	40
Construction and Material	3	23.08	–	–
Personal goods	2	15.38	–	–
Electronic and electrical equipment	–	–	1	20
Pharmaceuticals	1	7.69	–	–
Media	–	–	1	20
Chemicals	1	7.69	–	–
Total	13	100	5	100

Notes: The media company is engaged in the production of educational materials. See Appendix 1 for the details of companies in each industry
Source: Authors' own

Table 5 Summary of financial ratios used by index providers

Ratios	DJIM	FTSE	KLSEII
Liquidity ratio	$\frac{AR_i(t)}{MC_i(t)} < 33\%$	$\frac{AR_i(t)+C_i(t)}{TA_i(t)} < 50\%$	$\frac{C_i(t)}{TA_i(t)} < 33\%$
Interest ratios	$\frac{CSI(t)}{MC_i(t)} < 33\%$	$\frac{CSI(t)}{TA_i(t)} < 33\%$	$\frac{TI_i(t)}{PBT_i(t)} < 5\%$
Debt ratio	$\frac{TD_i(t)}{MC_i(t)} < 33\%$	$\frac{TD_i(t)}{TA_i(t)} < 33\%$	$\frac{TD_i(t)}{TA_i(t)} < 33\%$
Non-permissible ratio	Not applicable	$\frac{NPI_i(t)}{TR_i(t)} < 5\%$	$\frac{NPI_i(t)}{PBT_i(t)} < 20\%$

Source: Dergis and Marzban (2008), Sani and Othman (2013)
Note: Meanings of the terms used are provided in Appendix 2

The comparison of the companies based on qualitative sector screening shows the acceptability of all the samples by the different equity index providers. Therefore, all the companies are eligible for quantitative screening. This outcome is expected as Dergis and Marzban (2008) identify that only minor qualitative differences exist among equity providers. Appendix 1 shows a list of the companies, their core business and secondary activities.

Table 6 presents the results of the financial ratios calculated based on the formula adopted by the respective screening regulators. The result of KLSEII shows that in 2012, 84.62% of the companies have cash constituting less than 33% of their total assets. All three indices provide dissimilar results. Although DJIM and KLSEII adopt the same threshold, the liquidity ratio was different because of the different formula adopted.

Despite DJIM and FTSE employing the same interest threshold, more companies were able to meet up with FTSE standards in year 2012 and 2014 because FTSE uses total assets as its denominator which is relatively stable when compared with a DJIM's market capitalisation approach. Similarly, all three equity regulators adopt

Table 6 Analyses using financial ratios and thresholds set by index providers

		DJIM			FTSE			KLSE		
Ratio	*N*	Threshold	Freq.	%	Threshold	Freq.	%	Threshold	Freq.	%
2012										
Liquidity	13	<33%	9	69	<50	6	46	<33	11	84.62
Interest	13	<33%	7	54	<33	11	85	<5	7	53.85
Debt	13	<33%	6	46	<33	12	92	<33	12	92.31
NPI	13	NA	NA	NA	<5	13	100	<20	13	100
2013										
Liquidity	13	<33%	6	46	<50	8	62	<33	12	92.31
Interest	13	<33%	11	85	<33	12	92	<5	8	61.54
Debt	13	<33%	8	62	<33	13	100	<33	13	100
NPI	13	NA	NA	NA	<5	13	100	<20	12	100
2014										
Liquidity	13	<33%	5	39	<50	8	61	<33	12	92.31
Interest	13	<33%	12	92	<33	12	92	NA	9	62.23
Debt	13	<33%	6	46	<33	9	69	<5	9	69.23
NPI	13	NA	NA	NA	<5	13	100	<20	12	92.31

Notes: Freq. represents number of companies compliant according to the criteria of the index provider (i.e. DJIM, etc.)
Source: Authors' own

33% debt threshold, but a differing level of compliance was found due to the use of different estimators.

DJIM screens out companies that have any involvement with activities which are not Shari'ah-compliant at the qualitative stage; therefore no threshold is calculated. However, FTSE allows company a liberty of 5% NPI provided it is not the company's core business. The result is similar for both FTSE and KLSEII because both index providers adopt the same estimates. Overall DJIM adopts a more conservative screening measure. Due to inherent problem with harmonisation, we conducted out-of-sample analyses that are given in the following tables (Tables 7, 8, and 9).

4.1 Harmonisation Issues and the Solution

The out-of-sample result shows that it is difficult for companies to meet DJIM requirement. Generally, it is seen that the KLSEII accommodates more companies over the years. One hundred percent of the sample passes KLSEII liquidity test, while only 40% could meet the requirement of DJIM and FTSE. A wide variation is seen in the debt screening; while no company was able to meet DJIM requirement in all 3 years considered; the least percentage of companies endorsed by FTSE and KLSEII over the 3-year period is 60%. Both the out-of-sample and in-sample method show that a large number of companies can easily meet the NPI requirement of FTSE and KLSEII.

The report above considers case-by-case standards of the different equity providers. It is therefore necessary to estimate the number of companies that fulfils the overall criteria of each index provider to have an in-depth understanding of how much they differ from one another. Table 8 presents the number of companies that met the Shari'ah requirement of the index providers. The result shows that KLSEII accommodates the highest number of companies in all the years. This is not surprising as the adoption of stringent criteria will hinder Malaysia's aim of becoming an Islamic finance hub.

The ranking of out-of-sample result is like the in-sample estimates with KLSEII endorsing the largest number of companies followed by FTSE and DJMI in all years. It shows that most companies rejected by NSELII are given similar judgement when screened by other indices. Thus, the major differences are varying level of leniency in accepting companies.

Contrary to Khatkhatay and Nisar (2007) that the use of market capitalisation gives inconsistent result, this study found the adoption of market capitalisation to be more stable than the use of total assets. They explained that high volatility in the stock market might change the Shari'ah status of companies frequently. The result shows that DJIM which values firms based on their market capitalisation has a relatively stable number of approved companies over the years as compared to other methods. For the out-of-sample results, it consistently classified no company as Shari'ah-compliant, unlike the KLSEII which approved 60% in the first year and 40% in the second year. The consistency is also seen in the in-sample result as DJIM approved four companies in year 2013 and 2014. Conversely no other method had similar number of approved companies. This point shows that the adoption of

Table 7 Analysis of out-of-sample companies according to ratios and threshold set by index providers

		DJIM			FTSE			KLSE		
Ratio	*N*	Threshold	Freq.	%	Threshold	Freq.	%	Threshold	Freq.	%
2012										
Liquidity	5	<33%	2	40	<50	2	40	<33	5	100
Interest	5	<33%	2	40	<33	5	100	<5	2	40
Debt	5	<33%	0	0	<33	4	80	<33	4	80
NPI	5	NA	NA	NA	<5	5	100	<20	4	80
2013										
Liquidity	5	<33%	2	40	<50	2	40	<33	5	100
Interest	5	<33%	2	40	<33	5	100	<5	3	60
Debt	5	<33%	0	0	<33	3	60	<33	3	60
NPI	5	NA	NA	NA	<5	5	100	<20	3	60
2014										
Liquidity	5	<33%	1	20	<50	2	40	<33	5	100
Interest	5	<33%	3	60	<33	5	100	NA	3	60
Debt	5	<33%	0	0	<33	3	60	<5	3	60
NPI	5	NA	NA	NA	<5	5	100	<20	4	80

Note: NA means not applicable; Freq. represents number of Shari'ah-compliant companies
Source: Authors' own

Table 8 Analysis of least to most restrictive screens—sample companies

	DJIM			FTSE		KLSEII	
Ratios	*N*	Freq.	%	Freq.	%	Freq.	%
2012							
Liquidity	13	9	69	6	46	11	85
Liquidity and interest	13	4	31	6	46	7	53
Liquidity, interest and debt	13	1	8	5	38	5	38
Liquidity, interest, debt and NPI	13	**1**	**8**	**4**	**31**	**5**	**38**
2013							
Liquidity	13	6	46	8	62	12	92
Liquidity and interest	13	5	38	8	62	8	61
Liquidity, interest and debt	13	3	23	8	62	8	62
Liquidity, interest, debt and NPI	13	**3**	**23**	**8**	**62**	**8**	**62**
2014							
Liquidity	13	5	38	8	62	12	92
Liquidity and interest	13	5	38	8	62	9	69
Liquidity, interest and debt	13	3	23	6	46	7	54
Liquidity, interest, debt and NPI	13	**3**	**23**	**6**	**46**	**7**	**54**

Source: Authors' own

Note: Least restrictive (only liquidity screen) to most restrictive screen (liquidity and other three screens). (a) DJIM does not include NPI ratio in its process. (b) Number and percentage of companies that met the requirement of each index provider is written in bold text. (c) Freq. represents number of compliant companies according to selected screen

moving average market capitalisation is an effective measure in eliminating seasonal effects on DJIM screening decision. Also, the study disagrees with the conclusion of Pok (2012) that the DJIM is not a stricter criterion and that its estimators are what make it seem stricter. Apart from the effect of DJMI estimators, its stringent criteria rule out a number of companies at the qualitative state, thereby making it consider fewer companies than other screening regulators in the quantitative stage.

5 Level of Differences, Harmonisation and Way Forward

This case study analyses the differences of the world's leading Shari'ah equity screening criteria and provides an insight on how these differences affect the classification of equities into Shari'ah-compliant and non-Shari'ah-compliant. Financial ratios adopted by DJIM, FTSE and KLSE were calculated on NSELII Shari'ah-compliant companies, and it was found that a large percentage of companies in NSELII are approved by KLSE. Contrary to the findings that the use of market capitalisation provides inconsistent result, the result of DJIM was more consistent over time. Generally, the DJIM is found to have stricter restrictions than another index provider.

Table 9 Analysis of least to most restrictive screens—out-of-sample companies

		DJIM		FTSE		KLSEII	
Ratios	*N*	Freq.	%	Freq.	%	Freq.	%
2012							
Liquidity	5	2	40	2	40	5	100
Liquidity and interest	5	1	20	2	40	2	40
Liquidity, interest and debt	5	0	0	1	20	2	40
Liquidity, interest, debt and NPI	5	**0**	**0**	**1**	**20**	**2**	**40**
2013							
Liquidity	5	2	40	2	40	5	100
Liquidity and interest	5	1	20	2	40	3	60
Liquidity, interest and debt	5	0	0	1	20	2	40
Liquidity, interest, debt and NPI	5	**0**	**0**	**1**	**20**	**2**	**40**
2014							
Liquidity ratio	5	1	20	2	40	5	100
Liquidity and interest	5	1	20	2	40	3	60
Liquidity, interest and debt	5	0	0	0	0	2	40
Liquidity, interest, debt and NPI	5	**0**	**0**	**0**	**0**	**2**	**40**

Source: Authors' own

Note: DJIM does not include NPI ratio in its process. (a) Number and percentage of companies that met the requirement of each index provider is written in bold text. (b) Least restrictive (only liquidity screen) to most restrictive screen (liquidity and other three screens). (c) Freq. represents number of compliant companies according to selected screen

Although the range of differences among equity providers indicates the beauty of Islam, it shows how Islam permits flexibility among people and institutions in their unique environments based on social benefit. Notwithstanding, harmonisation of the different equity screening indices is important to promote the growth of global Islamic capital market. The confusion existing among investors will be reduced, and the citizen of a nation would not find the stocks of other countries less acceptable, thereby encouraging international investments. The findings of this study are expected to give understanding of the different equity screening providers to Islamic capital market stakeholders to enable them to arrive at a more synchronised regulation.

Due to limited number of companies included in the NSELII, the population of this study is small. Also, not all Islamic indices were examined, and this paper considered only three dominant Islamic indices. Future researchers should take this into consideration when selecting a benchmark for their studies and consider more indices to have a better understanding of the extent of the differences.

Appendix 1

Brief explanation of the sample

Industry	Company name	Core business	Secondary activities
Food producer	Cadbury	Manufacture and sales of refreshment beverages, confectionery and intermediate *Cocos*	Cocoa farming
	Nascon	Refining and sales of salt	Construction
	Nestle	Production of food and beverages	Health science
	UACN	Restaurant services, manufacturing, sales and distribution of food	Production of batteries, livestock feeds, chemicals
	Flour mill	Flour milling, production of pasta, edible oil and refined sugar	Power generation
Oil and Gas	Mobil	Marketing of petroleum products	Hydrant installation
	Seplat	Exploration and production of oil	Real assets
	Mrs	Manufacturing and marketing of refined oil	Lube blending plant, fuel terminals
	Forte	Manufacturing of petroleum products	Marketing of petroleum products
Construction and material	CCNN	Production and marketing of cement	Education
	Dangote Cement	Manufacturing and marketing of cement	Edibles transport, telecommunication
	Lafarge	Manufacturing and marketing of cement products	Construction and architecture
Personal goods	Unilever	Food, food ingredients, home and personal care products	Chemical production
	PZ	Manufacturing, distribution and sales of household brands	Electronics
Electronic and electrical equipment	Cutix	Manufacturing of electric cables and wires	Fossil fuels
Pharmaceuticals	GlaxoSmithKline	Manufacturing, marketing and distribution of consumer healthcare and pharmaceutical products	Consumer products
Media	Academy press	Printing of educational materials and general books	Mobilising science-based enterprises
Chemicals	CAP	Chemical and allied products	Coating business

Source: Authors' own table (2018)

Appendix 2

Meaning of abbreviations used in the study

$AR_i(t)$:	Accounts receivables of asset *i* at time *t*
$C_i(t)$:	Cash and cash equivalents of asset *i* at time *t*
$CSI(t)$:	Cash, cash equivalents, short-term investments of assets *i* at time *t*
$TA_i(t)$:	Total assets of asset *i* at time *t*
$TD_i(t)$:	Total debts of asset *i* at time *t*
$MC_i(t)$:	Market capitalisation of asset *i* at time *t*
$TR_i(t)$:	Total revenue of asset *i* at time *t*
$I_i(t)$:	Interest-bearing securities *i* at time *t*
$TI_i(t)$:	Total interest income of asset *i* at time *t*
$NPI_i(t)$:	Non-permissible income of asset *i* at time *t*
$PBT_i(t)$:	Profit before tax *i* at time *t*

Source: Authors' own

References

Abdul Rahman, A., Yahya, M., & Nasir, M. (2010). Islamic norms for stock screening, a comparison between the Kuala Lumpur Stock Exchange Islamic index and the Dow Jones Islamic market index. *International Journal of Islamic and Middle Eastern Finance and Management, 3* (3), 228–240.

Adam, N., & Abu Bakar, N. (2014). Shariah screening process in Malaysia. *Procedia-Social and Behavioural Sciences, 121*, 113–123.

Dergis, U., & Marzban, S. (2008). Review and analysis of current Shariah-compliant equity screening practices. *International Journal of Islamic and Middle Eastern Finance and Management, 1*(4), 285–303.

Htay, S., Abeedeen, Z., & Salman, S. (2013). Towards standardization of Shari'ah screening norms and practices. *International Journal of Humanities and Social Science Invention, 2*(11), 23–30.

Khatkhatay, M., & Nisar, S. (2007). Shari'ah compliant equity investments: An assessment of current screening norms. *Islamic Economic Studies, 15*, 27–76.

Pok, W. (2012). Analysis of Shariah quantitative screening norms among Malaysia Shariah-compliant stocks. *Investment Management and Financial Innovations, 9*(2), 69–80.

Sani, N., & Othman, R. (2013). *Revision of Shari'ah screening methodology the status of Shari'ah compliant companies in Malaysia*. In 3rd International Conference on Management Proceeding. Available at: www.internationalconference.com.my

Balqis obtained her MSc in Investment and Islamic Finance from the University of Nottingham Malaysia. She is currently working as an independent researcher in Malaysia and in giving financial advise to entrepreneurs who aims at financing their businesses the halal way. Her interests are Islamic capital markets, Islamic financial products, and education.

Mamunur Rashid received his PhD on Behavioural Finance from National University of Malaysia in 2014. He was awarded the PGCHE from the University of Nottingham in 2018. He is currently a Senior Assistant Professor of Finance in Universiti Brunei Darussalam. Prior to joining UBD, Mamunur taught Finance at Nottingham University Business School, The University of Nottingham (Malaysia Campus) since October 2012 until September 2018, and at East West University, Bangladesh (September 2005 - February 2012). His teaching areas include Islamic

Finance, International Finance, Corporate Finance and Financial Economics. Dr Mamunur was the founding deputy director of the Centre for Islamic Business and Finance Research at the University of Nottingham Malaysia Campus. Dr Mamunur is also an Associate Editor of International Journal of Islamic and Middle Eastern Finance and Management (Emerald). He is a Fellow of the Higher Education Academy, UK, and a member of Malaysian Finance Association since 2014. His research interest includes a broader investigation into the connection between values and performance in multi-cultural setting.

A Basic Comprehensive Accounting Package for *Musharakah*: Consolidation of Islamic and Conventional Practices

Umar Habibu Umar

Abstract

The current popular and universal accounting standard for the *musharakah* is Financial Accounting Standard (FAS) No. 4 issued by AAOIFI. However, this standard covers only recognitions, measurements and presentations of events and transactions in the financial statements of Islamic banks (IBs). Thus, this study consolidates conventional accounting practices relevant to partnership, AAOIFI's FAS No. 4 and the two *musharakah* standards developed by the Bank Negara Malaysia (BNM), with the view to producing a comprehensive accounting package for the *musharakah* that conforms to the *Shari'ah*. Basically, the study establishes that conventional accounts such as capital account, current account, income statement, revaluation account, realization account and cash account could be applied to *musharakah* with a view to providing a complete set of financial statements in line with the *Shari'ah* for the benefits of all the partners. But interest on drawings, interest on capital and interest on loan are the financial transactions found to be against the *Shari'ah*.

1 Introduction to the Concept of *Musharakah*

Musharakah is an Arabic word for partnership. It literally means "sharing" (Arshad & Ismail, 2010; BNM, 2010, 2015; Usmani, n.d.). In early literature of Islamic jurisprudence, the term *Musharakah* is also referred to as *Shirkah* (Arshad & Ismail, 2010; BNM, 2010, 2015; Usmani, n.d.). It is described as a contract that exists between two or more persons commonly referred to as partners, who combine their capital to an existing or a new business of a real estate or moveable asset, either on a

U. H. Umar (✉)
Department of Accounting, Northwest University, Kano, Nigeria

E. M. Ghazali et al. (eds.), *Management of Shari'ah Compliant Businesses*, Management for Professionals, https://doi.org/10.1007/978-3-030-10907-3_8

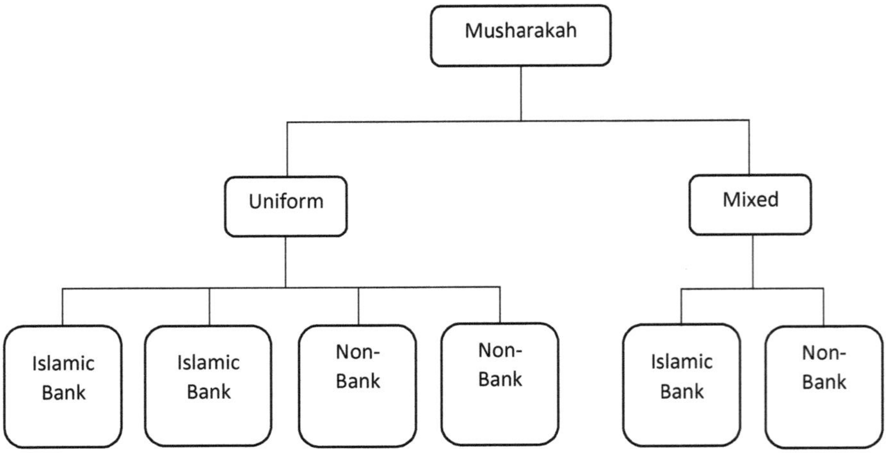

Fig. 1 Nature of the partners in musharakah. Source: Designed by the Author (2018)

temporary or permanent basis (BNM, 2010, 2015). This definition shows that *musharakah* exists between any two or more persons (not necessarily including the IB). However, the AAOIFI's definition as stated in its Financial Accounting Standard (FAS) No. 4 shows that *musharakah* is a partnership that occurs between IBs and their customers. The fact is that it could exist between two or more natural persons by combining their capital together to carry out a business. To sum up, it is a form of Islamic equity finance in which two or more persons (not necessarily including the IB) put together their capital in order to undertake a business in strict compliance with the *Shari'ah*. Figure 1 presents the nature of partners that could be involved in the partnership.

Figure 1 depicts the nature of the partners to the *musharakah* using two persons, being the minimum number of persons to form it. It could be seen that the partners in the *musharakah* are either uniform or mixed. The partners are IB and non-bank (NB). In this case, the NB is any individual (a natural person) or an organization other than IB. *Musharakah* is said to be uniform if all partners are either IBs or NBs, for example, if two or more IBs or Muhammad and Ja'afar contribute capital to engage in the business. In contrast, it is said to be mixed when, for example, an IB and its customer contribute capital to undertake the business.

Moreover, the need to sustain any form of *musharakah* business cannot be overemphasized in Islam. Provision of employment opportunities, redistribution of income, wealth maximization, business *zakah* maximization, *waqf* and discharging other corporate philanthropic activities among others are major reasons why the operations and practices of *musharakah* need to be sustained for poverty alleviation, welfare of *ummah* and economic growth and development.

2 Limitation of Contemporary Musharakah Accounting Standards

Accounting issues relating to the formation of partnership, admission of a new partner, retirement of a partner, preparation of annual financial statements and liquidation of the partnership are well known and documented in both local and international books of accounting. In addition, local and international accounting standards are developed to guide the preparation of such financial statements. International Accounting Standards (IASs)/International Financial Reporting Standards (IFRSs) are developed by the International Accounting Standard Board (IASB) to guide recognitions, measurements, disclosures and presentations of all transactions and events in the financial statements. These accounting standards are developed based on some principles, conventions and methods, some of which might contravene the *Shari'ah*. Consequently, the emergence of new modern Islamic banking and finance necessitates the creation of the Accounting and Auditing Organization for Islamic Financial Institutions (AAOIFI) to develop accounting, auditing and governance standards for Islamic financial institutions (IFIs) for treatments of events and transactions that have not been provided in the conventional standards. Thus, AAOIFI's standards are applied by the IFIs, especially the banks (Karim, 2001).

Currently, the only popular universal accounting standard for *musharakah* is AAOIFI's FAS No. 4. In spite of the fact that Islamic accounting protects the interests of the entire members of the society by ensuring fairness among them (Ahmed, 2012; Ather & Ullah, 2009; Hameed, 2000; Haniffa & Hudaib, 2010, 2011; Trokic, 2015), this standard (FAS No. 4) is only meant for the IBs. This standard does not cover recording partnership transactions and accounting treatments in the book of the client to the IB. Therefore, it is neither comprehensive to take care the accounting for the customers in *musharakah* with the IB nor *musharakah* where the IB is not a partner. Moreover, a research conducted through interview with Islamic accounting scholars in Malaysia reveals that AAOIFI's financial accounting standards are not as comprehensive as IASs/IFRSs and consequently IFIs adapt the IAS/IFRSs treatments of events and transactions that are not found in the AAOIFI's standards (Hameed & Yaya, 2005). This signifies that the conventional accounting practices could be adapted in the preparation of the financial statements of the IFIs, provided that they do not contravene the *Shari'ah*. This approach was actually used by AAOFI to develop accounting standards for Islamic financial institutions (Karim, 1995; Lewis, 2001). In other words, AAOIFI's standards are developed by substantial adaption of the conventional standards.

Moreover, although the IASs/IFRSs have been criticized for protecting self-interest with no emphasis on socio-economic justice (Hameed, 2000; Haniffa & Hudaib, 2011), they are for general application by firms in all industries with the exception of IAS 30 and IAS 41 (Afou, 2017; Hameed, 2007). By implication, the conventional accounting standards are almost applicable to every sector of the economy such as banking and finance sector, manufacturing sector, education sector, health sector, communication sector and agricultural sector among others.

3 Accounts for Musharakah

The key contents of conventional financial statements (such as statement of profit or loss, statement of financial position, statement of cash flow, etc.) are more useful to investors and other capital suppliers; nevertheless they are accepted to be integral part of Islamic accounting since the capital providers are part of the society (Hameed, 2000). In addition, Islamic accounting is not restricted to protecting the interests of the investors alone but rather the interests of the whole members of the society with fairness and justice. In order to prepare a complete set of financial statements, there is the need to keep proper records of the financial transactions. Keeping records for Islamic transactions is synonymous to the conventional counterpart (Butt & Hassan, 2011). Therefore, it is not wrong if the conventional source documents (cash receipts, bank statements, sales invoices, purchases invoices, credit notes, debit notes, payment vouchers, petty cash vouchers, bank pay-in-slips, cheque counterfoils, etc.), books of original entry (purchases journal, sales journal, returns inwards journal, returns outwards journal and journal proper), ledgers, etc. are kept with the view to keeping comprehensive records needed to prepare complete financial statements for the *musharakah*.

A. Capital Account

One of the important things in partnership is capital. Normally, the partnership is formed when different persons combine their wealth together to undertake a profit venture. According to AAOIFI's FAS No. 4 and Bank Negara Malaysia (BNM) (2010); Bank Negara Malaysia (BNM) (2015),[1] capital contribution to the *musharakah* could be made in cash or kind (any asset other than cash). In this case, the capital contribution in kind should be revalued at a fair value (market value).

The capital contributed by each partner is recorded in the capital account. In conventional practice, it is prepared in columnar form, that is, a column is created for each partner. There are two types of capital account: fixed capital account plus current account and fluctuating capital account (Wood & Sangster, 2002). Fixed capital account is the normal capital account into which the capital contributed by each partner is credited and debited to the cash/bank account or asset account (in the case of the contribution in kind). The balance of the capital remains constant for many years unless the partner brings additional capital or ceases to be a partner. Therefore, the fixed capital account is not going to be influenced by any profit or loss suffered during the financial year. These transactions that influence the capital of the partners are posted into the current account. The current account, as the name connotes, its balance normally changes (either increase or decrease) within the financial year. In this account, the benefits allocated to the partners such as share of profit, salaries, commission and interest on capital are credited to the account. On the other hand, drawings, interest on drawings, share of loss etc. are debited to the account. The account's balance can either be credit or

[1]For full details and explanations about the capital contribution in line with *Shari'ah*, see these references.

debit. While a credit balance is a surplus, a debit balance indicates that the partner is indebted to the business. The fluctuating capital account is opened if both fixed capital account and current account are combined in one account. Therefore, all debit and credit entries of the current account are correspondingly posted to the capital account.

It is recommended that both the fixed capital account and the current accounts should be opened concurrently in order to prevent the partners from reducing the actual capital they contribute (Wood & Sangster, 2002). In other words, keeping the two accounts can prevent the partners from reducing their contributed capital, especially as a result of excessive drawings.

From the Islamic point of view, the above transactions are valid except the interest on drawings and interest on capital. Charging a constant profit on an investment or any fixed return on the amount lent (because the lender does not bear any risk that might happen) is completely condemned by the *Shari'ah* except in the case of *murabaha* (Hameed, 2000). Therefore, fixed return on conventional bonds and preference shares as well as interest on leasing, notes receivables and notes payable are totally forbidden by the *Shari'ah* (Butt & Hassan, 2011). Similarly, the practices such as the futures and options, short sale, preferred stock, interest-based modern investment modes related transactions which are acceptable in conventional accounting are also rejected (Ather & Ullah, 2009). It is noteworthy that though nowadays Islam is the only religion that openly condemns interest, other religions like Christianity, Judaism and Hinduism reject it as well (Lewis, 2007).

B. Profit or Loss Account

One important issue to agree by the partners during the formation of the *musharakah* is the profit and loss sharing ratio(s). In conventional sense, the partners should agree on the ratio during the formation, but where there is no such agreement, Section 24 (1) of the Partnership Act (1890) regulates that both the profit and the loss should be shared equally. Conventionally, in most cases the same ratio is used to share both the profit and the loss, and it is allowed to fix or guarantee a certain amount of profit to any partner. This is totally condemned in Islam.

However, according to BNM (2010), the profit sharing ratio might depend on either the capital contribution or consensus of the partners. The partners are expected to agree on the profit sharing ratio before commencing the business; otherwise the business becomes unlawful (Usmani, n.d.).

Muslim jurists unanimously agreed that the loss suffered by partnership should be borne by the partners in the ratio of their capital contribution (BNM, 2010, 2015). In addition, other regulations for sharing the loss are (a) in any loss in capital suffered by the partnership as a result of misconduct, negligence or breaking partnership deed, such person responsible shall bear the loss whether an active partner or an employee of the business; (b) a partner can willingly bear a loss suffered by any other partner even if it is not stated in the partnership agreement; and (c) a non-partner can also accept to pay for the loss suffered by the partner among others (Usmani, n.d.). Similarly, the loss suffered by the IB as a result of misconduct or negligence of the other partner should be recognized in the financial statements of the IB as receivable amount from the responsible partner (AAOIFI, 2015).

The profit or loss to share is determined by preparing income statement (or statement of profit or loss account). The account has three sections: section 1 is for determining the gross profit; section 2 is where the net profit is ascertained; and finally, section 3 is used for sharing the profit or loss among the partners. The gross profit is the excess of the revenue over the cost of sales. The net profit is the excess of the gross profit over the total expenses. The first two sections are similar to the account for one-man business. Section 3 is called "Profit or Loss Appropriation Account" or simply "Appropriation Account", which is opened to share the net profit or loss among the partners. Transactions that are normally debited to the account are partners' salaries and commission, interest on capital and interest on loan, whereas net profit and interest on drawings are credited to the account. The difference between the two sides represents the profit or loss. The excess of the credit side over the debit side is the profit, which is shared by debiting the appropriation account and crediting the capital (or current) account. On the other hand, it is a loss if the total debit side is greater than the total credit side, and such amount should be shared by debiting the capital account and crediting the appropriation account.

C. Account for Changes in Partnership

Basically, the partnership is said to be changed as result of admission of a new partner into the business, withdrawal of a partner as a result of retirement or death and change in profit and loss sharing ratio. Upon the occurrence of any of these reasons, a new sharing ratio must to be established and the assets have to be revalued with the view to be fair to all the partners (which is a key objective of Islamic accounting). Revaluation of the asset often makes its value to either increase or decrease. The value of the asset is increased if its fair value is greater than the carrying amount (book value). On the other hand, the value is decreased if the fair value is less than its carrying amount.

Revaluation account is opened to accommodate the changes in the values of the assets. Any decrease in the value of an asset is debited to the account, whereas an increase in the value should be credited to the account. Revaluation expenses should also be debited to the account. The debit balance of the account represents a profit on revaluation, which should be shared by debiting the revaluation account and crediting the capital account, with the share of each partner. On the other hand, if it is a loss (credit balance), the amount should be shared by debiting the partners' capital account and crediting the revaluation account.

The accounting entries for a partner's withdrawal from the *musharakah* are to debit capital account of the partner and credit cash/bank account with the capital balance of the partner at the time of the withdrawal. But if a current account is operated, the balance has to be transferred from the current account to the fixed capital account with the view to arriving at the partner's capital balance. This is done by debiting the current and crediting the capital account (if a credit balance exists) or debiting the capital account and crediting the current account (if there is a debit balance).

In the case of the introduction of a new partner, the capital contribution in cash and in kind (at a fair value) would be debited to the cash/bank account and asset account, respectively, and credited to the new partner's capital account.

D. Account for Dissolution of *Musharakah*

According to BNM (2010, 2015), the partnership is terminated because of the following reasons: (a) consensus of the partners, (b) expiration of the tenure of the business agreed by the partners, (c) death of the partner(s) (especially the active), (d) incapacitation of the partners, (e) purchase of the whole business by a single partner or (f) illegality of the partnership. Similarly, these reasons are almost obtainable in the Partnership Act, 1890 (see Sections 32–35).

In Islamic finance, the total revenue from the disposal of the assets is used to settle liquidation expenses, total debts and, finally, the balance (whether profit or loss) which should be distributed among the partners. These are basically the same in the conventional practices as regulated by Section 44(b) of the Partnership Act, 1890.

The account to open for the dissolution of the partnership is called "Realization Account". Basically, carrying amounts of all the assets (except cash/bank), dissolution expenses and discount allowed to debtors are debited to the account, whereas sales proceeds from the disposal of the assets and discount received from creditors are credited to the account. A debit balance (profit) is shared by debiting the realization account and crediting the capital account. In contrast, if it is a credit balance (loss), it is shared by debiting the capital account and crediting the realization account. Any balance (whether debit or credit) in the partners' current account (if any) should be transferred to the capital account. Liabilities and dissolution expenses are paid by debiting their accounts and crediting the cash/bank account. And the amount received from debtors should be debited to the cash/bank account and credited to the debtors account. Then, to settle the partners, the partners' capital balances should be debited to the capital account and credited to the cash/bank account. To sum up, the necessary accounts to open for the dissolution of the partnership are realization account, capital account and cash/bank account.

However, it is worthy to note that if one of the partner becomes bankrupt (insolvent), that is, has a debit balance in the capital account which he could not settle from his personal wealth, such amount could be willingly settled by the partner(s) or someone outside the partnership (BNM, 2010, 2015). However, in conventional practice, it is mandatory to bear such loss as it is established in the case of Garner V. Murray (1904). In this case, it is ruled that solvent partners are responsible for the debit balance of the insolvent partner. The partners are expected to share the amount based on the agreed sharing ratio; otherwise, it should be shared according to their opening capital balances before the dissolution (Lee, 1973).

4 Conclusion

Musharakah (partnership) as a profit-loss sharing contract enjoys absolute and unanimous validity by all Muslim jurists. However, from accounting perspective, it enjoys little attentions from both practitioners and scholars. Thus, this study produces a basic comprehensive accounting package for *musharakah* through consolidation of conventional practices of accounting, AAOIFI's FAS No. 4 and two *musharakah* standards developed by BNM for the sustainability of the *musharakah*. It is established that apart from interest-based transactions such as interest on drawings, interest on capital and interest on loan, almost all the accounting entries posted into capital account, current account, income statement, revaluation account, realization account and cash account are valid for the application in the *musharakah*. These accounts need to be opened for the purpose of accountability in order to ensure continuous mutual understanding among the partners and successful implementation of the partnership agreements especially the ones that have financial implications. These could contribute greatly to the sustainability of the *musharakah*.

5 Limitations of the Study

This case study focusses on basic necessary accounts and accounting entries for the *musharakah*. It is noteworthy that these transactions are not exhaustive. The details of accounting issues such as recognitions, measurements, disclosures and presentations of events and transactions relevant to the *musharakah* have either inadequately or completely not discussed. In addition, goodwill, an intangible asset that emerges when there is change in partnership, has not been discussed in the chapter. Thus, an in-depth research needs to be conducted on its validity and methods of valuations in line with the *Shari'ah*.

References

Accounting and Auditing Organization for Islamic Financial Institutions (AAOIFI). (2015). *Accounting, auditing and governance standards*. Manama: AlMaiman Publishing & Distribution.

Afou, R. B. A. (2017). Knowledge of Islamic accounting among professionals: Evidence from the Tunisian context. *Journal of Islamic Accounting and Business Research, 8*(3), 304–325.

Ahmed, A. A. (2012). Accounting in Islamic perspective: A timely opportunity a timely challenge. *ASA University Review, 6*(2), 11–31.

Arshad, N. C., & Ismail, A. G. (2010). *Shariah* parameters for musharakah contract: A comment. *International Journal of Business and Social Science, 1*(1), 145–162.

Ather, S. M., & Ullah, H. (2009). *Islamic accounting systems and practices*. Retrieved November 13, 2017, from https://www.researchgate.net/publication/263809688/

Bank Negara Malaysia (BNM). (2010). *Draft of shariah parameter reference 4: Musharakah contract*. Retrieved June 15, 2017, from www.bnm.gov.my/guidelines/05_shariah/04_draft_shariah%20parameter_spr4.pdf

Bank Negara Malaysia. (2015). *Musharakah*. Retrieved June 15, 2017, from www.bnm.gov.my/guidelines/05_sharia

Butt, S. A., & Hassan, A. (2011). Valuation and accounting for redeemable corporate capital: An Islamic perspective. *Journal of Islamic Economics, Banking and Finance, 7*(66), 66–78.

Hameed, S. M. I. (2000). *The need for Islamic accounting: Perceptions of its objectives and characteristics by Malaysian Muslim accountants and accounting academics*. Ph.D, The University of Dundee.

Hameed, S. M. I. (2007). *IFRS vs AAOIFI: The clash of standards?* Retrieved December 10, 2016, from https://www.researchgate.net/publication/23779684/

Hameed, S. M. I., & Yaya, R. (2005). The emerging issues on the objectives and characteristics of Islamic accounting for Islamic business organizations. *Malaysian Accounting Review, 4*(1), 75–92.
Haniffa, R., & Hudaib, M. (2010). The two Ws of Islamic accounting research. *Journal of Islamic Accounting and Business Research, 1*(1), 5–9.
Haniffa, R., & Hudaib, M. (2011). A conceptual framework for Islamic accounting. In C. Napier & R. Haniffa (Eds.), *Islamic accounting series*. Cheltenham: Edward Elgar.
Karim, F. A. A. (1995). The nature and rationale of a conceptual framework for financial reporting by Islamic banks. *Accounting and Business Research, 25*(100), 285–300.
Karim, R. A. A. (2001). International accounting harmonization, banking regulation, and Islamic banks. *The International Journal of Accounting, 36*(2), 169–193.
Lee, G. A. (1973). *Modern financial accounting*. London: Thomas Nelson and Sons.
Lewis, M. K. (2001). Islam and accounting. *Accounting Forum, 25*(2), 103–127.
Lewis, M. K. (2007). Comparing Islamic and Christian attitudes to usury. In M. K. Hassan & M. K. Lewis (Eds.), *Handbook of Islamic banking* (pp. 64–81). Cheltenham: Edward Elgar.
Partnership Act. (1890). Retrieved Decemeber 15, 2017, from www.legislation.gov.uk/ukpga/1890/39/pdfs/ukpga_18900039_en.pdf
Trokic, A. (2015). Islamic accounting: History, development and prospects. *European Journal of Islamic Finance, 3*, 1–6.
Usmani, M. T. (n.d.). *An introduction to Islamic finance*. Retrieved December 15, 2017, from www.muftitaqiuusmani.com/
Wood, F., & Sangster, A. (2002). *Business accounting* (11th ed.). London: Pearson Education.

Umar Habibu Umar is a member of the Institute of Chartered Accountants of Nigeria (ICAN). He obtained BSc. and MSc. (Accounting) from Bayero University Kano, Nigeria. He has joined Northwest University Kano, Nigeria in 2013. Umar's major area of research interest is Islamic accounting and finance, especially Islamic inheritance accounting.

Converting Turkish Agricultural Credit Cooperatives into Islamic Financial Institution

Yusuf Dinc

Abstract

Central Union of Agricultural Credit Cooperatives (ACC) is a strong candidate to be the most significant and strategic actor in the interest-free financial sector in Turkey. Although it is currently an interest-based institution, ACC was first introduced to disentangle farmers from interest and usurers through its cooperation-based structure. In recent years farmers as its partners demanded interest-free financing and management reacted to meet the need. Thus a gradual conversion process is applied based on a unique concept. This study will first dwell on the emergence of ACC. The following sections will reveal an environmental analysis by comparing the conventional banking sector and Islamic banking with ACC. The concept for conversion is included in section 3. The last section will compare the ACC business model with those of conventional banking and Islamic banking. Results are reached that reveal ACC's legal structure and regulatory needs through the benefit that can be obtained by conversion and include proposals. This study is a pioneering work in terms of revealing the need for an interest-free conversion and setting forth a new concept needed over an existing example.

1 Introduction

Turkey is at the forefront with investments carried out in the field of Islamic finance. Turkey, with its energy import-based economy, sees Islamic finance as a strategic area for diversifying resources. By transforming this way, a 20% market share is

Y. Dinc (✉)
Islamic Economics and Finance Department, Faculty of Business Administration and Administrative Sciences, Istanbul Sabahattin Zaim University, Istanbul, Turkey
e-mail: yusuf.dinc@izu.edu.tr

E. M. Ghazali et al. (eds.), *Management of Shari'ah Compliant Businesses*, Management for Professionals, https://doi.org/10.1007/978-3-030-10907-3_9

anticipated for the Islamic finance sector. The number of actors multiplies by establishing Islamic banks with public funds. However, the current market share for Islamic finance is at 5% level.

Conversion of conventional actors into interest-free business model can bring an important alternative for taking paths appropriate to the targets. In this respect, Turkey's Agricultural Credit Cooperatives is significant in being able to develop the market through its strong capital structure and favorable business model. At the same time, they possess the modern-era institutionalized structure closest to the field of Islamic finance using the cooperative model.

According to Cooperatives in Developed Economies Report, the mid-nineteenth century found the emergence of cooperatives as an economic organization in the world. The creation of the Industrial Revolution brought economic and social problems such as rapid change and transformation, unemployment, internal migration, and the disruption of income distribution. These problems have reinforced the need for cooperatives. Cooperatives showed itself through the trend of consumption cooperatives that had been started primarily by workers in England. French production cooperatives, German tradesmen, and credit cooperatives followed England. Afterwards the cooperatives movement spread from these countries to other European countries and then to the whole world (Republic of Turkey's Ministry of Customs and Trade, 2013).

Cooperatives are generally separated into two types, agricultural and nonagricultural, and a significant portion of cooperatives (33%) is agricultural (Doğaner, Bülent, & Ocaklı, 2007). Agricultural cooperatives have a rather important place, especially in developing countries where farmers are the vast majority of the population (Pankobirlik Faaliyet Raporu, 2006).

Agricultural production's dependence on natural conditions can cause decreased productivity and bad years to be experienced in production. In such cases, farmers need loans. However, farmers have difficulty obtaining loans due to reasons such as lack of collateral, high default risk, and banks' unwillingness. As a result, farmers fall into the hands of moneylenders and have to give all or a significant portion of their production toward debt (Çıkın & Karacan, 1994). In order to solve the problems farmers face, agricultural credit cooperatives are needed that will provide them with interest-free loans.

The first cooperatives movement in Turkey began with the "Memleket Sandıkları" [Homeland Coffers], established by Ahmed Mithat Pasha during the Ottoman State (Demirtepe, 2003; Mülayim, 2013).

The coffer design was interest-free, the emergent purpose to also rescue farmers from the hands of usurers. Yet interest at this period of the Ottoman State was considered to be high "layered" amounts on paying back the loan; financial transactions were performed at around the inflation rate. The coffers later turned into the most entrenched financial institution (Hazar, 1990). It is still operating in interest-based model as Central Union of Agricultural Credit Cooperatives and started conversion into Islamic financial institution.

This study arrives at findings regarding the business model by analyzing the financial data and ratios of the ACC and then explains the conversion concept which is new and can be defined as balance sheet approach. Lastly, it comparatively discusses the business model and includes proposals. This analysis is important for the literature as it is one of the first to be developed over a sample in the sense of interest-free conversion.

2 Analysis of ACC

ACC's significance is essentially in being the most deeply established financial organization within the Turkish Republic. ACC, together with Ziraat Bank, which can be counted as the first domestic bank, hold an important place within the development of the Homeland Coffers. The ACC is a centralized agency, and by separating from Ziraat Bank in 1977, it has continued in its identity as an independent farmer organization by diversifying and strengthening its activities. Thus, it plays an active role in financing agricultural investments. Moreover, the business model, which does not drive ACC's profit objective, has significance within financial markets from this perspective.

ACC is the group with the strongest shareholder structure in Turkey, with currently around 1 million partners and 1600 cooperatives. ACC's assets exhibit strong growth. At the same time, ACC, which engages in investments in strategic areas, reinforce the role that farmers have in the economy through 14 subsidiaries. The structure, which is revealed through its possessed resources, provides employment to close to 11,000 people in total. The institution, which contributes to employment in the agricultural field through the financing it provides, supports the economy both on the side of supply and of demand.

ACC, which forms an active structure with the large amount of loans, continue to develop proportionally through its partnership structure on the side of resources. Holding 8.6% of the agricultural lending market, ACC is in the position of being the sector's one of the three largest actors.

The market-share success of ACC, which is surrounded by a competitive environment of banks, can be correlated with management performance. Opportunities exist for improving the success of ACC against rising performance. From this perspective, the interest-free business model is a powerful option through the alternatives related to being strengthened by resources.

2.1 The Asset Structure of ACC

ACC's financial data for the period of 2007–2016 have been presented and the findings interpreted. As seen in Fig. 1, the asset size amounting to 3 billion TRL at the beginning of the period reached 10 billion TRL at its end.

An average growth rate of 14% was achieved with this performance. In spite of its dependence on resources, the performance of active development is significant. Furthermore, growth in 2008–2009 and 2015–2016 was limited.

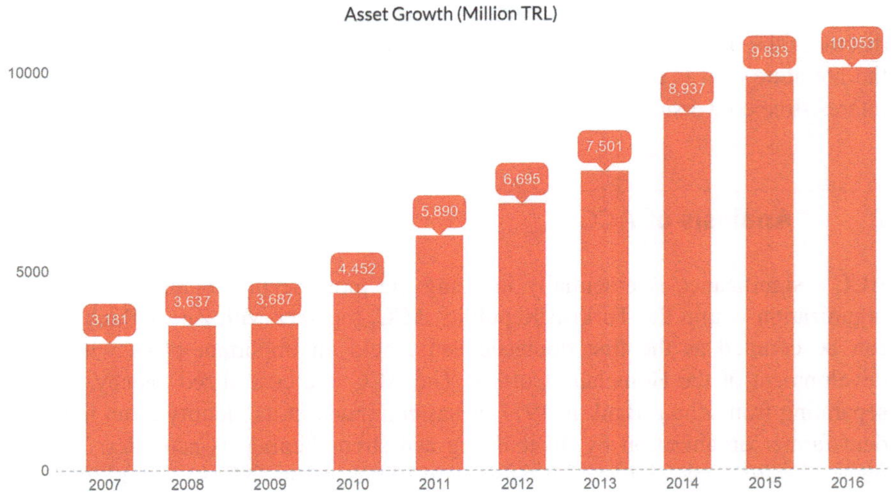

Fig. 1 Asset development (Data source: ACC)

Trade receivables are important items within the fixed assets of ACC. For the real sector, the shares of tangible fixed assets are expected to be high within the fixed assets. However, tangible fixed assets are not expected to get a high share in the structure of financial institutions. In this regard, the spreadsheets of ACC have the quality of financial institutions. The structure of tangible fixed assets/fixed assets can be seen in Fig. 2. However, due to the effect of depreciation and the absence of reevaluation, tangible fixed assets should be recognized as having the potential to offer greater values. Real estate belonging to organizations is seen to be predominant within the tangible fixed assets of ACC.

Key element on the assets is the credits. Of the loans provided by ACC, certain qualified agricultural loans are subject to subsidies at variable rates. Subsidies are applied only in terms of legal regulations and only on interest until the Law on Changes in Decrees on Certain Laws and Legal Judgment through Tax Laws was published on March 27, 2018 in the Official Gazette #30373.

Thus, the condition of subsidies being sole and only proposed to interest rates has been removed. In this respect, the maturity sale and profit share-based financings that ACC may implement are also taken in the scope of subsidies. This imposition, which in fact had made interest obligatory for farmers, also ends up this way. ACC has an opportunity to present interest-free financial models and to realize subsidized interest-free financing since the latest legislation.

2.2 The Liabilities Structure of ACC

When examined, ACC's resource structure is seen to be substantially grown from financial liabilities. Despite this, its leverage is limited compared to financial

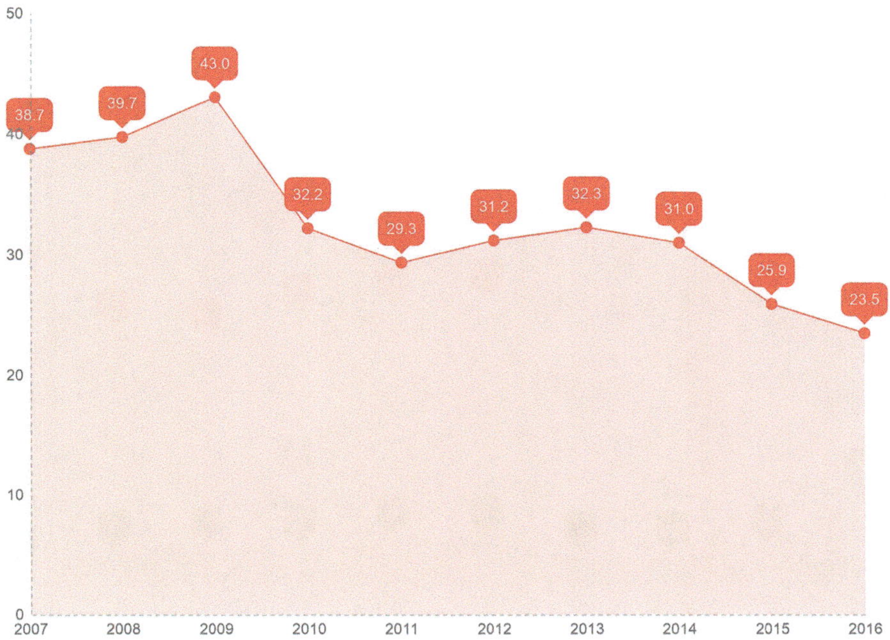

Fig. 2 Tangible fixed assets/fixed assets (Data source: ACC)

institutions. As for banking institutions, the leverage limit is defined by capital adequacy ratio (CAR) which is set to 8%, according to Article 45 of BL5411, generating the leverage as high as 12.5 times of equity. If calculations were made, ACC has a CAR value that no bank can attain. Figure 3 contains the liability breakdown. The share of equity capital within liabilities is around 36%.

When examining ACC's capital transactions, limited increase is seen. The basic source of increase is formed through shareholder records. Another source of capital increase is the additional cooperative shares collected after credit limit increases. ACC fundamentally has a unique structure that self-creates its own capital. This structure is more powerful than the effect of the oligopsony banking structure's handling of deposit/Islamic funds as an internal resource. Capital growth for 2007–2016 is shown in Fig. 4.

ACC is seen to have realized an average magnitude of capital at around 7% during the examined period. The capital growth structure is the factor in expanding the base of equity capital.

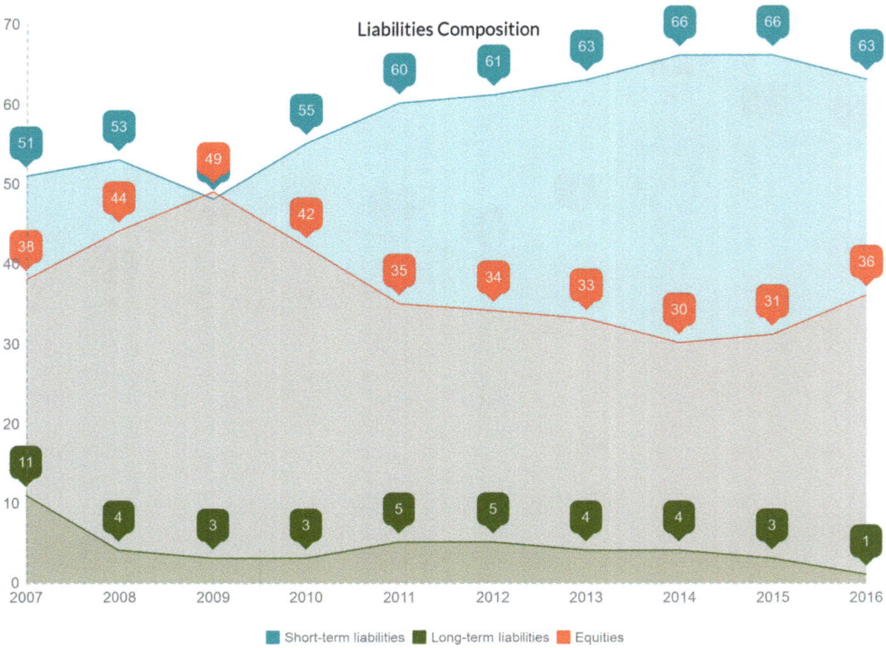

Fig. 3 Breakdown of liabilities (Data source: ACC)

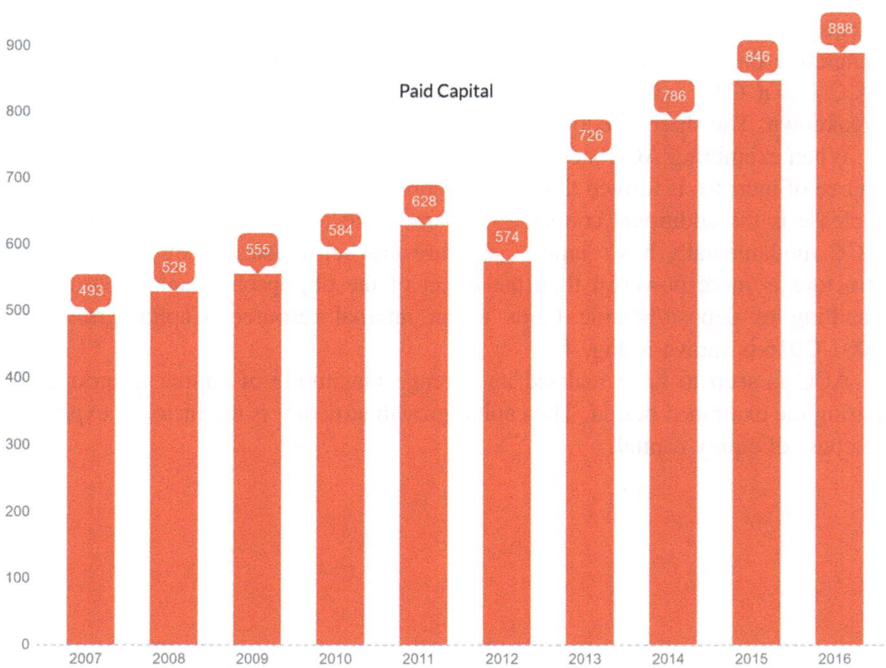

Fig. 4 Magnitude of capital (million) (Data source: ACC)

3 Analysis of the Agricultural Credit Environment

The ratio analyses show the basic characteristics of ACC to constitute distinct differences compared to other financial institutions. The main competitor for ACC is the banking sector. As a result, the performance of the banking sector has been examined as ACC's competition.

Asset portfolio development is considered one of the most important elements in the analysis. In accordance with this, Fig. 5 shows the correlation of asset growth in the banking sector with that of ACC to be weak. When considering the entire development trend of the sector separate from Islamic banking, similarities are reflected as seen from Fig. 6.

ACC's trend line resembles that of the sector in the period. Yet the trend of ACC is seen to remain under pronounced influence during the periods of both booms and boosts. In the business model, where borrowing is the key source, the banking sector's performance should be considered to be reflected in ACC over credit channels.

A similar effect can also be observed in Fig. 7. The trend line is seen to have separated from Islamic banking. However, a correlation is seen for the trend of ACC with the sector on booms and boosts, except that the structure, giving more specific reactions, is a representation of external dependence in terms of resources.

This effect is more evident in Fig. 8 where Islamic banking has been excluded from the graph.

In terms of the success of the credit portfolio, ACC is seen to exhibit a constantly improving trend, and in this respect the banking sector is seen to diverge in the face of this rising trend. Nonperforming loan (NPL) ratios are analyzed in Fig. 9. However, follow-up values at the beginning of the analyzed period should be noted as not within acceptable limits. Thus, providing recovery in a volatile economy is a remarkable achievement.

Being at a higher level than the banking sector's values is worth mentioning. Essentially, banks are able to show a lower nonperformance loan rate through the risks they pass on to asset management companies.

ACC does not remove assets from the balance sheet with this method. Banks, the determinant on this point, have customer relations, and ACC carries partnership relations. ACC's interest-free direction gives strength to these assessments.

When specifying nonperforming loans to agricultural loans, Fig. 10 shows ACC to exhibit better performance than Islamic banks at the end of the period. When considering receivables that have been transferred to asset management companies particularly in the sector, ACC is understood to have caught up to sector averages. However, expecting improvement is inevitable because the portfolio is concentrated on a single customer group.

On the side of resources, ACC has the feature of internal resource development through partnership shares. However, the number of partners, which dropped during the examined period, comes across as one of the obstacles in front of developments in this area.

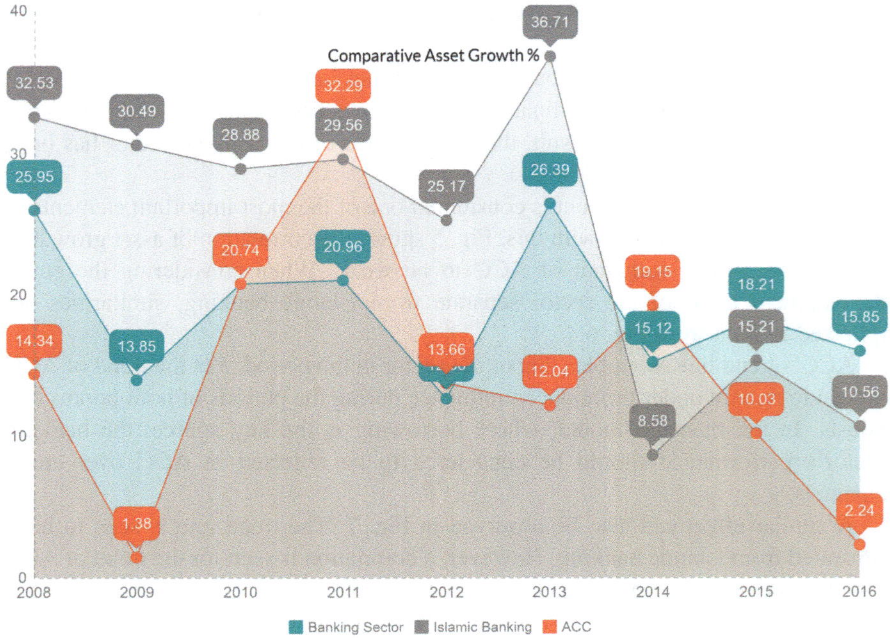

Fig. 5 Asset growth (Data source: ACC)

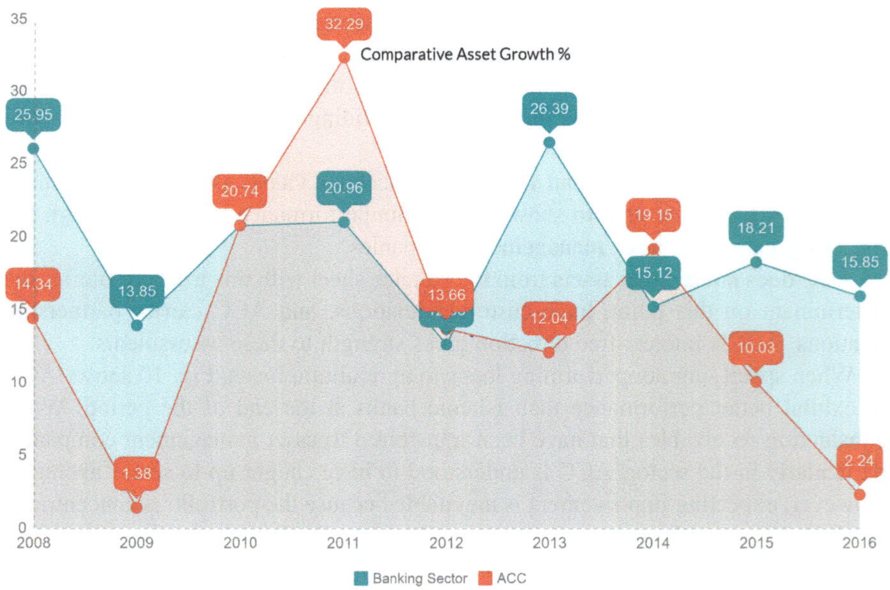

Fig. 6 Asset growth (sector and ACC) (Data source: ACC, Banking Supervision and Regulation Agency of Turkey (BRSA))

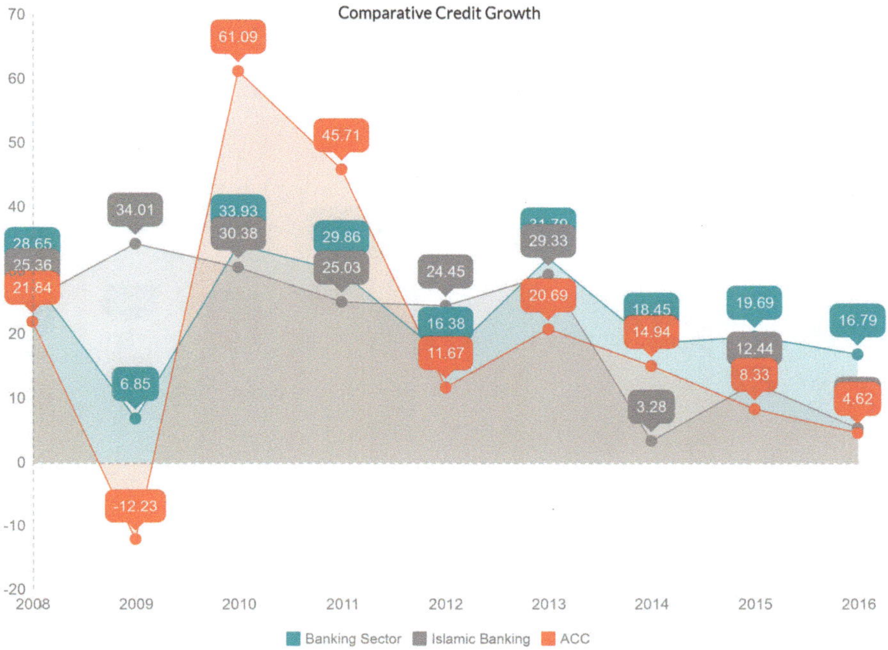

Fig. 7 Loan growth (Data source: ACC, BRSA)

When compared with the banking sector in Fig. 11, the development of partnership shares, representing a stable image, is generally provided from the additional shares obtained in response to limit increases. ACC is advantageous in terms of its deposit-like share increase without bureaucratic procedure.

In this sense, it can improve its equity constantly and at any time. As seen in Fig. 12, equity capital development exceeded the banking sector in the last annum of the examined period. ACC increases capital through limit increases in addition to the net profit to its equity, whereas banks can only increase their equity through profit.

This situation provides a unique and specific financial institutional structure. The advantages this situation provides in the area of banking are made out through the capital adequacy ratio.

Not being able to increase equity capital rapidly stands out as the most significant obstacle in front of interest-free finance development, whereas Islamic banks make a larger volume with smaller equity capital through the advantage of calculating methodology of the capital adequacy ratio (CAR).

This situation is visible in Fig. 13. As equity capital is unable to be increased, Islamic banking experiences difficulty in reaching the targeted 20% market share. In terms of equity capital, Islamic banks with their 3.6 billion TRL will get a 5% market share in the case of ACC being included in the field of interest-free banking. Asset size can reach a 7% market share. In this way, significant contributions can be presented to the Turkish economy in areas designated as strategic goals.

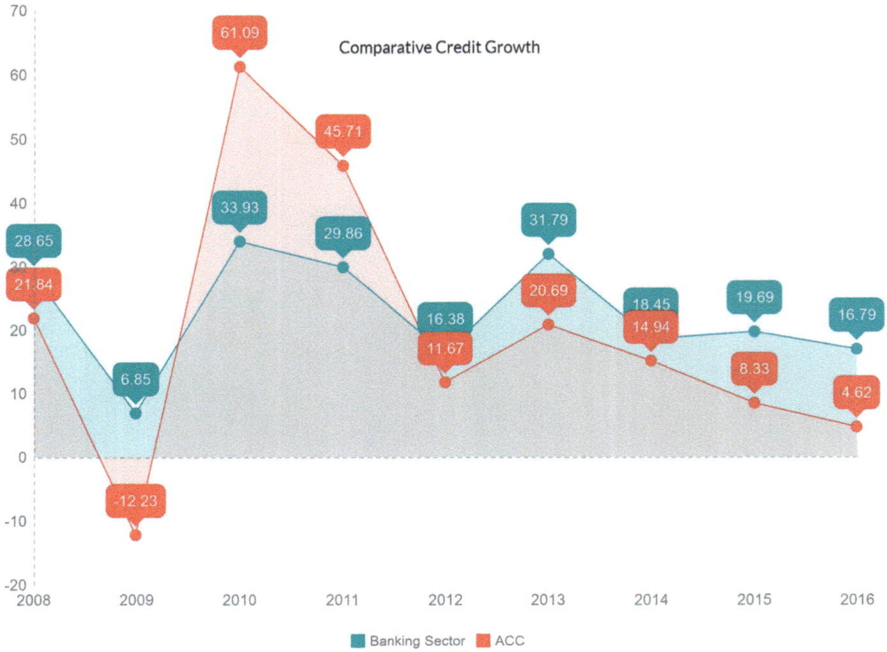

Fig. 8 Loan growth (sector and ACC) (Data source: ACC, BRSA)

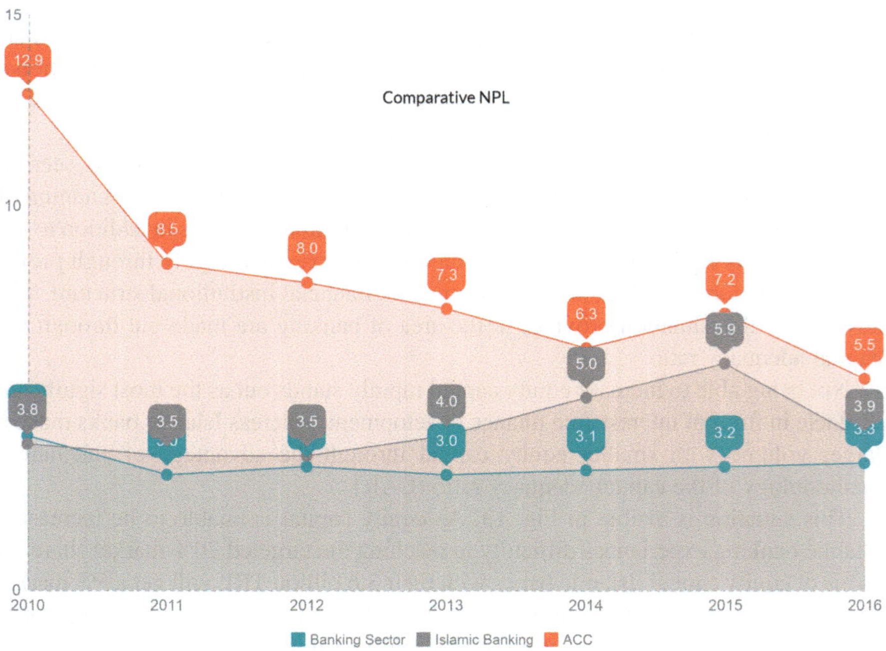

Fig. 9 Nonperforming loan ratios (Data source: ACC, BRSA)

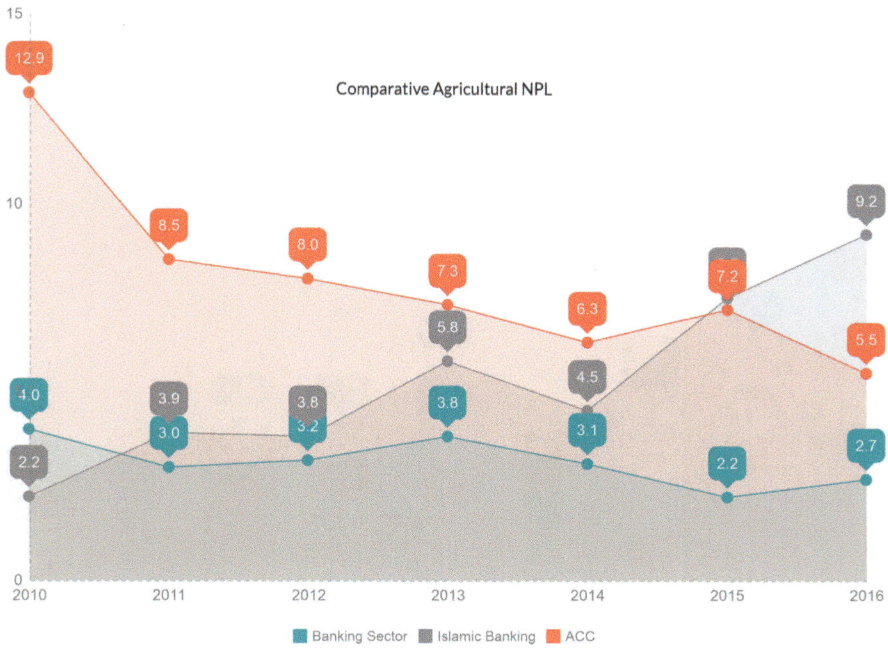

Fig. 10 The last 6 years of agricultural nonperforming loans (Data source: ACC, BRSA)

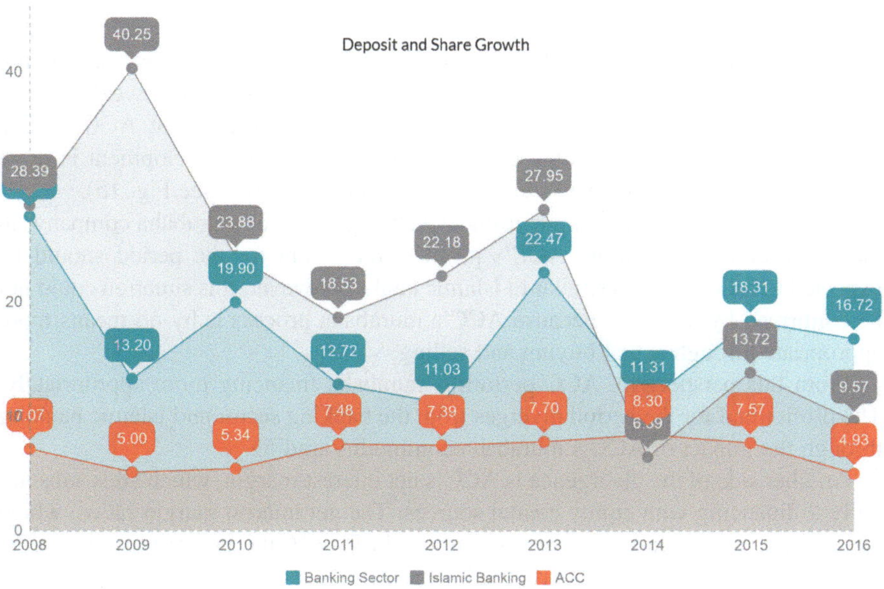

Fig. 11 Deposit/Islamic fund/partnership shares development (Data source: ACC, BRSA)

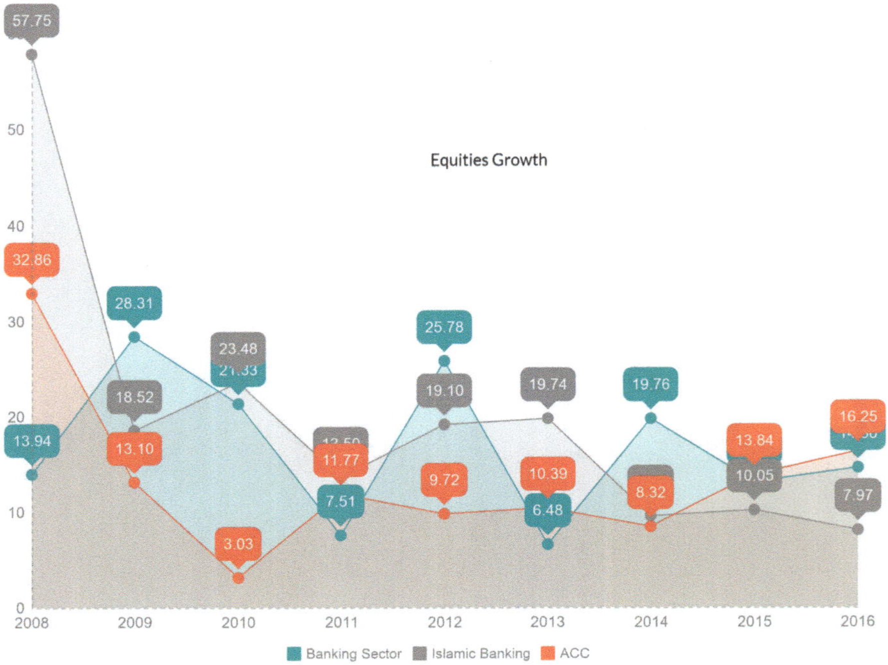

Fig. 12 Equity growth (Data source: ACC, BRSA)

When analyzing profit growth for the period, ACC's divergence from the banking sector can be examined in Fig. 14. The period's profit trend is seen to have developed in a direction opposite to the sector. The main distinction is that ACC, unlike financial institutions, possess the characteristic of producer. Development is more pronounced when Islamic banks are removed from the model (see Fig. 15).

Essentially, this relationship is from ACC being a type of murabaha company. In the scope of the evaluation, ACC's profit development for the period should be expected to follow a trend similar to Islamic banks. However, this situation could not be confirmed by the trend because ACC's murabaha process is by no means more appropriate through actual buying and selling.

From this perspective, ACC performs murabaha financing more appropriately. The profit trend for the period diverges from the banking sector and Islamic banking through the impact of ACC's murabaha commodity trading.

Another side of the divergence is ACC's net interest margin, which adds substantially to financing with equity capital sources. The net interest margin ratios, which have a very high value in the sector, lay out in Fig. 16 the profitability that ACC presents to investors when its original business model is made interest-free.

The asset profitability values also reveal the divergence of ACC from its nature as financial institutions. As seen in Fig. 17, ACC diverges from the banking sector in

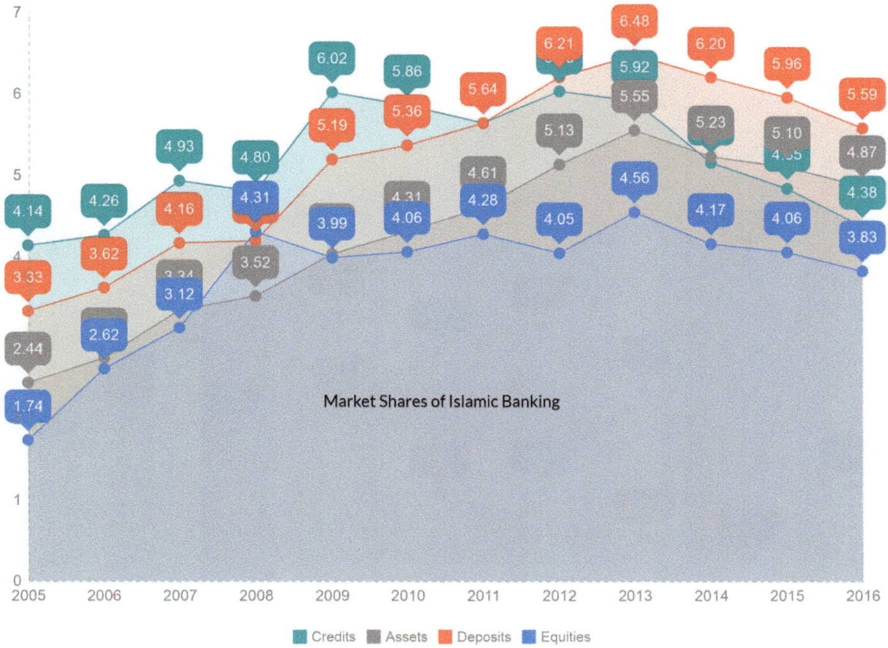

Fig. 13 Islamic banking market-share percentages (Data source: BRSA)

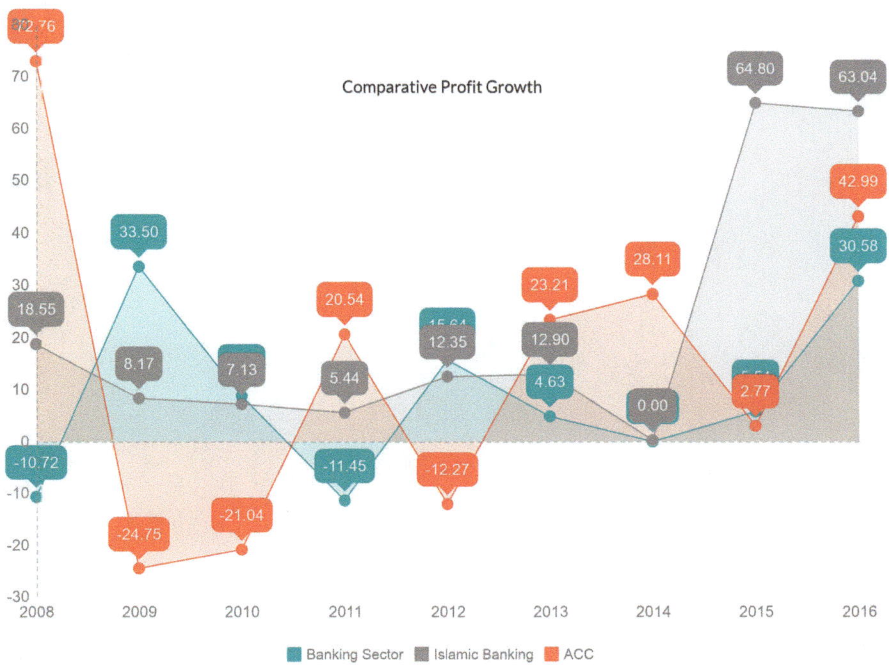

Fig. 14 Net profit development for the period (Data source: ACC, BRSA)

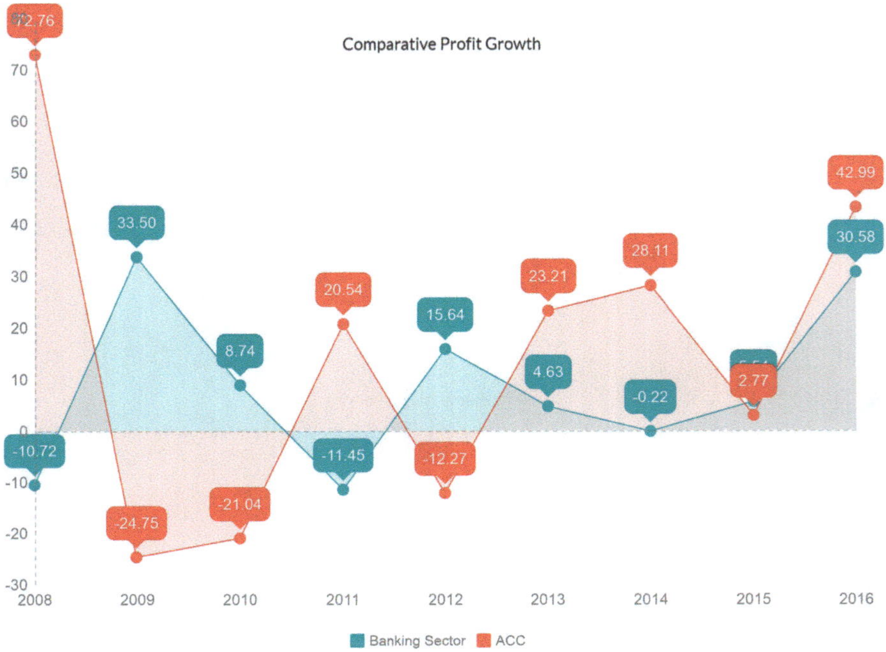

Fig. 15 Net profit development for the period (Data source: ACC, BRSA)

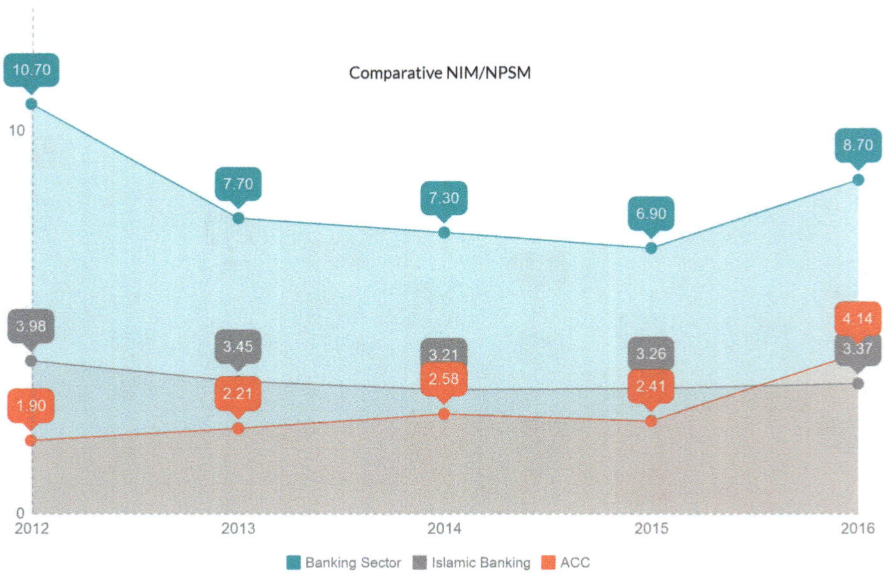

Fig. 16 Net interest margin (NIM) and net profit share margin (NPSM) comparison (Data source: ACC, BRSA)

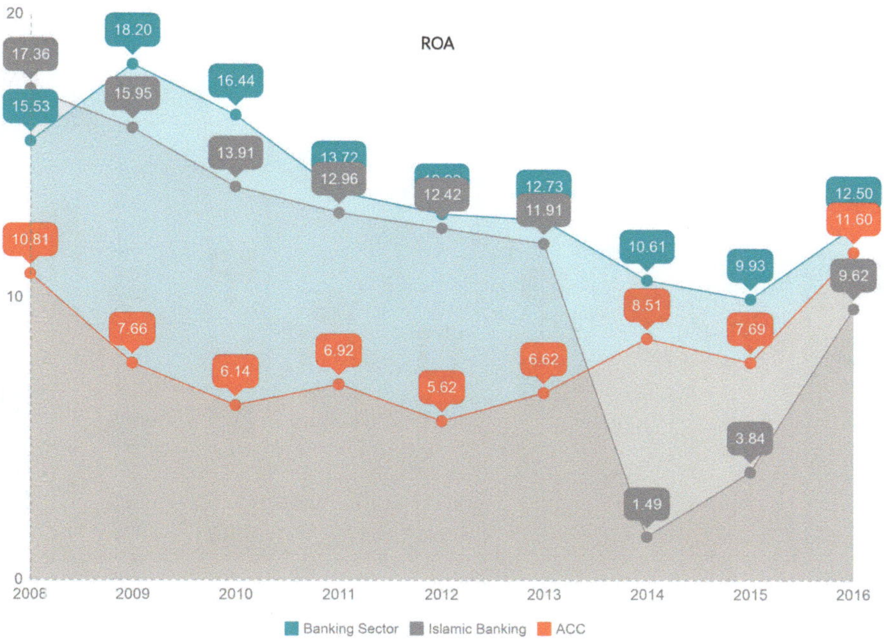

Fig. 17 Return on assets (ROA) comparison (Data source: ACC, BRSA)

terms of asset profitability. This case allows ACC to strengthen market shares through above-average profitability.

Business activities that nourish profitability do not cause farmers financial burden. Moreover, trade activities provide farmers support through guarantees such as goods purchasing. In this regard, ACC has the quality of being farmers' remedial partner. ACC has strong purchasing power and solutions to address what is needed.

While in terms of equity capital profitability, continuing ACC's activities using a leverage-free model in accordance with financial institutions is effective at lowering the trend's development (see Fig. 18). The banking sector manages a larger asset portfolio with less equity capital.

4 Conversion Concept

A couple of frameworks for conversion from conventional to Islamic financial institutions have been introduced. An each has its individual approach for conversion. For example, AAOIFI's Standard Number 6. Firstly, it focuses on conventional banks only. Secondly, it is based solely on qualitative principles. However, ACC is not a depository banking institution but a credit union for which the specific framework might be required. Moreover, the quantitative dimension could add more value for dealing with this type of institutions. Another framework is the one

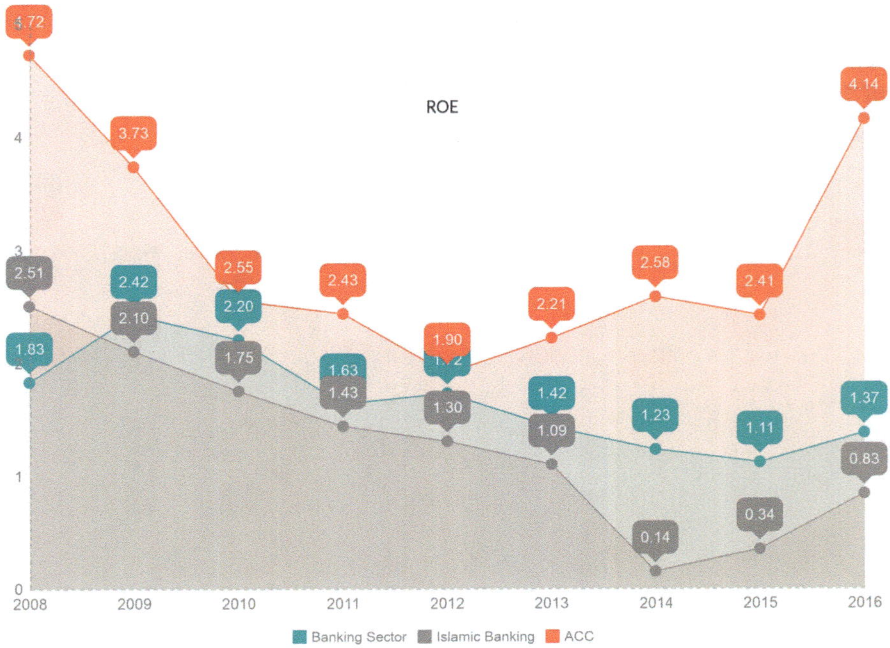

Fig. 18 Return on equity (ROE) comparison (Data source: ACC, BRSA)

recommended by State Bank of Pakistan's (SBP). Again, SBP's guidelines focus on depository institutions only. Unlike AAOIFI's standard, SBP gives more importance to quantitative criteria. Hence, combination of these two approaches could produce better results.

For the conversion of ACC into Islamic financial institution, we suggest the quantitative approach, which deals with both sides of balance sheet: assets and liabilities. Since ACC is not a depository institution, its balance sheet items cannot immediately be replaced by their Shariah compliant alternatives. Thus, a gradual conversion process is required. The aim of the ACC is to become a full-fledged Islamic financial institution rather than simply introducing an Islamic window which is relatively much easy for implementation (Sole, 2007).

4.1 Conversion of Assets

ACC plays a crucial role in financing the agricultural sector, which is the third largest and strategic component of the Turkish economy, offering its remedial partnership structures to farmers. It offers the farmers not only the quality input but also positively affects the output prices by rendering product purchase guarantees. Thus, using its financial models, the ACC indirectly reduces the cost of food items in the consumer basket, the share of which reaches 20–30% of total consumption.

Essentially, ACC offers two types of financing models: term loans and interest-free term loans. These financing models protect farmers' economic interests and offer loans of various types to meet farmers' needs related to its profession and livelihood.

The loans offered also separate into short term and long term, as they can be subject to cash-commodity distinctions. According to this, no type of loan offered in the form of currency is found other than *cash loans*. Medium-term loans are classified as *investment loans*, while short-term loans are classified as *business loans*. ACC provides credit to its partners in the identity of farmers. In the absence of partnership, they offer services to those making advance purchases. However, those advance purchasers registered as partners benefit from the advantage of corporation tax on profits obtained from the transaction by being thus registered.

A significant portion of those who prefer advance purchases remain obliged so for the purpose of avoiding interest-bearing loan treatments. The preference can be presented in this area through the interest-free subsidy regulation made in the last period.

Because the definition of agricultural subsidy made in Turkey in previous periods could only be applied to *interest*, ACC was unable to provide subsidies, even when utilizing the interest-free loans they provided to contribute to farmers' economic activities. In fact, in the case of removing the concept of *interest* from ACC's contracts, which are interest-free, a significant part of its activities lost the ability to provide subsidies to farmers. The importance of regulations regarding subsidies being brought to profit shares is great in terms of ACC's being interest-free. Table 1 includes ACC's current loans and interest-free model proposals.

4.2 Liabilities Conversion

Liabilities conversion has two aspects. First is fund collection which can be easily applied to the business model since it's a non-deposit structure. Mudarabah is a generally accepted model for Islamic fund collection. Since it is a farmers' cooperative, fund collection performance will always be better than banks that are incorporated companies. Therefore, it can manage a huge success with accepting deposits on the liabilities side.

Table 1 ACC' current loans and interest-free model proposals

Cash loan	Mudarabah Musharakah Istisna' Muzara'ah/Musaaqah Parallel Salam
Commodity loan	Murabaha
Insurance premium loan	Murabaha
Soil analysis loans	Murabaha
Remuneration loans	Ijarah
Mortgage loans	Murabaha
Agricultural vehicle-equipment loans	Murabaha/ijarah
Husbandry investment loans	Murabaha
Mortgage loans	Murabaha
Consumption loans	Murabaha
Interest-free term loans	Murabaha
The young farmer loan	Istisna'/Mudarabah Musharakah Muzara'ah/Musaaqah

Source: Authors' own table, 2018

Second credit received needs to be converted. ACC started to sign contracts with Islamic banks of Turkey to have musharakah funds to replace conventional credits. However, these banks do not have enough funds to replace the total amount of credits received from conventional banks. Moreover, ACC is not authorized to have foreign currency credits from any bank from abroad as well as the foreign Islamic banks. As a more appropriate solution in short term, sukuk issuance is a good option.

ACC has not to this day carried out the issuance of capital market instruments. The most important factor in this is the type of institution. Capital markets legislation defines issuing companies in the form of joint-stock companies but not cooperatives.

This binding condition of the legislation is fundamentally related to institutionalism and the principle of supervision. ACC is seen to have a very strong institutional structure organized at the level of a joint-stock company. Moreover, the advantageous environment formed from partnerships is open to the payers in terms of the required transparency.

The internal audit and control structure is strong and specialized. Clearly, no drawback exists in publicly offering a legal entity possessing an auditable and sustainable structure. However, the gaps in legislation should first be readdressed firsthand for issuance.

ACC still has a legal hurdle for public offerings in the interest-free domain. The issuers of sukuk (Islamic financial certificates), accordingly defined as lease certificates in the Turkish legal system, are the asset leasing companies. Resource institutions are defined as partnerships. In Article 3 Heading (ğ) of the Capital Market Board's Communiqué Series III No. 61.1 on Lease Certificates published in Official Gazette No. 28670 dated June 7, 2013, resource institutions are defined and ACC is not eligible.

ACC is seen to carry the identity of a financial institution when analyzing its activities and ratios. In this respect, legal regulations allowing for the ability of issuance should be performed in the Communiqué on Leasing Certificates.

In the case of legal regulations being completed, issuance of leasing certificates can be performed that define ACC in five different types. Resource diversification can be thus achieved. Determinations have been shared in Fig. 19 by preparing a SWOT analysis of ACC in light of this information and in the framework of the obtained findings.

As the SWOT analysis implies, the strengths of ACC as a potential Islamic financial institution overweigh its weaknesses, and the cooperative can benefit from responding to the opportunities and overcome its threats.

5 Comparing the ACC Business Model with the Banking System

Table 2 shows the comparison of ACC's business model with banking and Islamic banking. According to this, the basis of the business model in conventional banking is founded essentially on usury. While Islamic banks have adopted a business model based on profit and loss, ACC's business model offers a mixed structure.

ACC has the potential to make commercial profits because they participate in commercial activities. In addition, the business model offers a mixed structure because subsidies are established over interest rates.

Islamic banks use financing and risk as inputs, whereas conventional banks use deposit and the interest on their returns as inputs. This is because while the business model in conventional banking begins with resources, it starts with financing in Islamic banking. ACC, however, uses loans and the interest on its returns as inputs.

In terms of output, conventional banks are seen to generate interest and Islamic banks to produce profit/loss. ACC generates both profit/loss and interest as required by the mixed business model. The situation is also similar in terms of returns.

While conventional banks operate a single type of transfer mechanism, Islamic banks diversify theirs. ACC also offers an effective murabaha system, thus maintaining its mixed structure in this regard. In comparison with conventional banking whose transfer method is cash, Islamic banks possess a transfer method in the form of counterparty payments/capital or titles. Murabaha, which is essentially goods transfer, cannot go beyond counterparty payments in Islamic banks. In addition to the mixed model, ACC operates murabaha more effectively than Islamic banks. In comparison with banks that cannot participate in the buying/selling of commodities and real estate for commercial purposes as required by Article 57 of BL5411, ACC operates murabaha as a unique financing model because they are not subject to the binding provisions of BL5411.

While conventional banks carry the identity of contractor through the description of bank, Islamic banks are in the position of mudarib. Islamic banks represent the labor side as the mudarib in the mudarabah financing model of labor-capital partnership. As the owners of capital, Islamic fund owners make realizing their financings

STRENGTHS	WEAKNESSES
• In the subsidy program • Common network of branches • Specialization • Main solution partner of farmers • Institutions of interdependence • Ability to develop equity capital • Centralized and democratic structure • Strong insurance marketing ability • Murabaha-based business model • Partnership-based resource model • Offers cost benefit to partners • Unique legislative infrastructure • Above-average profitability and competitive advantage • Strong asset structure • Homogenous spread of risk • Ability to participate in commercial activities • Reduced transfer costs • High capital adequacy ratio • Large market shares	• Dependence on resources • Unable to develop common numbers • No FinTech investments • No authority to collect deposits • No deposit insurance • Unable to use leverage • Low return on equity capital • No access to international funding sources • No capital market instrument issuance • Low shares in animal husbandry • Interest-bearing debt • Limited cross-selling capability • Difficulties in sustaining collateral from partners • Partnership shares cannot be lured
OPPORTUNITIES	**THREATS**
• Partner base can be developed through FinTech investments • Providing product variety through interest-free finance models • Collaboration opportunities with Islamic banks over resources • Ability to issue Sukuk • Providing collateral through TMO-licensed storage contract • Integrate-able food sector relations • Opportunity for cooperation with public Islamic banks • Ability to develop products subject to cross-sales • Murabaha culture • Providing capital opportunities from interest-free financial institutions • Economies of scale in the banking sector • Opportunity to collaborate with other cooperatives • Interest-free finance law • Positive political outlook	• Alternative resources not being developed • Shortcomings in the Communiqué on Lease Certificates • Increased bank investment in agricultural financing • Land ownership problems • Banks domination in the area of FinTech • Few licensed depots • The relative long-term structure of investment financing • The partnership structure • Competitors' developments on market shares • Regulatory gaps in the interest-free area • No cooperative banking regulation

Fig. 19 SWOT analysis of ACC as financial institution. Source: Author

Table 2 Business model comparison

	Conventional	Islamic	ACC
Business model	Interest based	Profit based	Profit + interest based
Input	Deposit/ interest	Financing/risk	Credit/interest
Output	Interest	Profit/loss	Commercial profit/loss + interest
Yield	Interest	Profit/loss	Profit/loss + interest (subsidiaries)
Transfer mechanism	Credit	Goods/capital/titles	Goods/credit
Transfer type	Cash	Counterparty payments/ capital/titles	Goods/cash
Enterprise attribute	Bank	Mudarib	Cooperative
Institution income	Interest margin	Profit share	Commercial profit
Resource acquisition method	Deposit	Mudarabah	Credit/partner share
Fund disbursement method	Credit	Murabaha, musharakah, mudarabah, ijarah	Murabaha/credit
Institutional principles	None	Interest-free	Cooperation

Source: Authors' own table, 2018

possible by providing capital to Islamic banks. ACC obtains partnership shares through its description of cooperative as an interdependent institution.

In terms of earnings, conventional banks obtain interest margins. Islamic banks obtain profit shares. ACC achieves profit in terms of institutional earnings. The margin placed on interest is related to operational expenses.

In terms of resource acquisition method, conventional banks use deposits. Compared with ACC's model that uses partnership shares and loans, Islamic banks use the mudarabah model, and the resources they obtain are the capital. However, this capital is not about legal entities but about the profit/loss of the financings performed from the capital.

Islamic banks use the murabaha, mudarabah, musharakah, and ijarah models, compared with conventional banks who only offer the credit model in the use of funds. ACC uses the credit and murabaha models. Conventional banks do not have an institutional principle for business models. Islamic banks are based on the interest-free principle. Parallel with this, ACC is seen to establish its business model based on interdependence.

With these characteristics, ACC is a significant center of know-how. Aside from having a culture that participates in banking activities, they have the potential for being able to use these characteristics more effectively. Reinforcing its role within the economy by equipping ACC with the authority to raise funds is essential.

In this framework, ACC's existing activities apart from the interest-free termed financing model are understood to be carried out with interest due to legal and mandatory reasons. In fact, its current financial model is suitable to the base of interest-free finance. In practice, murabaha financings are seen performed more successfully and appropriately to its origins compared to interest-free banks. Assets being made interest-free will be realized through profit share subsidies.

Converting an interest-based institution to an interest-free institution is considered legitimate according to Islamic jurisprudence. Performing all future financings without interest is possible when all the legal and mandatory constrains are removed within the scope of the framework global or unique standards.

6 Results

This case study analyzes the conversion of ACC into an Islamic financial institution. The conversion concept is defined as a new approach different from already defined methods by AAOIFI or SBP. It is based on two-sided accounting principles which focus separately on assets and liabilities.

While determined suitable in accordance with Islamic jurisprudence as determined in AAOIFI Islamic Standards No. 6, ACC currently has insufficient legislative infrastructure for converting to an interest-free financial institution. In the case of encountering legislative issues, the emergent benefits that are unique need to be identified.

Aside from these, subjecting only subsidies in agricultural loans to interest has occurred as a regulation only because it was included among the impasses of economic secularism; ACC has the possibility of making its balance sheet assets interest-free.

Because the problem of interest concentrates on the side of liabilities through its current position and because the authority to collect funds being the basic problem in alternatives to credit dependency is only provided to banks, assessments are made around the standards of the banking sector. The model analyses conducted over financial data and comparisons have shown ACC to offer a mixed model. In this respect, it offers a structure convenient for shifting from usury to interest-free.

ACC still possess service diversity and the deepest sector knowledge in the world regarding the interest-free business model. Being appropriate to its institutional principles, they must return to its origins. The necessary legal regulations must be performed for having ACC become interest-free as it is based on the aim of freeing farmers and their assets from the domination of usurers and the stain of interest through interdependence and the first institutional structure in the struggle against usury and interest.

Bibliography

AAOIFI. (2012). Finans Kuruluşları İçin Faizsiz Bankacilik Standartları, Çev. Mehmet Odabaşı (Giriş ve 1–13, 15–19 ve 33. Standartlar) Doç. Dr. İshak Emin Aktepe (14 ve 20–32 ve 34–41. Standartlar), TKBB, İstanbul.

Akram, M., Rafique, M., & Alam, H. M. (2011). Prospects of Islamic banking: Reflections from Pakistan. *Australian Journal of Business and Management Research, 1*(2), 125.

Allen, F., & Santomero, A. M. (1997). The theory of financial intermediation. *Journal of Banking & Finance, 21*(11), 1461–1485.

Bayındır, S. (2005). Bir Finansman Yöntemi Olarak Kullanılan Sermaye Ortaklığının İslâm Hukuku Açısından Değerlendirilmesi (The Evaluation of Capital Partnership Used as a Financial Way from the Perspective of Islamic Law). *Usûl, 3*(2005/1), 139–157.

Bayındır, S. (2009). Asya Ve Afrika Kültürünün Dünyaya Bir Armağanı: Faizsiz Bankacılık. (A present from Asia and Africa Culture to the World: Interest-free Banking). *Icanas, 38,* 17.

Çıkın, A., ve Karacan, A. R. (1994). *Genel Kooperatifçilik. (Cooperatives in general).* İzmir: Ege Üniversitesi.

Demirtepe, N. (2003). Doğumunun 131. Yılında Ülkemiz Kooperatifçiliğinin Öncüsü Mithat Paşa ve Rusçuk. (Mithat Pasa and Ruscuk in the 131 anniversary of Turkish cooperatives). *Karınca,* 797.

Dinc, Y. (2015). *Gölge Bankacılıktan Regüler Bankacılığa Geçiş; Türkiye'deki Özel Finans Kurumları Örneği (Conversion from shadow banking to Islamic banking).* İstanbul: Beta.

Dinc, Y. (2017a). *Banka Pazarlaması ve Yeni Nesil Bankacılık (Bank marketng and new age banking).* Istanbul: Beta.

Dinc, Y. (2017b). Katılım Bankalarında Havuzlar ve Birim Hesap Değeri; Vade Uyumsuzluğu ve Fon Kullandırımı Üzerine Öneriler (Islamic banking pools and unit account value: Maturity mismatch and fund allocation), *Bankacılık ve Sermaye Piyasası Araştırmaları Dergisi,* Cilt:1, Sayı:2, 2017, ss. 9–21.

Dinc, Y. (2017c). *Tarım Kredi Kooperatifleri Analizi ve Tarım Katılım Bankası Avan Projesi (Analysis of Turkish agricultural cooperatives and Islamic agricultural banking project).* Istanbul: Beta.

Diyanet İşleri Başkanlığı, *İslam Ansiklopedisi (Islamic Encyclopedia),* Cilt 32-324/325

Doğaner, Y., Bülent, K., & Ocaklı, I. (2007). *Kapasite Geliştirme Programı Ortakların Eğitimi El Kitabı (Capacity increasing handbook),* Ankara.

El-Galfy, A., & Khiyar, K. A. (2012). Islamic banking and economic growth: A review. *Journal of Applied Business Research, 28*(5), 943.

Hammâd, N. (1996). *İktisâdî Fıkıh Terimleri (Islamic Terminology)* (trc: Recep Ulusoy), İstanbul.

Hanif, D. (2014). Differences and similarities in Islamic and conventional banking. *International Journal of Business and Social Sciences, 2*(2).

Hasan, Z. (2005). *Islamic banking at the crossroads: Theory versus practice.* In M. Iqbal & R. Wilson (Eds.), *Islamic perspectives on wealth creation* (pp. 3–20). London: Edinburgh University Press.

Hasan, Z. (2008). Credit creation and control: An unresolved issue in Islamic banking. *International Journal of Islamic and Middle Eastern Finance and Management, 1*(1), 69–81.

Hazar, N. (1990). *Kooperatifçilik Tarihi (Cooperatives history).* Ankara: Türk Kooperatifçilik Eğitim Vakfı.

Mansoor Khan, M., & Ishaq Bhatti, M. (2008). Islamic banking and finance: On its way to globalization. *Managerial Finance, 34*(10), 708–725.

Mülayim, Z. G. (2013). *Kooperatifçilik.* Ankara: Yetkin Yayınları.

Parasız, İ. (2007). *Modern Bankacılık Teori ve Uygulama (Modern banking theory and application).* Bursa: Ezgi.

Rosly, S. A. (2005). *Critical issues on Islamic banking and financial markets.* Kuala Lumpur: Dinamas.

Saunders, A., Cornett, M. M., & McGraw, P. A. (2006). *Financial institutions management: A risk management approach*. New York: McGraw-Hill/Irwin.
Shah, S. F., Raza, M. W., & Khurshid, M. R. (2012). Islamic banking controversies and challenges. *Interdisciplinary Journal of Contemporary Research in Business, 3*(10), 1018–1026.
Siddiqi, M. N. (1983). *Banking without interest*. The Islamic Foundation, Leicester, UK. Volker Ninehouse review.
Sole, M. J. (2007). Introducing Islamic banks into conventional banking systems (EPub) (No. 7-175). *International Monetary Fund.*
Usmani, M. T. (2004). *An introduction to Islamic finance*. Karachi: Maktab Maa'rul Quran.
Wilson, R. (2008). Innovation in the structuring of Islamic sukuk securities. *Humanomics, 24*(3), 170–181.
Zaki, F., & Hussainey, K. (2015). Conversion into Islamic banks: Jurisprudence, economic and AAOIFI requirements. *European Journal of Islamic Finance, 3*, 1–8.

Reports/Statistics

BRSA, İnteraktif Aylık Bülten (Bulletin), Gelişmiş İstatistik.
BRSA, Bültenler (Bulletin), Bankadışı Mali Kuruluşlar Bülteni.
European Association Of Co-Operative Banks 2015 Annual Report.
Gümrük Ticaret Bakanlığı. (2013). *Gelişmiş Ülkelerde Koop Uygulamaları Raporu, Report on cooperatives in developed economies.*
Pankobirlik. (2006). *2006 Annual Report.*
State Bank of Pakistan, Guidelines for Conversion of a Conventional Bank into an Islamic Bank.
TBB, Annual Report.
TBB, Bankalarımız 2011 (Banks).
TBB, Bankalarımız 2012 (Banks).
TBB, Bankalarımız 2013 (Banks).
TBB, Bankalarımız 2014 (Banks).
TBB, Bankalarımız 2015 (Banks).
TBB, Bankalarımız 2016 (Banks).
TCMB. (2016). Türk Lirası Mevduat ve Döviz Tevdiat Hesapları (Turkish Lira Accounts)
TIM. (2016) Ekim Sektörel Bazda Yıllık İhracat Rakamları (Export Report).
TUİK. (2017) Temel İstatistikler (Basic Statistics).
TUİK, 31 Ocak 2013 tarih ve 15843 sayılı Türkiye İstatistik Kurumu Düzeltilmiş Haber Bülteni (Bulletin).
TUİK, 12 Temmuz 2016 Tarih ve 21605 sayılı TUİK-EGM Haber Bülteni, SGK, Aylık Bülten.
TUİK, Dış Ticaret İstatistikleri (Bulletin).
World Council of Credit Unions (WOCCU), 2015 (Stats).

Legislations

18.04.1972 Kabul 28 Nisan 1972 Tarih 14172 sayılı Resmi Gazete'de yayımlanan 1581 Tarım Kredi Kooperatifleri Ve Birlikleri Kanunu (ACC Law).
16.12.1983 tarih ve 83/7506 sayılı Bakanlar Kurulu Kararı (Ministry Resolution).
1.11.2005 tarih ve 25983 mükerrer sayılı Resmi Gazete'de yayımlanan 5411 sayılı Bankacılık Kanunu (Banking Act).
1.11.2006 tarihli ve 26333 sayılı Resmî Gazete'de yayımlanan Bankaların Kredi İşlemlerine İlişkin Yönetmelik (Credit Law).
06.03.2007 Tarih ve 26454 Sayılı Konut Finansmanı Sistemine İlişkin Çeşitli Kanunlarda Değişiklik Yapılması Hakkında Kanun (Mortgage Law).

04.11.2012 Tarih ve 28457 Sayılı Küçük ve Orta Büyüklükteki İşletmelerin Tanımı, Nitelikleri ve Sınıflandırılması Hakkında Yönetmelikte Değişiklik Yapılmasına Dair Yönetmelik (SME Law).
30.12.2012 tarih ve 28513 sayılı Resmi Gazete'de yayımlan 6362 Sayılı Sermaye Piyasası Kanunun (Capital Markets Law).
07.06.2013 Tarih ve 28670 Sayılı Resmi Gazete'de yayımlanan Seri III No:61.1 Kira Sertifikaları Tebliği (Rent Certificates and Asset Rental Companies Act)
14.02.2011 Tarih ve 27846 Sayılı Resmi Gazete'de Yayımlanan 6102 Sayılı Türk Ticaret Kanunu (Turkish Trade Act).
10.03.2017 Tarih ve 26458 sayılı Resmi Gazete'de yayımlanan Banka Kartları Ve Kredi Kartları Hakkında Yönetmelik (Debit and Credit Card Law).

Yusuf Dinc started his banking carrier at Albaraka Turk Participation Bank in 2007 with the investor relations department. Dinc later worked for Trakya University as Assistant Professor from 2016 to 2017. He has books, essays, and researches on banking, shadow banking, and Islamic banking. He has been working as associate professor at Istanbul Sabahattin Zaim University since 2017.

Part II

Islamic Marketing and Management

Cradling Two Worlds: Tanamera

Mohan V. Avvari and Anita Chakrabarty

Abstract

Tanamera is a brand that cradles two worlds in producing and marketing a range of personal care products for the natural premium personal care segment as well as the Halal consumer segment. It is a family-owned brand, founded by three siblings in 1995, and produces and markets a range of natural and eco-friendly traditional Malay wellness products including tropical spa treatments and personal care products for the premium segment. As part of their efforts to establish and grow their brand initially, the entrepreneurs had to market their products internationally especially in Europe because of the low acceptance of natural products as well as low appreciation for homegrown brands in the Malaysian market. In recent years, however, the tides have changed, and natural products are widely accepted as consumers are concerned about the safety of the products as well as its effects on the environment and their surroundings. At the same time, globally there has been a greater demand for Halal products including personal care products. In view of the current market scenario of rising consumer demand for Halal products and the rising number of competitors in the Halal product category and the natural personal care market, from both ethnic and regional brands and global brands, Tanamera has to decide whether to continue to cradle the two worlds in terms of appealing to both the Halal and the premium natural personal care segments.

M. V. Avvari · A. Chakrabarty (✉)
Nottingham University Business School, University of Nottingham Malaysia, Semenyih, Selangor, Malaysia
e-mail: anita.chakrabarty@nottingham.edu.my

E. M. Ghazali et al. (eds.), *Management of Shari'ah Compliant Businesses*, Management for Professionals, https://doi.org/10.1007/978-3-030-10907-3_10

1 Introduction

Tanamera is a Halal, groundbreaking Malaysian firm producing and marketing natural and eco-friendly traditional Malay wellness products which include tropical spa treatments and personal care products. The company has a global presence that spans 14 countries with key markets in Germany and Europe. The company behind the brand which started in 1995 began as a small family business evolving to a contract manufacturer for other brands before its journey to its current position as an international brand. All its products are manufactured in their production plant in Kuala Selangor, Malaysia, using age-old traditional ingredients. Tanamera products include hair care, body care, face care, massage oils and teas based on locally found flora and fauna such as lemongrass, ginger, hibiscus and coconut oil. The brand's product range can be broadly divided into Tanamera Professional Range, Tanamera retail offerings, Tanamera Post-natal care, Tanamera Green Hotel Amenities and Tanamera wellness services. A famous product range of Tanamera is the unique Malay traditional postnatal care products passed down by the practice of midwives of the past packaged in new convenient avatar for the mothers of today. The company has won numerous accolades and local awards, including the best Home Spa products award in 2009, Malaysian Wellness Awards and the prestigious Japanese G-Mark award in 2005. Tanamera is also certified by the Vegetarian Society and has received the Good Manufacturing Certification by the Ministry of Health, Malaysia, with Halal certification from the Department of Islamic Development Malaysia (JAKIM).

Tanamera is eco-friendly using recyclable packaging material and does not do any animal testing, with all natural plant actives, without artificial perfume, colourings and preservatives. Its current growth has been thus far fuelled by its natural retail products and its spa products especially in foreign markets. They also have a postnatal range of products with initiatives in expanding services in the postnatal range. The brand has recently partnered with Mexter Health Care services to provide postnatal massages at the premium LYC Mother and Child care centre in an upscale location in the capital of Kuala Lumpur (LYC Mother and Child Care Centre, 2018).

The time has now come for the company to evaluate its efforts and directions it has taken so far. The founders have to make decisions on their next phase of growth because of two reasons. First, the natural personal care product market is facing many competitors from established global firms and regional and local firms. This includes natural products in the personal care industry based on ethnic roots. Second, the group's success in its overseas markets for natural products may not be easily replicated in markets that are looking for Halal products. Equally, the number of competitors in the Halal personal care market has grown with products that appeal to the millennials concerned about the products they use from a religious point of view, globally. In this scenario, how should Tanamera cradle the two worlds between the premium natural personal care products targeted at the natural product segment and the Halal consumer segment, whilst considering new growth directions and entering new markets locally, regionally and globally?

2 The Natural Personal Care Industry

Till date, there is no official or legal definition for the natural personal care industry in terms of what it constitutes and how a product can be considered natural. In general, the personal care industry is subject to regulations that govern various products in terms of its safety for use. In the United States of America, personal care products fall under the Federal Food, Drug and Cosmetic Act (FD&C Act) and the Fair Packaging and Labeling Act (FPLA). In Europe, all personal care products must comply with the EU Cosmetics regulations 1223/2009. Many natural products however use the term "organic" in their products. The organic label is regulated by the US Department of Agriculture (USDA) which means it has to be farmed using methods that promote cycling of resources, promote ecological balance and conserve biodiversity.[1] Synthetic fertilisers, growth hormones, drugs, sewage sludge, irradiation and genetic engineering are not to be used. The organic label specifically implies that organic labelled products have to be certified including food products, beauty and personal care products. In 2009, Natrue[2] (an organisation based in Europe) offers their certification of natural personal care products for the European markets. In the global personal care industry, however, no single authority has developed a universal definition of natural cosmetics or personal care products; hence for various categories of products, the term natural entails the lack of chemicals, preservatives or dangerous ingredients where suited and often combined with the term organic. For example, AVEDA is famous for their shampoo which emphasises their "naturally derived" ingredients and formulated without parabens, phthalates and sodium lauryl sulphate. A trailblazer in natural cosmetics and personal care,[3] The Body Shop, had taken it further and provided products with natural ingredients and no animal testing and is ethically sourced. However, other personal care giants such as Nivea, however, somewhat modestly refrain from making too many claims, emphasising 95% natural ingredients in some of their pure and natural range of personal care products.[4] Therefore, it is relatively difficult to judge the level of "naturalness" in a product category from its label alone unless the brand or product is accredited by global, government or accreditation bodies.

The global natural and organic personal care market is expected to rise at an annual growth rate by 8.8% between 2016 and 2024, accounting for market value of US$11.5 billion in 2017 (Research and Markets Report, 2017). Key market players in the natural and organic personal care industry include established players in the industry such as Loreal SA, Kao Corporation, Kiehl's, Johnson and Johnson Consumer Inc., The Hain Celestial Group, Natura Cosméticos S.A., Estée Lauder Companies Inc. and Procter and Gamble amongst others. Natural spa product players who are globally famous include Jurlique, Malie Organics, Intelligentnutrients and Dr. Hauschka. In the current

[1] https://www.usda.gov/topics/organic

[2] https://www.natrue.org/

[3] https://www.aveda.com/

[4] https://www.nivea.com.au/

Table 1 Selected natural personal care brands from India, China and Korea

India	China	Korea
Biotique	Herborist	Innisfree
VLCC	Wei	Blithe
Juicy Chemistry	Innoherb	Glow
Soul Herbs		Isoi
Khadi Naturals		Whamisa
Nyassa		Belif
Raw Rituals		Aromatica

Note: Authors' own table (2018)

environment, however, players include regional and ethnic-based players such as those from India and China, and more popularly known are Korean personal care brands. Table 1 provides some of the more established natural personal care brands from India, China and Korea.

3 The Halal Personal Care Industry

Halal personal care means that the personal care products are free from ingredients which are forbidden by the Islamic law and thus considered pure and clean. Hence, these products which include cosmetics do not contain any animal-derived material, such as blood from any animal, pork and pork-based ingredients or alcoholic components in the manufacturing process and also in their packaging (Research Nester, 2018). The Halal personal care industry which includes Halal cosmetics is expected to reach USD54,164 million by 2022, from USD20,247 million in 2015, with an average growth rate of 15.2% (Allied Market Research, 2018). It is a growing lucrative industry targeting Muslim consumers in Europe, the Middle East, Africa, South Asia and South East Asia.

Key players in the global Halal personal care market include established key players such as Loreal, Proctor and Gamble, Colgate and Palmolive as well as Unilever. In the Southeast Asian region, brands such as Martha Tilaar from Indonesia were one of the pioneers in promoting the traditional personal wellness product category from Indonesia targeted towards the indigenous consumers in both Malaysia and Indonesia. Halal personal care products in Malaysia are plentiful, with both local and global brands competing in a market consisting of around 61% Muslims.[5] Global brands such as Unilever have pursued Halal certification in their popular brands such as Dove, Lifebuoy, Sunsilk, Clear and Tresemmé. Local Malaysian brands such as Safi and Nourish Organics, Aurawhite Beauty, Ronasutra, Vida Beauty, D'Herbs and Sendayu Tinggi are popular in Malaysia and nearby countries. Malaysian Halal cosmetics such as SimplySiti, Dida and Pretty Suci have also become very popular in niche segments consisting of Muslim women in Malaysia who are looking for trendy Halal products.

[5]Department of Statistics Malaysia (2010). Malaysian Population and Housing Census.

4 Background of Tanamera

In 1995, three siblings in Malaysia started a company with a makeshift factory to produce their dream products which are non-toxic and natural, based on their Malay traditional heritage. Natural according to them means green or environmentally friendly products which are marketing catchwords of today. The family used natural products, based on homegrown Malay traditional remedies and herbs used to soothe, beautify and heal.

The three siblings, Faridah, Fauziah and Faisal, completed the construction of their RM 1.5 million GMP certified natural products factory in the year 1999. With this natural product factory, they were able to formulate, design and manufacture for companies such as Cosway, Amway and Revel, all in Malaysia and abroad. However, these products were not their own brand, and it took some time before their dream could materialise. Fortunately for them, they did not have to wait too long. The family established FA Herbs Sdn. Bhd. in 2000, which established them as a contract manufacturer for other firms and leading to the creation of Tanamera, the brand.

In Malay, the word Tanamera literally means Red Earth.[6] Tanamera's business concept revolves around the provision of a range of spa products/services and accessories, based on raw materials which are sourced from tropical regions. The inception of the brand allowed the siblings to experiment in the formulation and design of a natural product range. Their first products were natural herbal soaps and essential oil mists, targeted at the needs of those looking for natural products. They were not willing to compromise on their principles of creating natural products, including the packaging which was made of unbleached recycled paper. No toxic chemicals, artificial colours or fragrance are used in Tanamera products.

4.1 International Expansion

Tanamera began exporting to various EU countries (Germany, Sweden, Denmark, Spain, Austria, Portugal, the UK) and Russia in 2003. The government had a big role to play in its international foray through various agencies in supporting and assisting small business like Tanamera in their growth and/or internationalisation efforts. Trade promotion agencies such as MATRADE, MARA and SMIDEX played a key role in Tanamera's international expansion efforts, in terms of helping to develop domestic distribution network ties and international marketing and providing grants for expansion and promotion especially in the European markets in its early days (Chakrabarty, Avvari, & Saqib, 2014).

The firm's initial participation in trade fairs and exhibitions led to their first international foray. It was here that their current German distributor came across Tanamera's products and decided to try selling it in Germany. The international

[6] http://www.tanamera.com.my/

foray encouraged the extension of their product line which proved to lead to their successful expansion in other European markets.

Business partners aided Tanamera's rapid overseas expansion as a network of global distributors carried out international sales. Partner selection was a careful process. The company worked only with partners who shared the same values as Tanamera's management team. Business partners were pivotal in shifting the strategic direction of the company from natural products to the spa market. This strategic realignment strengthened its foothold in the European market. Foreign sales contributed towards 100% of its total sales turnover. Now, Tanamera products are available in 15 countries including Germany, Denmark, the UK, Russia, Japan, Maldives, Czech Republic, Vietnam and China (Alias, 2017; Top 10 Malaysia, 2017).

4.2 The Domestic Market and Tanamera's Offering

Whilst the natural eco-friendly products of the brand were readily accepted by the European markets, the homegrown company's early experience in the Malaysian market was not an easy one. The Malaysian market reception of the brand in the early days was far from welcoming. Malaysian consumers did not understand the natural concept and even the brown paper packaging when they were first introduced. The products were also premium priced; hence the unprepared Malaysian market was concerned about why natural products were expensive. The very idea that local, natural products were premium priced was also considered an oxymoron. Tanamera had to venture out of the country to be accepted in their own (Chakrabarty et al., 2014).

Luckily, the tide has turned since then. Natural and green products have become important features of personal care products. Customers are now more concerned about their health and safety, shunning toxic and chemically laden products. Furthermore, the brand by the enterprising Malay siblings is a premium brand, produced and marketed based on Halal principles—crucial features for the growing segment of the educated, well-travelled Muslim customer. The Halal customer looks for Halal certification to ensure that the product is produced at the highest level of purity in its ingredients and its manufacturing process. It assures consumers that the brand shares the same religious values or perspectives. On the other hand, the Halal certification more than the natural characteristic of the brand may act as a "hygiene factor" rather than a "motivator", and whilst its presence might not offer a great benefit for the brand, in contrast its absence could severely reduce its ability to penetrate Muslim consumer markets (Butt, Rose, Wilkins, & Ul Haq, 2017). For Tanamera, its natural ingredients may have won over the European markets, but its future growth may be attributed to its Halal certification.

Tanamera products consist of hair care, body care, face care, massage oils, essential oils and herbal teas. They were also the first Malaysian personal care brand to have a full suite of postnatal products, including bath soaps and scrubs, massage oils and postnatal massage services firmly entrenched in the traditional Malay culture for postnatal care for mothers. Ingredients for the products consist of locally found raw materials such as ginger, coconut oil, basil and hibiscus. The pricing for the items is premium to emphasise the quality of the products and its ingredients and manufacturing process. The products are sold online via their own online shop. Their products can also be found in their own stores in popular shopping malls such as the Garden's Mid Valley, Sogo and the Starling Mall. Their professional range of products are found in various spas as well as their own spa in Malaysia.

Tanamera's offering in the market is distinguished into several categories. First is the Tanamera Professional Range which is offered in spas and wellness centres. Tanamera retail offerings are found in their retail outlets in key locations, malls and airports. Tanamera Postnatal care range is also found in retail locations but also provided through postnatal care services. Tanamera Green Hotel Amenities is a range that has been developed for distribution to hotels, which equally promotes the natural and wellness concept of the brand. Finally, are the Tanamera wellness services, with their own branded spas in Langkawi and Kuala Lumpur.

In Malaysia, both Tanamera spas and its range of products are promoted using their own website.[7] Their brand and its success are often showcased via local television shows targeted at the Malay Muslim customers, newspapers, general health and beauty magazines in various languages (see footnote 1) as well as on YouTube reviews[8,9] and recommendations from online bloggers, particularly for its postnatal products (see footnote 2).

5 The Challenge for Tanamera

Tanamera has made great inroads into their foreign market with the natural products and now in the Malaysian market to win over local customers. Their earlier experience highlighted the relative immaturity of the market with regard to local products and natural products. The Malaysian market unlike other country markets did not believe that their own brands are equivalent to or better than competitive brands from Europe or the USA. This phenomenon may have inadvertently led to the brand's success in its overseas markets especially in the initial years of its inception. In this case, the brand was very fortunate to have gained the opportunity to establish itself in the German market because the Malaysian market was less appreciative of its natural characteristic and suspicious, because it was homegrown.

In tandem with global trends, Malaysian customers are now equally receptive of natural products, which may explain the rise of Korean brands or could have been caused by the rise of natural Korean brands, such as Innisfree. On the other hand, the Halal personal care industry in Malaysia has exploded in the past few years with both global, regional and local personal care players vying for space in the lucrative industry.

[7]https://tanamera.com.my/tanamera-news/

[8]https://www.youtube.com/watch?v=_jBjsNySka4/

[9]https://www.youtube.com/watch?v=EsdIcSNLzss&t=479s/

Tanamera's particularly unique postnatal care services have also been well received in the local market. For the founders, the market context can be construed as cradling two worlds, pursuing the premium natural customer segment for their products whilst cradling the Halal segment. Whilst the Halal personal care market is growing, with Muslim customers globally choosing products true to the Halal principles, the natural personal care line has also grown with many global and regional Asian brands coming on board for customers who are concerned about their health and safety.

In this competitive environment, the founders have to consider whether the current marketing strategy is suitable for the long run. The founders have a range of products, and its postnatal products may be unique to their brand as other more contemporary brands do not pursue this category of products within their portfolio. Furthermore, they have online sales, spas and pop-up stores as well as a retail outlet in Malaysia, apart from their postnatal service outlets.

Internationally they have carefully selected partners, which distribute and market their products especially in the professional range to spas. Therefore, decisions must be made at this juncture, about how Tanamera can continue to establish themselves and grow in the local, regional and global markets, as other natural and Halal brands from different countries and established global players increase in the Halal global market. In the current market context with many Halal, natural and ethnic or regional brands, the founders have to consider the source of their next phase of growth locally, regionally and globally. The founders also have to consider the extent to which the brand can continue to prosper in their existing markets and how it will be perceived in its existing markets in comparison with other brands, all of which claim to be natural and/or Halal. Furthermore, the brand has to now consider whether the strategy of cradling the two worlds is a strategy they should pursue as they decide upon the strategy for their next phase of growth.

References

Alias, A. (2017). *Produk Tanamera Ke 14 Negara.* Accessed July 13, 2018, from https://www.bharian.com.my/bisnes/usahawan/2017/12/358328/produk-tanamera-ke-14-negara/

Allied Market Research. (2018). Report on Halal Cosmetics Market by Product Type (Personal Care Products, Color Cosmetics, and Fragrances), Application (Hair Care, Skin Care, Face Care, and Beauty Care), and Distribution Channel (Online and Offline)—Global Opportunity Analysis and Industry Forecast, 2014–2022. Accessed June 25, 2018, from https://www.alliedmarketresearch.com/Halal-cosmetics-market/

Butt, M. M., Rose, S., Wilkins, S., & Ul Haq, J. (2017). MNCs and religious influences in global markets: Drivers of consumer-based Halal brand equity. *International Marketing Review, 34*(6), 885–908.

Chakrabarty, A., Avvari, V. M., & Saqib, S. (2014). Exploring drivers of internationalization of SMEs in an emerging economy—Case studies from Malaysia. *The Journal of International Marketing Strategy, 2*(1), 13–27.

LYC Mother and Child Care Centre. (2018). Accessed June 25, 2018, from https://www.lychealth.com/

Research and Markets Report. (2017). *Report on global natural and organic personal care market size, market share, application analysis, regional outlook, growth trends, key players, competitive strategies and forecasts, 2018 to 2026*. Accessed June 30, 2018, from https://www.researchandmarkets.com/research/x6vj53/global_natural?w=5/

Research Nester. (2018). *Report on Halal cosmetic product market: Global demand, growth analysis & opportunity outlook 2023*. Accessed July 15, 2018, from https://www.researchnester.com/reports/Halal-cosmetic-product-market-global-demand-growth-analysis-opportunity-outlook-2023/207/

Top 10 Malaysia. (2017). *Taking the bull by the horn*. Accessed June 30, 2018, from http://top10malaysia.com/main/taking-bull-horn/

Mohan V. Avvari is Associate Professor at the Nottingham University Business School in Malaysia. His teaching and research interests are in Strategy and Innovation—with special interests in Sustainability Oriented Business Strategies. He has published about 40 research papers and is on the editorial panel for regional research journals. He has served as a resource person for workshops organised by UN-ESCAP, UNESCO, etc.

Anita Chakrabarty is the Deputy Director of MBA programmes at Nottingham University Business School, University of Nottingham Malaysia. She has a PhD from University of Nottingham, Masters of Marketing (University of Northumbria at Newcastle). Anita is also a Human Resource Development Fund certified trainer and Fellow of the Higher Education Academy (UK). Her teaching and research interests are mainly in the field of consumer behaviour, marketing strategy and marketing services. She has a particular interest in customer value co-creation.

Halal Dietary Supplement Products in Malaysia

Norhazwani Mohamed Asri and Azmin Azliza Aziz

Abstract

The demand for halal products including food and beverage, pharmaceuticals and dietary supplement has significantly increased due to the religious obligations of Muslims. The case study takes a broad look at the factors influencing the consumption of dietary supplements such as vitamins and minerals and specifically at the rising demand for halal dietary supplements by Muslim consumers in Malaysia.

1 Introduction

"Halal" originates from the Arabic word which means "permissible" or "lawful" in Islamic law. Basically, it is regularly applied to permissible food and drinks. As a Muslim, finding halal is obligatory which not only limited for food or drinks but also for everything regardless of whatever they need, such as pharmaceutical products, cosmetics, clothing, entertainment, or even in any business activity. Halal is something permitted, which means that no restrictions exist and it is allowed by Allah, the lawgiver (Battour & Ismail, 2016; Mustafar & Borhan, 2013). There are numerous verses in Quran that mentions about halal as a way of life, with one of them from chapter "The Role of Cash Waqf in Poverty Reduction: A Multi-country Case Study" verse 168, which is translated as "O mankind! Eat of that is lawful and wholesome in the earth, and follow not the footsteps of the devil. Lo! He is an open enemy for you". This

N. M. Asri (✉)
International Islamic College, Kuala Lumpur, Malaysia
e-mail: norhazwani@iic.edu.my

A. A. Aziz
University of Malaya, Kuala Lumpur, Malaysia

E. M. Ghazali et al. (eds.), *Management of Shari'ah Compliant Businesses*, Management for Professionals, https://doi.org/10.1007/978-3-030-10907-3_11

verse indicates that the halal concept is universal and humans are prohibited to involve in any forbidden way in their life. In other words, in Islam everything is lawful except the things which are prohibited based on the Quran and Sunnah précised by Prophet Muhammad SAW (Riaz & Chaudry, 2003).

On the other hand, the opposite of halal is "haram", which means prohibited or unlawful. Allah SWT has absolutely forbidden anyone and enforced the punishment in the hereafter as well as a legal penalty in this world for those who were engaged with haram practices (Al-Qaradawi, 1999). It was also revealed in chapter "The Role of Cash Waqf in Poverty Reduction: A Multi-country Case Study" verse 173 of Quran which states that "He hath forbidden you only carrion, and blood and swine flesh, and that which hath been immolated to (the name of) any other than Allah. But He who is driven by necessity, neither craving nor transgressing, it is no sin for him. Lo! Allah is Forgiving, Merciful".

In Malaysia, the halal industry is governed by the Department of Islamic Development Malaysia (JAKIM) which began in the year 1974. JAKIM was established to ensure the status of halal on consumer food products and goods in the country. Besides JAKIM, Halal Industry Development Corporation (HDC) also undertakes the developmental roles for the halal industry. This organization has identified four key halal industry sectors as the drivers of growth under the Halal Industry Master Plan, specifically specialty processed foods, cosmetic and personal care, halal ingredients and animal husbandry. In producing products, manufacturers need to observe the guideline which was prescribed under the General Guidelines on the Production, Preparation, Handling and Storage of Halal Food. This guideline is to ensure that their practices are halal compliant based on the requirement of the Malaysian Halal Standards for Good Manufacturing Practices (GMP) and Good Hygiene Practices (GHP), which is one of the most recognized halal logos in the world. Meanwhile, Malaysia has also introduced a new standard which is known as the Malaysian Standard MS 2424:2010 (P): Halal Pharmaceutical—General Guidelines, which is focused on the supply chain management of medicines and health supplements, from the processing to handling, packaging, labelling, distribution, storage and display.

Moreover, according to industry reports 2007, the Malaysia External Trade Development Corporation (MATRADE) stated that the value of medicines exported from this country reached RM678 millions which is mostly from the Middle East to cater the market demand on halal pharmaceuticals and healthcare. Following this, in April 2011, the Industry Standards Committee on Halal Standards (ISCI) in collaboration with the expertise from government and industry bodies release halal pharmaceutical and medicine guidelines which are in line with the practices of "Malaysian Standard". However, it is voluntary; the Ministry of Health is not necessary to approve any halal logo stickers or other signage on packaging, although the porcine and bovine materials need to be disclosed for procurement purposes.

According to Euromonitor International (2015), the market growth for vitamins and dietary supplement products in Malaysia has shown tremendous performance, in which the retail sales have increased from RM940.4 million (USD248.3 million) in 2005 to RM1.9 billion (USD572.6 million) in 2014. It represents a compound annual growth rate (CAGR) of 7.0% over the past years. Obviously, this shows that the intake of dietary supplement products has become trendy among Malaysians, most probably due to the increased awareness of healthy living.

2 Dietary Supplementary Product and the Type of Users

Dietary supplement product can be categorized into several types such as vitamin, mineral, fatty acid, amino acid, dietary fibre, medicine and herbal or traditional supplement (Bee & Wan, 2016; Imai, Nakamura, Ando, & Shimokata, 2006). According to Radimer et al. (2004), supplement can be referred to as multivitamins, single vitamins, single minerals, herbal supplements, oil supplements and any other dietary supplementation consumed by the users. Imai et al. (2006) define dietary supplementary user as a person who took any dietary supplement at least once in the previous year. Basically, there are three groups of users; "daily users" is for the users consumed the dietary supplement once a day, "weekly users" representing those who take it once a week, and "seldom users" representing those who only take it less than once a week.

2.1 Knowledge and Perception

According to Bellinger, Castro and Mills (2004), knowledge is how to apply data and information, which can answer "how" questions and relates with deterministic process. It is more about how the people solve the issue or make any decision based on data and information gathered. Generally, it can also refer to the facts, feelings, or experiences faced by an individual or a group of people (Abd, Asrarhaghighi, & Abd, 2015).

Knowledge is very important to Muslim consumers in choosing a product, including dietary supplements. A study by Sadeeqa and Sarriff (2014) found that the level of knowledge among pharmacists towards issues surrounding halal pharmaceutical is good. It is because they need to answer the questions from the patients regarding the source of ingredients in a prescribed medicine. They also concluded that better knowledge of the patients on halal pharmaceuticals will lead to better perception towards halal pharmaceuticals (Sadeeqa & Sarriff, 2014). However, Abd and Abd (2015) found that the religiosity factor is more influence on behaviour of Muslim consumers as compared to halal knowledge. Therefore, the product manufacturers should emphasize on the procedure of halal certification in producing their product, since it can influence the attitude of consumers to consume the product. In order to make the process of halal certification more efficient, Mashitoh, Rafida and Alina (2013) said that the government should encourage the participation from the related body such as industries and non-governmental organizations to participate in the process, so that it may not burden government agencies such as JAKIM only in enforcement and surveillance activities.

2.2 Attitude and Intention

Knowledge is a crucial factor for both Muslim marketers and consumers. For the former, they must be aware that food which mixed with diseased animals or those which do not follow the Islamic process of slaughter is prohibited according to Shariah (Abd & Abd, 2015). For the consumers, especially Muslims, knowledge may influence their attitude and consequently their purchasing intention, which is based on the familiarity of the food product rather than checking the halal labelling on the packaging (Hamdan, Mat Issa, Abu, & Jusoff, 2013). Sadeeqa, Sarriff, Masood, Saleem and Atif (2013) also found a positive relationship between the attitude and intention of pharmacists in their study. They highlighted that any prescription given to the patient should depend on the patient's attitude and intention. The patient should know the ingredients of their medications, and hence, it is the responsibility of the healthcare provider to inform the patients about it, although about 90% of the patients are aware about the issue. Moreover, for halal medication, the public must be provided with halal medicine and drugs with clear "halal" logo on the packaging.

3 Conclusion

The demand and consumption trend of dietary supplement products is fast growing among Malaysian consumers as many are now health conscious. The hectic and sophisticated lifestyle means that many consumers are not able to fulfil their daily nutrient requirements. Moreover, the increasing medical expenses for chronic disease treatments have also influenced this trend. Due to these factors, many people tend to rely on dietary supplement products to improve or at least maintain their health condition.

Nevertheless, due to religiosity, Muslims are obliged to check on the halal status of the dietary supplements before consuming them. The context of halal is not only concern with the ingredients of the product such as pork- and alcohol-free, but the entire production process of the product must also be *halalan toyyiban*. Obviously, any food or drink which lies within the grey area and does not fall clearly under halal or non-halal category is classified as "*syubhah*", alternatively called questionable or dubious. In this category, until the status becomes clear, Muslims should avoid consuming *syubhah* food or drinks (hdcglobal.com). For this reason, JAKIM and other government bodies are coming together to prepare the requirements to meet up with the halal standard.

It is important for Islamic bodies, practitioners and researchers to understand the factors that contribute to the intention of consuming halal dietary supplement product. As such, Islamic bodies such as JAKIM can come out with initiatives to create awareness and spread knowledge on what is meant by halal, among consumers through various programmes, public events as well as reading materials. In fact, this knowledge should be exposed to children starting from primary school by introducing it into schools' curriculum. On the other hand, manufacturers could improve the perception of these products by ensuring that the halal status of their products is met, throughout the whole supply chain process.

Studies on halal dietary supplement products are relatively scarce as compared to studies on halal food, halal cosmetics and halal pharmaceuticals. Thus, the literature on this topic is quite limited. As studies on halal dietary supplement product are limited, future research could focus on various perspectives of this topic. For example, it would be interesting to look into the factors that influence the consumption of halal dietary supplement product among chronic patients. Moreover, the traditional dietary supplement product such as *jamu*, which are manufactured traditionally by local people especially in rural areas, should also be studied, in order to examine whether the practice of *halalan toyyiban* are met.

In order to achieve the efficiency of the halal standard management, research looking at the effectiveness of monitoring system from the enforcement body should also be conducted. With competent monitoring systems, the standards for halal requirement can be sustained, and Malaysia can be a role model for other Muslim countries.

References

Abd, R. A., & Abd, R. S. (2015). Assessing knowledge and religiosity on consumer behavior towards halal food and cosmetic products. *International Journal of Social Science and Humanity, 5*, 10–14.

Abd, R. A., Asrarhaghighi, A., & Abd, R. S. (2015). Consumers and halal cosmetic products: Knowledge, religiosity, attitude and intention. *Journal of Islamic Marketing, 6(1)*, 148–163.

Al-Qaradawi, Y. (1999). *The lawful and the prohibited in Islam (Al-Halal wal haram fil Islam)*. Indianapolis, IN: American Trust Publications.

Battour, M., & Ismail, M. N. (2016). Halal tourism: Concepts, practices, challenges and future. *Tourism Management Perspectives, 19*, 150–154.

Bee, Y.G., & Wan N.W.K. (2016). *Traditional health supplements in Malaysia*. Accessed June 24, 2018, from http://www.krinstitute.org/Working_Paper-@-Traditional_Health_Supplements_in_Malaysia.aspx

Bellinger, G., Castro, D., & Mills, A. (2004). *Data, information, knowledge, and wisdom*. Accessed June 24, 2018, from http://www.systems-thinking.org/dikw.htm

Euromonitor International. (2015). London: Euromonitor International. Accessed June 24, 2018, from http://www.euromonitor.com/

Hamdan, H., Mat Issa, Z., Abu, N., & Jusoff, K. (2013). Purchasing decisions among Muslim consumers of processed halal food products. *Journal of Food Products Marketing, 19*, 54–61.

Imai, T., Nakamura, M., Ando, F., & Shimokata, H. (2006). Dietary supplement use by community-living population in Japan: Data from the National Institute for longevity sciences longitudinal study of aging (NILS-LSA). *Journal of Epidemiology, 16*(6), 249–259.

Mashitoh, A. S., Rafida, A. N., & Alina, A. R. (2013). Perception towards halal awareness and its correlation with halal certification among Muslims. *Middle-East Journal of Scientific Research, 16*, 01–04.

Mustafar, M. Z., & Borhan, J. T. (2013). Muslim consumer behavior: Emphasis on ethics from Islamic perspective. *Middle-East Journal of Scientific Research, 18*(9), 1301–1307.

Radimer, K., Binderwald, B., Hughes, J., Ervin, B., Swanson, C., & Picciano, M. (2004). Dietary supplement use by US adults: Data from the National Health and Nutrition Examination Survey, 1999–2000. *American Journal of Epidemiology, 160*, 339–349.

Riaz, M. N., & Chaudry, M. M. (2003). *Halal food production*. New York: CRC.

Sadeeqa, S., & Sarriff, A. (2014). Assessment of knowledge, attitude and perception among hospital pharmacist regarding halal pharmaceuticals. *Journal of Applied Pharmaceutical Science, 4*(05), 080–086.

Sadeeqa, S., Sarriff, A., Masood, I., Saleem, F., & Atif, M. (2013). Knowledge, attitude and perception regarding halal pharmaceutical among general public in Malaysia. *International Journal of Public Health Science, 2*(4), 143–150.

Norhazwani Mohamed Asri received her MBA specialized in Islamic Banking and Finance from International Islamic University Malaysia (IIUM), Malaysia and is currently a lecturer at School of Management, International Islamic College, IIUM, Kuala Lumpur, Malaysia. Her teaching areas includes Islamic banking and finance and also other business administration subjects. At the moment, she is involved with research in area of Islamic banking and Halal related studies.

Azmin Azliza Aziz received her PhD in Operations Research from the University of Warwick UK and is currently a senior lecturer at the Faculty of Business and Accountancy, University of Malaya, Kuala Lumpur, Malaysia. Her research interest includes the area of transportation optimisation, logistics and halal related studies. Dr. Azmin Azliza Aziz can be contacted at aazliza@um.edu.my.

Impact, Perception and Challenges Due to Halal Certification: The Case of Zulaikha Shop

Ahmad Rafiki

Abstract

The *Halal* certification is a label that indicates compliance with Islamic principles. This certification should be applied by all enterprises in various industries including food. The *Halal* food market is fast developing and growing in many countries. This case aims to explore the impact, perception and challenges of *Halal* certification in a shop named Zulaikha in Medan, in North Sumatera, Indonesia. The *Halal* certification has had a huge impact on Zulaikha's business, resulting in increased sales and gaining the trust of Muslim consumers. Today, the owner of Zulaikha has become a successful entrepreneur in the *Halal* food industry in Indonesia. A small survey was conducted to examine customers' perceptions towards *Halal* certification. The responses of the respondents are in line with the findings of previous studies. Meanwhile, the challenges faced by owners/managers associated with regard to the *Halal* certification are discussed in this study. It is hoped that this case study would be a source of inspiration for other entrepreneurs in starting and running their own Halal-certified ventures. The lessons learnt in this study would also be useful for various stakeholders to address issues related to *Halal* certification.

1 Introduction

Halal certification is normally issued for all types of products and services ranging from food to travel, hospitality, education, tourism, pharmaceuticals, cosmetics, personal care, entertainment, edutainment and fashion (Isabelle & Laurent, 2015).

A. Rafiki (✉)
Department of Business Administration, University College of Bahrain, Janabiyah, Bahrain

E. M. Ghazali et al. (eds.), *Management of Shari'ah Compliant Businesses*,
Management for Professionals, https://doi.org/10.1007/978-3-030-10907-3_12

Based on a report on the Global Islamic Economy[1] in 2016, the global Muslim market was estimated at around 16.6% of the global expenditure, which amounts to around US$1173 billion. The revenues for Halal-certified food and beverage products globally have been estimated at around US$415 billion.

Factors that could influence a Muslim's decision in applying *Halal* certification for their organisation include religious teachings, competency, costs, experience, commitment, rules and regulation, profit, trend, quality, human capital, bureaucracy, incentives, satisfaction, achievement and facilities. These are also considered as the challenges related to *Halal* certification for the owners or managers of various enterprises. The most important factor is the influence of religion. Religion plays an important role in an individual's cognitive capability, in influencing consumer behaviour and attitudes (Jusmaliani & Nasution, 2009). Khraim (2010) concludes that religion plays a crucial role in understanding consumers because it significantly influences consumption due to linked taboos and rules. Meanwhile, *Halal* is a religious concept that shapes feelings and attitudes in Muslims' consumption (Hanzaee & Ramezani, 2011).

In this case study, the author attempts to elaborate the literature on *Halal* certification, with special reference to the Zulaikha shop, accompanied by a discussion on consumers' perceptions, impact and challenges of *Halal* certification. The case study examines the development of *Halal* certification in Medan in Indonesia (the city where the Zulaikha shop is located). This is a unique case where an initiative of having *Halal* certification brings *barokah* or blessing from Allah SWT and sharing prosperity to the rest of the society as experienced by the owner of Zulaikha shop.

2 Halal Certification

The authenticity of *Halal* products is based purely on the product assurance provided by the label (Jabar, Ishak, Johar, & Wahid, 2014; Mohamad, Baharuddin, & Ruskam, 2015; Tieman, Ghazali, & Van der Vorst, 2013), and that label is the *Halal* certification. The *Halal* certificate is a document issued by an Islamic organisation (Hanzaee & Ramezani, 2011) to inform and reassure the consumers that the products are *shariah* compliant. It is as a symbol of quality, which assures that the product is natural, safe, healthy, clean and green in all aspects of slaughtering, storage, display, preparation, hygiene and sanitation. The obligations concerning the *Halal* process and consumption of *Halal* products are clearly mentioned in Al-Qur'an in many verses such as Al-Maidah 5: 3–4; 88; Al-Baqarah 2:168; 173; 219; Al-An'am 6:121; and An-Nahl 16:67.

Halal certificates fall into two types: a site registration certificate which signifies that a production facility is *Halal* certified but which cannot be used to guarantee goods produced and the *Halal* product certificate covering the ingredients and the manufacturing process used (Hanzaee & Ramezani, 2011). Meanwhile, according to

[1]https://ceif.iba.edu.pk/pdf/ThomsonReuters-stateoftheGlobalIslamicEconomyReport201617.pdf

Razalli, Yusoff and Roslan (2013), the *Halal* certification practices should be measured by 12 items, including (1) *Halal* documentation, (2) management responsibility, (3) raw material, (4) location, (5) exterior area, (6) premise, (7) facility, (8) tools and equipment, (9) staff characteristic, (10) staff policy, (11) pest control and (12) waste management. It is vital for the owners/managers to understand all the above information before they can meet all requirements related to *Halal* certification process.

The *Halal* certification process starts with the selection of an organisation or a product that meets the standards and requirements set by the authorised bodies. Many countries, like Singapore, Indonesia, Brunei and Malaysia, have government-approved *Halal* programmes, whereas the predominantly food-exporting countries have their own independent certification bodies. Those authorised bodies should endeavour to verify and ensure accurate *Halal* labelling in order to protect Muslims' consumers as well as to promote a fair trade. Among the credible *Halal* certification bodies are the Halal Food Authority (HFA) in the UK; the Islamic Food and Nutrition Council of America (IFANCA); the Halal Food Council International (HFCI), the Australian Federation of Islamic Council (AFIC), the Federation of Islamic Association of New Zealand (FIANZ), the Islamic Religious Council of Singapore (MUIS), the Bureau of Food, Drugs and Cosmetics Research of the Indonesian Ulama Council (LPPOM-MUI) and the Central Islamic Committee of Thailand (CICT); and the Department of Islamic Development (Jabatan Kemajuan Islam Malaysia) (JAKIM) in Malaysia.

In the case of Indonesia, the LPPOM-MUI has appointed 40 *Halal* certifier bodies. Unfortunately, despite an increase in the application of *Halal* certification every year since 2005 in Indonesia, the registration is not that impressive with 63% of products without any *Halal* certification, while only 51,000 out of 123,000 registered products were labelled with the *Halal* logo.[2] The *Halal* certification organisations play a crucial role, not only as a link between the producer and the *Halal*-sensitive consumer but also functions as a supply chain partner in the producer's value chain (Annabi & Ibidapo-Obe, 2017).

The increasing number of applications for *Halal* certifications in Medan, especially for food products, is an indication that the consumers' awareness for such certification are also increasing. With regard to the issuance of *Halal* certification in Medan city, a total of 197 certifications will expire between 17 February 2018 and 18 January 2020. Table 1 provides details of 197 certifications by their product category.

Meanwhile, the increasing number of recent studies on *Halal* certification indicates that the interests and concerns of researchers are increasing. There are many aspects related to *Halal* certification which are being continuously discussed in many countries, especially the Islamic countries. A summary of studies on *Halal* certification from 2011 to 2017 is shown in Table 2.

[2]Retrieved from: http://www.bicg.org/bicg.php?sectionID=16 on 19/06/2011. Bali: Bali International Consulting Group

Table 1 Certified food Halal products by MUI of Medan city

Business product	Total number of companies	Business product	Total number of companies
Cake	37	Bread/bakery	13
Cake—Bika Ambon	5	Catering/restaurant	40
Coffee	11	Crisps/snacks/ chocolate	42
Ice cream	1	Processed food—meat/chicken	7
Sauce/ketchup/honey	5	Frozen food/fish	2
Salt	1	Coconut milk	2
Flavour/food Colouring/paste	9	Processed drink/syrup	15

Source: MUI Medan, 2018 (https://muimedan.or.id/beranda/info-halal/)

3 Case Context

Medan city is the capital city of North Sumatera province, which acts as the gateway to the Western part of Indonesia and is the third largest city in the country. As an important commercial and economic hub of Indonesia, Medan is growing tremendously with its economy mainly based on trade, services, production and manufacturing, and natural including tobacco, rubber, palm oil, tea and coffee. Meanwhile, the people of the city consist of several religions and ethnic groups as given in Table 3.

Despite the diversity in religion and ethnicity, the application of Halal certification is increasing by around 13% every year.[3] The Muslim consumers are the ones promoting the importance of *Halal* certifications, while Islamic educational institutions also proactively create awareness among their students.

4 Zulaikha Company Profile

Zulaikha shop is located in Medan and sells Bika Ambon and layer cakes, besides other snacks. Besides Zulaikha, there are other shops in Majapahit Street (see Fig. 1) in Medan that sells sweets, snacks and cakes. Most people will come to this street to buy the "oleh-oleh" cake or other gifts, especially Bika Ambon. This delicacy is a typical gift that is normally bought if visiting Medan and popular throughout Sumatra, as well as in Malaysia, Brunei and Singapore. There are shops that have been there for more than two decades such as ATI, Rica, Acai and Ratna, but the most popular is Zulaikha which is relatively new as it has been in the market only for 5 years.

[3]http://www.halalmui.org/mui14/index.php/main/go_to_section/59/1368/page/1

Table 2 A summary of studies on Halal certification from 2011 to 2017

Year	Author(s)	Findings
2011	Rajagopal et al.	The concept of Halal is familiar to the students; however, their awareness and knowledge of Halal-certified products are extremely low
2012	Marzuki et al.	It promotes the importance of restaurant managers to have knowledge on Muslims' dietary restrictions, sensitivity and religious practices. Halal certification signifies that it has some attributes that make it unique and conforming to the Islamic dietary rules
2013	Razalli et al.	There are 12 items of Halal certification practices that affect hotel performance. The facilities and staff policy have significant effects, while other ten practices were found to have no effect on hotel performance
2014	Shariff and Lah	A controversy on the integrity of Halal certification issued by the respective religious authority in the originating country. It is against the process that has been implemented in Malaysia
2014	Noordin et al.	The strategic approach towards Halal quality management that addresses the operational efficiency of the Halal food certification system using the Malaysian Halal certification
2017	Annabi and Ibidapo-Obe	A failure to adopt holistic Halal terminology which implies that within the UK Halal cosmetics industry, manufacturers may not be working within agreed standards for Halal product integrity
2015	Prabowo et al.	Halal certification in food service industry gains low interest from industries. There are hampering factors in various perspectives and offers some suggestions to overcome issues accordingly. Lack of socialisation and information have led to the lack of knowledge and awareness
2016	Ab Talib and Abdul Hamid	Proper application of resources, in this case Halal certification, could positively influence logistics performance. The governmental factors act as the moderator between the Halal certification-logistics performance relationship or could directly influence logistics performance
2016	Henderson	It reviewed the importance of Halal food for Muslim tourists and its regulation and certification. Malaysia and Singapore operate regulatory schemes for Halal food which relatively advanced. Provision of Halal food is a competitive advantage for destinations positioned as Muslim-friendly
2016	Rafiki and Wahab	The business experience, motivation, training and education have a significant relationship with the obtainment of Halal certification
2017	Ab Talib	There are motivations of implementing Halal food safety certification. The internal motivations concern a firm's internal processes, people and the available resources, while the external motivations relate to a firm's external elements such as government intervention and market pressure
2017	Othman et al.	A positive relationship between knowledge, attitude, sensitivity to government policy regarding the Halal certification process on the organisation's performance

Source: Author's own Table (2018)

Table 3 Religion and race profile of Medan city in 2017

Religion	Total	Percentage (%)	Race	Total	Percentage (%)
Islam	1,661,260	69.53	Batak	790,233	34.39
Christian	476,402	19.94	Javanese	780,169	33.03
Catholic	42,640	1.78	Chinese	255,431	10.65
Hindu	11,386	0.47	Minangkabau	211,728	8.60
Buddha	197,490	8.26	Malay	185,680	6.59
Confucianism	460	0.018	Acehnese	76,455	2.78
Total	2,389,016	100	Others	89,320	3.95
			Total	2,389,016	100

Source: BPS—Central Agency on Statistics (2017)

Fig. 1 Majapahit Street, Medan (Author's own image, 2018)

The owner of Zulaikha shop is Hajjah Mariani. She was a former pharmacist who worked in one of the national pharmaceutical companies for about 35 years before she started her own business on August 6, 2003. Starting the new venture, selling Bika Ambon cakes was not an easy job for her initially, and she never imagined that she would become a successful entrepreneur one day. She saw that during Muslim Eid festival, many Muslims were queuing to buy Bika Ambon from non-Muslim shops. She thus decided to sell the product during Eid and started with eight boxes. This later went up to 200 boxes, and she was able to compete with the competitors. She now employs 70 employees compared to just 3 at the beginning. Mariani's route to success lies in her ability to predict the market and producing Bika Ambon with seven flavours, besides selling other products including layer cake, cake rolls, brownies, fruit syrup, etc. All of her products are her own recipes. Unintentionally, she was applying a differentiation strategy in her business. She never compromised with the quality of products, and this ultimately convinced consumers who came back again and again.

In the beginning, Mariani collaborated with a number of people including the pedicab drivers. For introducing and promoting her business, she would give the pedicab drivers a free Bika Ambon cake and drinking water. She never ignored the importance of mouth-to-mouth promotion and also carried out personal marketing through her friends/colleagues. She implemented cheap, efficient and effective ways to promote her business. The lesson here is that it is extremely important to create and maintain relationships or networks in business.

Hajjah Mariani also came up with a unique supermarket concept by providing a packing service for tourists who intended to send it by courier to other places. With the support of her family, she always tries to learn innovative ways to meet the demands of consumers and improve her products and services.

Hajjah Mariani started the business with a capital of Rp.10 million (US$689) and became the first Muslim entrepreneur to sell Bika Ambon. Slowly her sales improved without any losses. As a result, many banks offered her loans. However, she was not interested in taking loans and proudly said: 'I want to stand on my own feet'. She felt that by taking loans, she would be bound to other parties. Although many people asked her to expand her business by opening branches in other towns, Mariani decided to open shops only in Medan. The reason was simply because her Bika Ambon was typical of Medan and might taste different in other places.

Hajjah Mariani considers herself a true servant of Allah SWT, blessed with abundant fortune. She is dedicated to contribute and share her wealth with the less fortunate and with society, by paying zakat and giving alms to the mosques as well as sponsoring *da'wah* (sermon) activities. Taking care of her employees is also on top of her priority by providing them good places to live and often coaching/guiding them in their work place.

5 Issues and Analysis

5.1 The Impact of Halal Certification

When Zulaikha obtained its *Halal* certification, it had a huge impact. Following in their footsteps, many Muslim shops on the same street in Medan now carry the *Halal* certificate as well. In the past, Bika Ambon was only sold by the Chinese shops, and it was not clear whether the cakes had ingredients prohibited for Muslims. After Zulaikha entered the market with *Halal* products, both Muslim and non-Muslim consumers are buying Zulaikha's products. Today, Zulaikha shop sells an average of at least 1000 boxes a day of Bika Ambon alone (not including other products such as Layer cake, etc.). At a price of IDR 60,000 (US$4.14) per box, they earn around IDR 60 million (US$4137) in a day or IDR 1.8 billion (US$124,137) in a month. This is the collection from just one shop (see Fig. 2). Zulaikha is now expanding their business through online promotions and sales. During Eid holidays, the sales can

Fig. 2 The Zulaikha shops (two shop lots) (Author's own images, 2018)

increase by 2–5 times as compared to the normal daily sales, and they sometimes cannot take any more orders.

By producing *Halal* food, Muslims expect to get *barokah* (blessing) from God—they believe that He will multiply the benefits to those who are committed and consistent in the Islamic practices. This is evident in this case, where it has brought happiness and satisfaction to all stakeholders including the owners, customers, suppliers as well as the government.

5.2 Perception of Halal Certification

A small survey was used to explore consumers' perception about *Halal* certification in general. Convenience sampling technique was used, and 90 respondents were asked to fill up the short questionnaires. The instruments were adapted and derived from the previous studies by Ahmed, Al-Kwifi, Saiti and Othman (2014), Ali, Xiaoling, Sherwani and Ali (2017), Aziz and Vui (2012) and Awan, Siddiquei and Zeeshan (2015), on consumers' expectations of *Halal* products. Below is the Table 4 of the respondents' profile.

As shown in Table 4, 37.7% of respondents were Zulaikha's customers for the first time, and the rest of 73.3% have purchased Zulaikha's products more than once. This indicates that Zulaikha's products are well known by consumers, especially by those who live in Medan. The repeat purchase indicates that the shop has been successful in satisfying the costumers. It is interesting to note that 44.4% of the respondents has been buying Zulaikha's products for the last 3–5 years, while only 15.6% have been Zulaikha's customers for less than a year.

Meanwhile, 57.8% of respondents are between 21 and 40 years old, and 42.2% of them are more than 41 years old. This shows that Zulaikha's products are liked by a wide range of customers from different age groups, especially with the variety in tastes and flavours. Moreover, a majority (73%) of the respondents earn an income of IDR 5,000,000 with only 11.1% of respondents earning less than IDR 2,500,000.

Table 4 Demographic data ($n = 90$)

Respondents' profile	Percentage (%)
1. Is it the first time purchasing Zulaikha's products?	
Yes	37.7
No	73.3
2. How long have you been Zulaikha's customer?	
<1 year	15.6
1–3 years	17.8
3–5 years	44.4
>5 years	22.2
3. Ages of respondents	
20–30	24.5
31–40	33.3
41–50	31.1
>51	11.1
4. Income profile	
<IDR 2,500,000	11.1
IDR 2,500,000–4,999,999	15.6
IDR 5,000,000–7,499,999	28.9
IDR 7,500,000–9,999,999	22.2
IDR >10,000,000	22.2
5. Educational profile	
Elementary school	8.9
Junior/senior high school	35.6
Undergraduate (diploma/bachelor)	42.2
Post-graduate (Master/MBA/PhD)	13.3

Source: Author's own Table (2018)

This may indicate that Zulaikha's products are bought by higher-income customers, who are concerned with the quality of ingredients and *Halal*-certified products. 42.2% of respondents have an undergraduate degree, while 8.9% of respondents are with elementary school certificate. Having a well-educated group of customers indicates that they are well informed with regard to the best products in the market as they have the ability to access and compare product information. Knowledge is important when it comes to the decision-making process.

Below are the discussion of each statements in Table 5:

86.7% of respondents agreed that *Halal* certification is a symbol of quality, while only 2.2% of them disagreed with the statement. *Halal* certification was considered as a symbol for quality because it is a certification for a complex assessment of the food production process (Razalli et al. 2013). It is a label that can serve as the outcome of a quality assurance scheme (Verbeke, Rutsaert, Bonne, & Vermeir, 2013) and as an assurance that the products meet Islamic guidelines.

92.2% of respondents agreed that *Halal* certification delivers trust on products, while only 1.1% of them disagreed with the statement. Trust on the authenticity of *Halal* is purely based on the product assurance (Abdul, Ismail, Hashim, & Johari,

Table 5 A survey on perception of Halal certification ($n = 90$)

Statements	Scale				
	Strongly agree	Agree	Neutral	Disagree	Strongly disagree
1. Halal certification is a symbol for quality					
Percentage (%)	44.5	42.2	11.1	1.1	1.1
2. Halal certification delivers trust on products					
Percentage (%)	42.2	50	6.7	1.1	0
3. Choosing product with Halal logo because of religious influence					
Percentage (%)	24.4	28.9	6.7	22.2	17.8
4. Price of products carry Halal certification is expensive					
Percentage (%)	3.3	6.7	17.8	30.0	42.2
5. Halal certification is not important for me					
Percentage (%)	3.3	3.3	8.9	40.0	44.4
6. Halal certification is only for Muslim consumers					
Percentage (%)	8.9	11.1	13.3	31.1	35.6
7. Halal certification only for Muslim shops					
Percentage (%)	5.6	5.6	8.9	37.8	42.2
8. The sales of shops are increasing when selling products with Halal certification					
Percentage (%)	26.7	33.3	11.1	17.8	11.1
9. Halal certification is a trend					
Percentage (%)	4.4	6.7	10.0	36.7	42.2
10. Halal certification must genuinely be issued by authorised bodies					
Percentage (%)	47.8	35.6	8.9	4.4	3.3

Source: Author's own Table (2018)

2009), and the trust on the *Halal* label is critical for sustaining business (Zailani, Arrifin, Wahid, Othman, & Fernando, 2010).

53.3% of respondents agreed that they choose products with a *Halal* logo because of religious influence, while 40% of them disagreed with the statement. Even though there are other factors influencing the choice of *Halal* logo besides religion teachings, it is the most important. *Halal* quality is informed by religious perceptions and its legislative requirements (Verbeke et al., 2013).

47.8% of respondents disagreed that the price of products with *Halal* certification is expensive, while 10% agreed with the statement. Although the enterprises had invested quite a significant amount of money to apply for *Halal* certification, it doesn't mean the owner/managers could increase the prices of products.

84.4% of respondents disagreed that '*Halal* certification is not important for me', while 6.6% of respondents agrees with the statement. As the majority of respondents are quite educated, they are aware of the importance of *Halal* certification. Ali, Marzuki and Halim (2012) asserted that *Halal* logo has positive perception with the quality in food purity, safety and cleanliness.

66.7% of respondents disagreed that '*Halal* certification is only for Muslim consumers', while 20% of respondents agreed with the statement. It is for all people as a practice of the dietary habits and preferences (Wilson & Liu, 2011).

80% of respondents disagreed that '*Halal* certification is only for Muslim shops', while 11.2% of respondents agreed with the statement. For example, even though the UK is not a Muslim country, many enterprises have opted for *Halal* certification (Annabi & Ibidapo-Obe, 2017; Elseidi, 2017). This is similar in other European countries with supportive policies for *Halal* products are created.

60% of respondents agreed that the sales of shops are increasing after selling products with *Halal* certification, while 28.9% of respondents disagreed with the statement. *Halal* certification as an Islamic brand maintains and enhances strategic value that brings prospects.

78.9% of respondents disagreed that *Halal* certification is a trend, while 11.1% of respondents agreed with the statement. According to Shafie and Othman (2006), the *Halal* logo is more meaningful and important than carrying ISO or similar certification for a lot of consumers.

83.4% of respondents agreed that *Halal* certification must be issued by authorised bodies, while 7.7% of respondents disagreed with the statement. This statement relates to an issue of fake certification, so most consumers are worried about this issue. The authenticity of *Halal* certification provides assurance about the product purity (Jabar et al., 2014; Mohamad et al., 2015).

6 Halal Certification Challenges

Indonesia has a wide diversity in terms of demographic profile and market characteristics as compared to other countries. Thus, the challenges of applying and issuing the *Halal* certification may vary from other countries. Below are the challenges that are faced by the owners/managers in the food sector in Medan:

(A) *Bureaucracy*

The government needs to create policies that encourage manufacturers, producers and owners to apply for *Halal* certification. Multiple dealings and delays in responses should become a concern. With the integration of food channels and supply chains, this will create transparency, trust and attraction among stakeholders. The rules and regulations on business systems must support the *Halal* certification process. The applicants want simple and easy processes.

(B) *Costs*

The standard cost per certificate is up to IDR 5 million for medium-sized companies and IDR 2.5 million for small companies. However, the cost excludes the accommodation and insurance expenses, which normally depend on the size of the company. The government actually gains income from the taxpayers, including the enterprises who apply for the *Halal* logo, and thus governments can play a role by providing incentives to the enterprises to decrease their financial burden.

(C) *Facilities*

The public or private sector contributes by providing facilities to those who have interests in understanding *Halal* certification; however, it has rarely happened. The appropriate platforms can boost the awareness and development of *Halal* certification.

(D) *Human Capital*

Human capital issues relate to the capability and acceptance of people towards *Halal* certification. The educated consumers could probably understand the benefits of *Halal* certification besides seeing it as a religion obligation. Public and private institutions, particularly Islamic education institutions, should find ways to teach owner/managers as well as others which lack knowledge about *Halal* certification.

The reluctance by the employees to attend training sessions will directly create difficulties in understanding technical matters, for instance, the documents/forms to be prepared, completed and submitted to auditors, etc. and the information to be reported and uploaded. Moreover, the business experience of managers is needed to face issues that emerge when dealing with the certification process.

(E) *Enforcement*

The agencies who are responsible for the issuance of *Halal* certification have difficulties to monitor and evaluate the enterprises. The lack in number of officers that are appointed to carry out enforcement was seen. The expectation of the *Halal* integrated systems is to ensure a deliverance of *Halal* quality products; however, some companies may abuse the process technically. The awareness programmes and frequent reminders are needed to prevent such abuses from occurring, including the avoidance of misunderstandings by explaining that *Halal* certification is meant for both Muslim and non-Muslim producers/consumers.

7 Conclusion

The impact of *Halal* certification is clearly shown with the benefits received by Zulaikha, both materially and spiritually. The commitment, consistency and innovativeness of the owner have contributed to her success. This case also reveals the clear benefits of implementing Islamic business practices. The certified *Halal* products bring values, quality as well as other spiritual benefits to the customers and producers.

Perception of customers on *Halal* certification is aligned with the meaning and characteristics of *Halal* concept that complies with the *Shariah*. It is imperative that the five challenges related to *Halal* certification should be addressed for development purposes in the future. Coordination, collaboration and attention by all stakeholders are needed to see improvements. This may take a long time and complicate dealings. As for comparison and summary, Table 6 points out the expectation of Muslim consumers on the *Halal* products and its certification process.

Table 6 A summary of Muslim consumer view and Halal certification process

Muslim consumer standpoint on Halal product	Halal certification process
1. Products must be produced without any forbidden ingredients	1. Halal accreditation should be done with an Islamic association with a good international reputation
2. Products must prove to be in the interest of the consumers' health and wellbeing	2. All processes must comply with requirements under the *Shariah*
3. Products must be clean and hygienic and have supply chain integrity	3. All ingredients must be checked as to their suitability to be certified Halal. All ingredients must be certified Halal before the product can be certified Halal
4. Products must benefit those who produced them	4. Any Haram (unlawful products) must be processed in separate facilities and never come into contact with Halal certifiable products
5. Products and the materials that make up these products must be traceable from the origin, to have total confidence	5. Halal and products considered Haram can never be stored together

Sources: Rahman (2009) and Sungkar (2007)

References

Ab Talib, M. S. (2017). Motivations and benefits of Halal food safety certification. *Journal of Islamic Marketing, 8*(4), 605–624.

Ab Talib, M. S., & Abdul Hamid, A. B. (2016). Can Halal certification influence logistics performance? *Journal of Islamic Marketing, 7*(4), 461–475.

Abdul, M., Ismail, H., Hashim, H., & Johari, J. (2009). Consumer decision making process in shopping for Halal food in Malaysia. *China-USA Business Review, 8*(9), 40–47.

Ahmed, Z. U., Al-Kwifi, O. S., Saiti, B., & Othman, N. B. (2014). Consumer behavior dynamics of Chinese minorities. *Journal of Technology Management in China, 9*(1), 6–23.

Ali, R., Marzuki, S. Z. S., & Halim, R. A. (2012). The awareness towards Halal logo attributes among customers of Halal certified restaurants: An exploratory study. In B. Alserhan (Ed.), *2nd Global Islamic Conference* (pp. 307–313). Abu Dhabi: Global Islamic Marketing Association.

Ali, A., Xiaoling, G., Sherwani, M., & Ali, A. (2017). Factors affecting Halal meat purchase intention: Evidence from international Muslim students in China. *British Food Journal, 119*(3), 527–541.

Annabi, C. A., & Ibidapo-Obe, O. O. (2017). Halal certification organizations in the United Kingdom: An exploration of Halal cosmetic certification. *Journal of Islamic Marketing, 8*(1), 107–126.

Awan, M. H., Siddiquei, N. A., & Zeeshan, H. (2015). Factors affecting Halal purchase intention – Evidence from Pakistan's Halal food sector. *Management Research Review, 38*(6), 640–660.

Aziz, Y. A., & Vui, C. N. (2012). *The role of Halal awareness and Halal certification in influencing non-Muslim's purchase intention.* In 3rd International Conference on Business and Economic Research (3rd ICBER 2012), Proceedings paper 1,819, Bandung.

BPS. (2016, 2017). *Indikator Ekonomi Indonesia Tahun 2016.* Jakarta: Biro Pusat Statistik.

Elseidi, R. I. (2017). Determinants of Halal purchasing intentions: Evidences from UK. *Journal of Islamic Marketing, 9*(2), 1–31.

Hanzaee, K. H., & Ramezani, M. R. (2011). Intention to Halal products in the world markets. *Interdisciplinary Journal of Research in Business, 1*(5), 1–7.

Henderson, J. C. (2016). Halal food, certification and Halal tourism: Insights from Malaysia and Singapore. *Tourism Management Perspectives, 19*(2), 161–164.

Isabelle, A., & Laurent, T. (2015). Building holistic brands: An exploratory study of Halal cosmetics. *Journal of Islamic Marketing, 6*(1), 109–132.
Jabar, F. A., Ishak, M., Johar, N., & Wahid, S. N. S. (2014). A study on the relationship between awareness and knowledge of Muslim retailers toward Halal cosmetic products. In *Proceedings on the International Conference on Science, Technology and Social Sciences (ICSTSS)* (pp. 383–388). Singapore: Springer.
Jusmaliani, J., & Nasution, H. (2009). Religiosity aspect in consumer behaviour: Determinants of Halal meat consumption. *ASEAN Marketing Journal, 1*, 1–11.
Khraim, H. (2010). Measuring religiosity in consumer research from an Islamic perspective. *Journal of Economic & Administrative Sciences, 26*, 52–78.
Marzuki, S. Z., Hall, C. M., & Ballantine, P. W. (2012). Restaurant managers' perspectives on Halal certification. *Journal of Islamic Marketing, 3*(1), 47–58.
Mohamad, A. A., Baharuddin, A. S., & Ruskam, A. (2015). Halal industry in Singapore: A case study of nutraceutical products. *Sains Humanika, 4*(2), 35–40.
Noordin, N., Md Noor, N., & Samicho, Z. (2014). Strategic approach to Halal certification system: An ecosystem perspective. *Procedia – Social and Behavioral Sciences, 121*, 79–95.
Othman, B., Shaarani, S. M., & Bahron, A. (2017). The influence of knowledge, attitude and sensitivity to government policies in Halal certification process on organizational performance. *Journal of Islamic Marketing, 8*(3), 393–408.
Prabowo, S., Abd Rahman, A., Ab Rahman, S., & Abu Samah, A. (2015). Revealing factors hindering Halal certification in East Kalimantan Indonesia. *Journal of Islamic Marketing, 6*(2), 268–291.
Rafiki, A., & Wahab, K. A. (2016). The human capital and the obtainment of Halal certification. *Journal Islamic of Marketing, 7*(2), 134–147.
Rahman, H. A. (2009). *Halal agro-industry supply chain*. World Food Shortage Conference – Series II, 9–10 July, Putra World Trade Center (PWTC), Kuala Lumpur.
Rajagopal, S., Ramanan, S., Visvanathan, R., & Satapathy, S. (2011). Halal certification: Implication for marketers in UAE. *Journal of Islamic Marketing, 2*(2), 138–153.
Razalli, M. R., Yusoff, R. Z., & Roslan, M. W. M. (2013). A framework of Halal certification practices for Hotel industry. *Asian Social Science, 9*(11), 316–326.
Shafie, S., & Othman, N. (2006). Halal certification: An international marketing issues and challenges. *Journal of Marketing Research, 15*, 565–575.
Shariff, S. M., & Lah, N. (2014). Halal certification on chocolate products: A case study. *Procedia – Social and Behavioural Sciences, 121*, 104–112.
Sungkar, I. (2007). Developing the Halal value proposition from farm to folk. In *Proceedings of the 3rd Malaysian International Agro-Bio Business Conference*, 12–13 July, Kuala Lumpur.
Tieman, M., Ghazali, M. C., & Van der Vorst, J. (2013). Consumer perception on Halal meat logistics. *British Food Journal, 115*(8), 1112–1129.
Verbeke, W., Rutsaert, P., Bonne, K., & Vermeir, I. (2013). Credence quality coordination and consumers' willingness-to-pay for certified Halal labelled meat. *Meat Science, 95*(4), 790–797.
Wilson, J. A. J., & Liu, J. (2011). The challenges of Islamic branding: Navigating emotions and Halal. *Journal of Islamic Marketing, 2*(1), 28–42.
Zailani, S., Arrifin, Z., Wahid, N. B., Othman, R., & Fernando, Y. (2010). Halal traceability and Halal tracking systems in strengthening Halal food supply chains for food industry in Malaysia (a review). *Journal of Food Technology, 8*(3), 74–81.

Ahmad Rafiki is an Assistant Professor in the Department of Business Administration of University College of Bahrain. He obtained his BBA in Marketing from UiTM, Malaysia, master's in management from IIUM and PhD from USIM. He is a Certified Islamic Marketer (CIMA) from IIMA. He had published a number of articles in refereed journals, is in the editorial advisory boards and is reviewer of several reputable international journals.

Was the Boycott of McDonald's Malaysia Religiously Motivated?

Ezlika M. Ghazali, Dilip S. Mutum, Meenatharisni Sundramohana, and Priscila Valdivieso

Abstract

In August 2014, McDonald's Malaysia found themselves in the middle of a marketing crisis, after Palestinian supporters in Malaysia called for a national boycott of the fast-food chain through an online campaign. The 'Boycott McDonald day' turned into violent demonstrations outside the outlets of two McDonalds, which resulted in a loss of around 80% of revenue, and other outlets deciding to close for the day. This case study examines the background and issues involved and the actions taken by McDonalds to deal with this crisis.

1 Company Background

When brothers Dick and Mac McDonald opened a hamburger restaurant in San Bernardino, California, in 1940, they never imagined the magnitude of prominence and growth the company would achieve. From humble beginnings, the brothers

E. M. Ghazali (✉)
Faculty of Business and Accountancy, Department of Marketing, University of Malaya, Kuala Lumpur, Malaysia

University of Malaya Halal Research Centre (UMHRC), Kuala Lumpur, Malaysia
e-mail: ezlika@um.edu.my

D. S. Mutum
Nottingham University Business School, University of Nottingham Malaysia, Semenyih, Selangor, Malaysia

M. Sundramohana · P. Valdivieso
Faculty of Business and Accountancy, University of Malaya Graduate School of Business, University of Malaya, Kuala Lumpur, Malaysia

E. M. Ghazali et al. (eds.), *Management of Shari'ah Compliant Businesses*, Management for Professionals, https://doi.org/10.1007/978-3-030-10907-3_13

concentrated their menu on limited choices, namely, burgers, fries and beverages, which gave them an advantage by focussing on quick service as well as quality.

Fifteen years later, a work visit by salesman called Roy Kroc sparked the beginning of what the world would ultimately come to recognise as a fast-food global phenomenon. Kroc was absolutely fascinated by the effectiveness of the processes and grabbed the opportunity presented to him when the McDonald brothers were looking for a new agent. He took over the operations and purchased the exclusive rights to the brand name—McDonald's, 6 years later. With a flair for marketing, Kroc soon realised that the McDonald's system he founded could be expanded and implemented beyond the US borders.

Kroc had a prominent vision to create a restaurant system that revolved around uniformity in preparation and consistency in high-quality food. He also put a lot of weight on the idea that burgers, fries and beverages should taste the same regardless of the outlet it was prepared. To accomplish this vision, he chose a distinctive path—encouraging both suppliers and franchisee to buy into this concept that they will not be working for McDonald's, and instead working for themselves together with McDonald's—the start of the franchise business model. His ideology, 'In business for yourself, but not by yourself', was based on the principle of a three-legged stool, with each representing McDonald's franchisees, suppliers and employees, respectively. He strongly believed that one without the other would result in a weak business structure. To ensure high-quality product specifications, several quality centres worldwide were designed to make sure that the standards are consistently met.[1]

Be it Mickey-D's (USA), McDee (New Zealand) or Macca's (Australian), McDonald's has become part of a global culture. Over time, the company has successfully penetrated global markets, making them the leader of the fast-food industry serving an average of 70 million customers wide-reaching on a daily basis. McDonald's revenue reached its highest peak in 2013 with US$28.11 million, and there are now more than 40,000 McDonald's restaurants worldwide.[2] Despite providing a standard menu, they also accord geographic and cultural variations to suit targeted local customers—emerging from a strategic point of view of thinking globally but acting locally.

One of the main catalysts of a consumer's behaviour is culture, and McDonald's goes to great extents to carefully localise their food menu by creating new choices according to local culture and traditions. Over the years, it has offered consumers numerous menu variations which cater to different cultural and religious customs all around the world. For instance, in order to penetrate the Indian market, they introduced custom burgers such as the Maharaja Mac and Spicy Paneer Wrap. India is also the only country where they do not serve beef or pork, besides offering several vegetarian options. Other examples include McPaltas in Chile—a burger with avocado paste; teriyaki Mac Burger in Japan, a pork burger glazed with Teriyaki sauce; bulgogi burger in South Korea, sliced meat with bulgogi sauce;

---

[1]https://www.mcdonalds.com/us/en-us/about-us/our-history.html

[2]https://www.statista.com/statistics/208917/revenue-of-the-mcdonalds-corporation-since-2005/

etc.[3] Similarly, McDonald's has adapted their products based on Malaysian culture. With a Muslim population of around 61.3%,[4] McDonald's places high importance on offering strictly "Halal" menus that is certified by the Department of Islamic Development Malaysia (JAKIM). Another offering unique to Malaysia is *Bubur Ayam*, a Malaysian-style porridge with chicken strips garnished with fried shallots, spring onions and chilies. McDonald's Malaysia also brings out limited-time-only products during the different festive seasons, such as the Prosperity Burger, consisting of beef or chicken patties covered in black pepper sauce, during the Chinese New Year.

2 The Arab (Palestine)–Israel Conflict

The Israel–Palestine conflict is several decades old and started when huge numbers of Jews began arriving in Palestine starting in the late 1800s. We will not go and try explain the complex roots of the conflict, which is outside the scope of this case. However, the conflict has had far-reaching consequences including the death of thousands of innocent civilians. There are no indications that there is going to be any solution to this conflict in the near future.[5]

This conflict has had many chapters, and one of the most important is the conflict in the Gaza strip, which has become a flashpoint in the Israel–Palestine conflict. Gaza is one of the most densely populated areas in the world and a blockade of the strip has been maintained by Israel and Egypt since 2007. There have been three major conflicts since Hamas was voted into power in the Gaza Strip. The most notable was the 2014 Gaza war which started on 8 July 2014.[6] Rocket attacks, missiles as well as fighting on the ground, left over 2200 people killed (most of them Palestinians) and many others injured, with severe damage to buildings and infrastructure in the Gaza strip. A ceasefire was agreed between the parties on the 26th of August 2014.

3 The Malaysian McDonald's Boycott

The Palestinian–Israeli conflict has resulted in consumer boycotts all over the world, especially targeted at Israeli companies and products as well as those which were assumed to be linked to Israel in some way. This has actually resulted in a movement

[3]http://www.foodnetwork.co.uk/article/crazy-meals-mcdonalds-menus-around-world/list-page-4.html

[4]Malaysia Demographics Profile 2016. Retrieved November 26, 2016 from http://www.indexmundi.com/malaysia/demographics_profile.html

[5]https://www.bbc.co.uk/newsround/20436092

[6]https://www.bbc.com/news/world-middle-east-28252155

called to the Boycott, Divestment and Sanctions (BDS) movement.[7] This Palestinian-led movement has grown from strength to strength and promotes various forms of boycott against Israel including Israeli products and even engaging with Israeli-linked organisations. Consumers in many parts of the world have responded to this call and have decided to boycott any product or company liked to Israel, as a way of expressing anger against Israel's perceived oppression of Palestinians.[8] Many lists of Israeli products and companies that support Israel have been circulating on social media as well as on website and other media to promote the boycott of Israel.[9]

The definition of boycott and boycotting behaviour according to Friedman (1999, p. 4) is 'the attempt by one or more parties to achieve by urging individual consumers to refrain from making selected purchases'. When consumers develop feelings of hostility towards a country, one of the common reactions is to boycott the products related to the country. One of the companies affected was McDonald's. McDonald's was included in this list, and it was alleged that the company channelled their profit to Israel. One of these publications alleged that the company is a major corporate partner of the Jewish United Fund and that the company received recognition in 2000, as a first tier corporate partner to the cause of Zionism (Jewish nationalism).[10]

The calls for a consumer boycott of Israel spread rapidly to Malaysia, a market with a large Muslim population, mainly spread by a number of non-governmental Islamic organisations, especially over social media.[11] In Malaysia, the call for a boycott was most likely due to a feeling of solidarity with the Palestinians, most of whom are Muslims. As past research has indicated, religion certainly influences consumer behaviour (Ahmad, Rahman, & Ab Rahman, 2015; Mathras, Cohen, Mandel, & Mick, 2016; Sood & Nasu, 1995). An online campaign called to boycott McDonald's restaurants nationwide on the 8th of August 2014 from 7 a.m. indefinitely.[12] What started as a call to boycott McDonald's products ultimately resulted in violent acts outside some of the McDonald's outlets. Two of the most affected outlets from the violence were in Kerteh and Dungan, in the eastern state of Terengganu.[13] In addition, it was reported that McDonald's staff suffered from harassment, threats and verbal abuse.[14] McDonald's reported 80% loss of revenue on the day and some material

[7] https://bdsmovement.net/what-is-bds

[8] https://boycottisraeltoday.wordpress.com/boycott-israel/

[9] http://www.inminds.com/boycott-mcdonalds.php

[10] http://vpm.org.my/bds/32-why-boycott-mcdonalds

[11] https://globalvoices.org/2014/08/15/how-the-boycott-mcdonalds-campaign-for-gaza-is-hurting-some-muslims-in-malaysia/

[12] http://www.malaysiandigest.com/features/509889-why-boycott-israel-needs-to-happen-now.html

[13] https://says.com/my/news/what-happens-when-malaysians-choose-to-boycott-mcd-s

[14] http://www.straitstimes.com/asia/se-asia/mcdonalds-malaysia-says-staff-harassed-and-abused-over-gaza-conflict

losses due to acts of vandalism. To prevent any untoward accidents and cases of abuse, some of the restaurants closed the operations for the rest of the day. In some McDonald's outlets, security guards were hired to protect the restaurants. Other restaurants that didn't face any protests outside the establishments also reported significantly lower number of consumers. It should be pointed out that even though many Malaysian costumers supported the boycott, many were against the vandalism and the abuse targeted at the employees.

4 Implications to Consumer Brand Loyalty

The McDonald's boycott created a lot of negative publicity, and the McDonald's brand in Malaysia was clearly hurt as a consequence. This was not surprising as research has indicated that religious boycotts can have significant impacts on both corporate profits and brand image (Abosag, 2014). Even though the financial repercussions of the boycott on the performance of McDonald's Malaysia was not clear,[15] there is some evidence based on information provided by various outlet administrators that the number of customers were lower than the normal, during the boycott. It is highly likely that sales would have dropped as a result. In addition, it is also highly likely that the McDonalds boycott had a negative impact on the loyalty of their customers by creating negative perception about the brand due to the negative word-of-mouth via social media.

5 McDonald's Fights Back

To battle against the global boycott, McDonald's in different countries approached the issue with different tactics, mainly short term in nature and related to the magnitude of the boycott. One of the key decisions made was to detach themselves from this emerging controversial matter by amending their franchise policy by banning the opening of outlets at any Israel Settlement beyond the Green Line borders.[16] This particular tactic was taken into account by many other global brands as well so as to avoid negative responses by consumers.

In Malaysia, McDonald's took a number of steps. First of all, they took out an advertisement in Sinar Harian, one of the prominent Malay newspapers.[17] This indicates that the management was targeting the Malay (Muslim) consumers and their main aim was to show that the boycott actually hurts the local workers who rely on McDonald's to earn a living. A one-page long advertisement addressed to

[15]http://corporate.mcdonalds.com/content/dam/AboutMcDonalds/Investors%202/2015%20Annual%20Report.pdf

[16]McDonald's Boycotts The Settlements. Retrieved from The Daily Beast: http://www.thedailybeast.com/articles/2013/06/26/mcdonald-s-boycotts-the-settlements.html

[17]http://www.marketing-interactive.com/mcdonalds-malaysia-places-ad-fight-boycott/

Malaysians emphasised the impact on domestic economy and the fact that this boycott will only jeopardise the livelihood of Malaysian staff and management team, 85% of whom were Muslims.[18] It was also highlighted that the company offered business prospects to more than 50 local suppliers, who in turn provided employment to over 2500 locals. They added that they were in the planning stage to expand to 500 restaurants countrywide, creating over 11,500 new job opportunities. Thus, the boycott would hinder this plan and in fact harm the local economy.

> The real victims of these allegations are friends, workers and families who are the subject of discrimination and our franchisees who are working to make a living.—McDonald's Malaysia

Another tactic exercised by McDonald's was to respond to the false speculation in a professional manner before it was blown out of proportion. They also insisted and denied the claims that they were funding Israeli operations in Gaza. They highlighted that they were not involved in political activities, violence or oppression. They also released a statement on their Facebook page mentioning that McDonald's has been unfairly targeted and as a consequence, some of their staff had to endure harassment, verbal abuse and threats. They also reminded the nation to fall back on values and to respect one another.[19]

McDonald's also publicly highlighted their charitable contributions and their responsibility towards the community in various newspaper advertisements. They expressed pride for being a committed and concerned charitable organisation for the past three decades in Malaysia by noting that Ronald McDonald's House of Charity had contributed over RM11 million to aid 20,000 unfortunate children and also their collaboration with University Kebangsaan Malaysia Medical Centre for families with patient's who could not afford to pay for surgery. The 'Prosperity Gives back' campaign also managed to collect about RM900,000 for charity. All these corporate social responsibility (CSR) activities were widely publicised in the mass media.[20]

6 Concluding Thoughts

This case study elucidates how religious sensitivities propelled McDonald's consumers in Malaysia, specifically from the Muslim community, to boycott the company. The 'Boycott McD Malaysia' protests resulted in aggressive demonstrations which disrupted operations, resulting in some outlets to be closed for several days, with staff harassed and their property vandalised. During the crisis, consumers who felt strongly about the whole issue expressed their dissatisfaction in

[18]http://www.themalaymailonline.com/malaysia/article/real-victims-are-malaysians-says-mcdonalds-ad-pleading-against-local-boycot

[19]https://www.facebook.com/notes/mcdonalds/media-statement-by-mcdonalds-malaysia/10152531458431998/

[20]http://www.prweek.com/article/1307071/mcdonalds-fights-back-islamist-boycott-threat

the marketplace, indicating a change in their purchase behaviour and their loyalty towards McDonald's.

The rebuttal tactics used by McDonald's was clearly successful, and the company made a good recovery. The company's decisive response is a perfect example on how a company should respond to this type of crisis, by immediately coming out with strong statements refuting the claims and highlighting the possible impact of the boycott to the Malaysian domestic economy, as well as upholding their charitable contributions. While it may not regain loyalty from all the boycotters, the fight back definitely helped McDonald's to come out of the crisis with flying colours.

References

Abosag, I. (2014). The influence of religiously motivated consumer boycotts on brand image, loyalty and product judgement. *European Journal of Marketing, 48*(11/12), 2262–2283.

Ahmad, A. N., Rahman, A. A., & Ab Rahman, S. (2015). Assessing knowledge and religiosity on consumer behavior towards halal food and cosmetic products. *International Journal of Social Science and Humanity, 5*(1), 10.

Friedman, M. (1999). *Consumer boycotts*. New York: Routledge.

Mathras, D., Cohen, A. B., Mandel, N., & Mick, D. G. (2016). The effects of religion on consumer behavior: A conceptual framework and research agenda. *Journal of Consumer Psychology, 26*(2), 298–311.

Sood, J., & Nasu, Y. (1995). Religiosity and nationality: An exploratory study of their effect on consumer behavior in Japan and the United States. *Journal of Business Research, 34*(1), 1–9.

Ezlika M. Ghazali is affiliated to the Department of Marketing, Faculty of Business and Accountancy, University of Malaya, Kuala Lumpur, Malaysia. She is also currently attached to the Business and Commercialisation Division, University of Malaya Halal Research Centre. Her research interests include switching barriers, augmented-reality marketing, online retailing, sustainable marketing and social entrepreneurship. Ezlika has widely published in journals including *Information Technology and People*, *Journal of Retailing and Consumer Services*, *Internet Research*, *Electronic Markets* and others.

Dilip S. Mutum is Associate Professor of Marketing with Nottingham University Business School, University of Nottingham Malaysia. His research interests include digital consumption and sustainable marketing. Dilip has also advised various organisations on strategic marketing issues. His research work has been published within a range of publications—both in print and online.

Meenatharisni Sundramohana was an MBA student at the University of Malaya Graduate School of Business, University of Malaya, Kuala Lumpur, Malaysia. She is currently working with Ramsay Sime Darby Health Care, Ara Damansara, Malaysia, and involved in customer relations.

Priscila Valdivieso was an MBA student at the University of Malaya Graduate School of Business, University of Malaya, Kuala Lumpur, Malaysia.

Cadbury and the Porcine DNA Crisis

Ezlika M. Ghazali, Dilip S. Mutum, Mardiana Md Radzi, and Wei-Pin Woon

Abstract

On 23 May 2014, Malaysian newspapers reported that samples of two Cadbury products in Malaysia, namely, Cadbury Dairy Milk Hazelnut and Cadbury Dairy Milk Roast Almond, tested positive for traces of porcine DNA by the Ministry of Health Malaysia. This was a serious issue in a country with a large number of Muslim consumers. As soon as the news came out, the Malaysian Department of Islamic Development suspended the halal certification of two Cadbury chocolate products that allegedly contained porcine DNA. This case study examines the issues and the response of the company to the crisis. It highlights the importance of the role of swift public relations in crisis management. It also highlights the fact that sustainable marketing is not just about profits and that companies need to take all stakeholders into account.

E. M. Ghazali (✉)
Faculty of Business and Accountancy, Department of Marketing, University of Malaya, Kuala Lumpur, Malaysia

University of Malaya Halal Research Centre (UMHRC), University of Malaya, Kuala Lumpur, Malaysia
e-mail: ezlika@um.edu.my

D. S. Mutum
Nottingham University Business School, University of Nottingham Malaysia, Semenyih, Selangor, Malaysia

M. Md Radzi · W.-P. Woon
Faculty of Business and Accountancy, University of Malaya Graduate Business School, University of Malaya, Kuala Lumpur, Malaysia

E. M. Ghazali et al. (eds.), *Management of Shari'ah Compliant Businesses*, Management for Professionals, https://doi.org/10.1007/978-3-030-10907-3_14

1 Introduction to Cadbury, the Company

Cadbury was established by John Cadbury in England in 1824. Cadbury started his business by selling tea, coffee and chocolate drinks. On 1831, Cadbury and his brother Benjamin opened a factory in Crooked Lane and started commercial scale production. They developed the business until 1861 then handover it to Cadbury's sons George and Richard. During that period, George took care of production and purchasing, while Richard was in charge for marketing and after sales. By 1905, Cadbury introduced their first Dairy Milk chocolate. The company successfully differentiated themselves from other products in the market by adding higher proportion of milk within the recipe. Within 10 years, the chocolate became the company's best-selling product.

Cadbury was a constant constituent of the FTSE 100 on the London Stock Exchange from the index's 1984 inception until the company was bought over by Mondelez International (originally Kraft Foods) in 2010. The company has its headquarter in Uxbridge, West London, and has operations in over 50 countries internationally.

1.1 Cadbury Malaysia

Cadbury Confectionery Malaysia Sdn. Bhd. operates as a subsidiary of Mondelez International, Inc. Their factory is located at No. 8, Persiaran Raja Muda, Seksyen 15, 40200 Shah Alam, Selangor, Malaysia. The brand has a long history in Malaysia and has been selling cocoa products for over 40 years in the country. Their product range in Malaysia includes bars (Dairy Milk Hazelnut, Dairy Milk Roast Almond, Dairy Milk Black Forest, etc.), bags and boxes (Choclairs Original, Choclairs Blueberry, Choclairs Raisin Rush, etc.), and biscuits (Fingers). At the time of the crisis, the Asia-Pacific region (which includes Malaysia) accounted for 15% of Mondelez International's US$35 billion (RM112.7 billion) business, with about three quarters of its annual revenue generated from the biscuits, chocolate and gum and candy categories.

2 The Porcine DNA Crisis

Malaysia is a multi-racial and multi-cultural country with over 30 million population. About half of the population are ethnic Malays, followed by Chinese, Indians and other ethnic groups. According to the constitution, Islam is the official religion of the country, and all Malays are Muslims. Muslims are strictly not allowed to consume pork even there is only a doubt or suspicion, and the news that Cadbury chocolates were contaminated was a really serious issue. Many Muslim consumers reacted negatively upon the contamination news as Cadbury is a household name in Malaysia. Many of them were extremely concerned, and this was highlighted by the high volume of search as indicated by Google trend, with the popular keywords searched in Malaysia during the crisis, including 'Cadbury halal' and 'Cadbury babi (Note: babi is Bahasa Malaysia for pork)'.[1] To make the matter worse, the news went viral on social media even though it was just a rumour, and there was no official confirmation or any official statements by the Malaysian authorities. Cadbury's Facebook page was flooded with enquiries demanding clarification on the matter and even derogatory comments.

An in-depth interview of 16 Malaysian consumers was particularly interesting as it revealed that most of them first heard about the rumours via social media, and more specifically via Facebook. They were shocked when the news came out, as Cadbury is a popular brand in Malaysia. One of the participants mentioned feeling cheated while another was furious. They all stopped buying Cadbury products until the Government finally announced the news that there was no contamination.[2]

According to an MOH staff, who was a part of the investigating team, the samples were part of monitoring sample for Food Act requirements by the Malaysian MOH.[3] The Food Act of Malaysia does not require checks for porcine DNA, but analysis was done as part of competency training for the lab staff, which was considered necessary for future accreditation or for analysis of emergency samples. It should be highlighted that the MOH lab was not accredited for porcine analysis or any other Halal-related analysis. The Department of Chemistry Malaysia is the only lab accredited for Halal testing by the Department of Islamic Development Malaysia (JAKIM). Moreover, there was no requirement for labelling of any of the samples sent to the MOH lab in order to maintain anonymity of the samples and avoid bias. However, there had been concerns that should any legal issue arise; the integrity of samples would be disputed as there was no sample identification. It became an issue because the sample was clearly labelled with the Cadbury name. There is a possibility that other samples were detected with porcine contamination in the past but did not go viral because as they were not that famous or popular as compared to Cadbury.[4]

The news led to calls for boycott and even *jihad* or holy war, against the brand and Mondelez International, by various Islamic groups who claimed that the brand had gone against Islamic religious tenants.[5] It was reported that if the boycott were to take place in Malaysia, about 800 stores selling all products made by Cadbury, Mondelez and US food giant Kraft worth $19 billion would be affected.[6]

The news soon garnered the attention of international media. BBC, Reuters and The Huffington Post were some of the international news outlets which reported on

[1] http://poxse.com/brand-review/how-cadbury-malaysia-recover-their-market-reputation-against-porcine-dna

[2] In-depth interview with consumers.

[3] In-depth interviews with MOH staff.

[4] In-depth interviews with MOH staff.

[5] http://www.themalaymailonline.com/malaysia/article/after-pig-dna-uproar-cadbury-says-working-to-ensure-products-are-halal-comp

[6] http://www.reuters.com/article/us-malaysia-cadbury-idUSKBN0E90RO20140529

the issue.[7,8] The uproar on the porcine contamination spread beyond Malaysian shores with Saudi Arabia and Indonesia launching investigations for pork DNA contamination in Cadbury products sold in the countries.[9]

Worried about the possible impact of the issue on law and order, JAKIM also urged 'the public not to speculate on the nature of the issue but allow the right authoritative body to conduct further investigations'.[10] In Putrajaya, JAKIM said the official decision on the halal status of the samples would be made and announced within the next 7 days pending results of the analysis by the Chemistry Department.

3 Cadbury Crisis Management

Due to the overwhelming negative public response and the extent of international interest towards the issue, Cadbury took several proactive steps to lessen the impact.

Cadbury utilised various communication channels to spread words on their commitment to investigate and mitigate the issue. One of the main channels they utilised was social media. As Facebook was where the news first broke, Cadbury used the same medium to connect to consumers and reassure them with regard to the issue. Cadbury had already started to address consumers' concerns early in the crisis by informing them about the ongoing investigation that had taken place to get to the bottom of the issue.

Although the contamination was not confirmed, Cadbury immediately recalled the two suspected batches containing the porcine DNA, which were Cadbury Dairy Milk Hazelnut, batch number 200813M01H I2 with expiry date on 13 November 2014, and Cadbury Dairy Milk Roast Almond, batch number 221013N01R I1 with expiry date on 15 January 2015.[11] The move was made as precautionary step to preserve the image of the brand and to show consumers they were serious in rectifying the issue.

Following the withdrawal of the chocolates, Cadbury Malaysia voluntarily invited Department of Islamic Development Malaysia (JAKIM) to test their products. JAKIM's monitoring and halal enforcement team went to Cadbury factory in Shah Alam to collect test samples on 26 May 2014.

On 30 May 2014, the first official press statement was released while the investigation was still ongoing. The press statement in dual languages (Bahasa Malaysia and English) was put up on their Facebook page as well as on their website. In the statement, Cadbury stressed on the 'Halalness' of their products and that they would

[7]http://www.huffingtonpost.com/2014/05/28/cadbury-malaysia-muslims-pork-halal_n_5404555.html

[8]http://www.bbc.com/news/business-27663857

[9]http://www.aljazeera.com/news/middleeast/2014/06/saudi-arabia-tests-cadbury-chocolate-pork-20146153245207534.html

[10]https://www.thestar.com.my/news/nation/2014/05/26/cadbury-halal-seven-days/

[11]http://www.thestar.com.my/news/nation/2014/05/24/cadbury-choclate-porcine-dna

continue to work with the Malaysian authorities to ensure that their products would strictly adhere to the Halal requirements as stipulated by JAKIM. They also pledged to produce quality products that meet Malaysian consumers' requirements and expectations.

4 Post-Crisis Management

The official test results were released shortly on the 2nd of June 2014, and JAKIM verified that the products complied with Islamic Law and the Malaysian Halal Standard, which is approved by JAKIM's halal certification panel.[12] On the differing results between the tests carried out by the Health Ministry and JAKIM, Minister in the Prime Minister's Department Datuk Seri Dr. Jamil Khir Baharom clarified that the former had not collected the samples from the factory and that the contamination might have happened elsewhere.

JAKIM cleared Cadbury from any porcine contamination on 3 June 2014 and reinstated its halal certification on 6 June 2014. Following this, Cadbury immediately issued its official press statement to share the news with the public, reaffirming that their products were Halal. The statement was also posted on their website and Facebook fan pages.

In order to reach a wider consumer base, they also made use of YouTube. The company uploaded video clips explaining the procedures taken to ensure that high quality and Halal requirements were met. The video was released in both Bahasa Malaysia and English and entitled 'Cadbury Chocolates, Made in Malaysia for Malaysians' and 'Coklat Cadbury, Buatan Malaysia Untuk Rakyat Malaysia', respectively. They also revamped their website in July 2014 as an ongoing effort to repair their brand reputation. The newly revamped website included all information regarding the issue, press releases issued by Cadbury and authorities, as well as steps taken to rectify it. Apart from that, Cadbury launched series of marketing messages and promotions to regain its lost image and credibility. Its Facebook fan page was consistently filled with advertisements promoting the halal status of its products. Cadbury took one step further by organising the first ever Joy Shop Sales at Centro Mall, Klang from 5 to 7 September 2014. During the sales, consumers enjoyed up to 70% discount on great selection of Cadbury chocolates. It was reported nearly 7000 consumers attended the event.[13] Quoting Tan Chian Pang, the Head of Chocolate, of Cadbury Malaysia, 'Year 2014 has been particularly tough for Malaysia and we at Cadbury wanted to rekindle moments of joy by creating a one-stop Joy Shop for consumers to purchase their favourite Cadbury chocolate'.

[12]https://www.thestar.com.my/news/nation/2014/06/02/no-pig-dna-in-cadbury-chocolate-jakim/

[13]http://my.mondelezinternational.com/Newsroom/2014-Press-Releases/Cadburys-first-ever-Joy-Shop-Sale-attracted-7000-consumers

The consumers interviewed were divided on how they perceive the effectiveness of Cadbury's crisis management.[14] About half of them believed Cadbury had done their best to mitigate the issue, while the rest thought that Cadbury could have done better in terms of the response speed in addressing consumers' concerns over the issue. To quote a participant's opinion on the matter: 'Despite the issues, I am sure that Cadbury has done their very best to get the trust back from the consumers. Therefore, I perceived (sic) that they have stepped up on their quality control and strictly ensure that all Halal requirements are to be met'.

Despite the debate, majority of the consumers seem to have a better perception towards the brand and have continued to support the brand after the crisis ended. Only a few interview participants still had some reservations about the Halal status of Cadbury products and reported that they were no longer buying their products.

The source of the Cadbury contaminations has never been identified. However, the damage control responses including public relation campaigns, undertaken by the company to dampen the level of damage to its brand as well as the proactive measures, were successful. Mondelez Malaysia won the Gold Award at the 2015 PR Week Asia-Pacific Awards held in Hong Kong, for its handling of the Halal crisis.[15]

The crisis had other consequences from a policy perspective as well. The MOH had a dialog with JAKIM to examine the roles of the two Malaysian regulatory bodies. Thus, it was decided that MOH should solely focus on analysis related to food safety, while JAKIM would focus only on Halal-related issues. The person who leaked the information to the press and the public was never identified. Following this crisis, all MOH staff were required to re-sign the secrecy and confidential agreements.

5 Concluding Thoughts

For any company, small issues can rapidly grow to dangerous unmanageable levels, if not managed promptly and can ultimately tarnish the image of the brand and the company. Once the fire has started burning, the flames are difficult to put down, and it can prove extremely hard to regain the consumers' trust afterwards. According to Sheth, Sethia and Srinivas (2011), assessment of business results should be based not only on economic performance but should take into account the environmental and social impact as well or what is known as a 'triple bottom line' responsibility. Sustainable marketing takes into account the social and environmental perspectives, besides economic results, and emphasises the importance of stakeholder orientation, and as Ghazali and Mutum (2016) have highlighted, Islamic marketing is compatible with the concepts of ethical and sustainable marketing. The case has several parallels

[14]In-depth interviews with consumers.

[15]https://www.thestar.com.my/business/business-news/2015/07/04/mondelez-bags-gold-for-cadbury-campaign/

with the Halal food crisis faced by Ikea Malaysia (Mutum & Ghazali, 2014), where a prompt response from Ikea saved the company from a potential PR disaster.

References

Ghazali, E., & Mutum, D. S. (2016). Islamic marketing: Compatibility with contemporary themes in marketing. In D. S. Mutum, M. M. Butt, & M. Rashid (Eds.), *Advances in Islamic finance, marketing, and management: An Asian perspective* (pp. 217–226). Bingley: Emerald Group Publishing.

Mutum, D. S., & Ghazali, E. (2014). Ikea Malaysia and the Halal food crisis. In D. Mutum, K. S. Roy, & E. Kipnis (Eds.), *Marketing cases from emerging markets* (pp. 31–33). New York: Springer.

Sheth, J. N., Sethia, N. K., & Srinivas, S. (2011). Mindful consumption: A customer-centric approach to sustainability. *Journal of the Academy of Marketing Science, 39*(1), 21–39.

Ezlika M. Ghazali is affiliated to the Department of Marketing, Faculty of Business and Accountancy, University of Malaya, Kuala Lumpur, Malaysia. She is also currently attached to the Business and Commercialisation Division of the University of Malaya Halal Research Centre. Her research interests include switching barriers, augmented-reality marketing, online retailing, sustainable marketing and social entrepreneurship. Ezlika has widely published in journals including *Information Technology and People*, *Journal of Retailing and Consumer Services*, *Internet Research*, *Electronic Markets* and others.

Dilip S. Mutum is Associate Professor of Marketing with Nottingham University Business School, University of Nottingham Malaysia. His research interests include digital consumption and sustainable marketing. Dilip has also advised various organisations on strategic marketing issues. His research work has been published within a range of publications—both in print and online.

Mardiana Md Radzi was an MBA student at the University of Malaya Graduate School of Business, University of Malaya, Kuala Lumpur, Malaysia.

Wei-Pin Woon obtained his MBA from the University of Malaya. He is currently working as a sales executive at Mercedes-Benz Malaysia.

Can Siti Khadijah Telekung Overcome Cultural Differences in the UK?

Dilip S. Mutum and Ezlika M. Ghazali

Abstract

The telekung is a two-piece religious garment unique to Southeast Asia, namely, Malaysia and Indonesia, worn by Muslim women specifically for prayers. It is usually loose and is worn over the normal clothing. By emphasising premium quality and comfortable fitting as their unique value proposition, Siti Khadijah® became the leading brand of prayer apparel for Muslim ladies in Malaysia. The company is looking to expand to other markets including Indonesia and more recently into the UK market. However, the UK market presents certain issues the company has not faced in either the Malaysian or Indonesian markets. This is mainly to do with cultural differences between Muslims of different ethnic backgrounds.

1 Company Background

Siti Khadijah Apparel (SKA) was established in 2009 in Bangi in the state of Selangor, Malaysia. It began its business selling the woman prayer outfits (telekung) under the brand name of Siti Khadijah®. The company has now expanded to more

D. S. Mutum (✉)
Nottingham University Business School, University of Nottingham Malaysia, Semenyih, Selangor, Malaysia
e-mail: dilip.mutum@nottingham.edu.my

E. M. Ghazali
Faculty of Business and Accountancy, Department of Marketing, University of Malaya, Kuala Lumpur, Malaysia

University of Malaya Halal Research Centre (UMHRC), University of Malaya, Kuala Lumpur, Malaysia

E. M. Ghazali et al. (eds.), *Management of Shari'ah Compliant Businesses*, Management for Professionals, https://doi.org/10.1007/978-3-030-10907-3_15

than ten branches all over Malaysia and one in Jakarta, Indonesia.[1] According to Muhamad Munzir Aminuddin, Director of Marketing and Sales for SK, his mother, Padzilah Enda Sulaiman the founder of Siti Khadijah Apparel, had problems finding a comfortable prayer outfit and would alter every telekung. She realized that other Muslim ladies in Malaysia would be facing the same problem as well. She spent about 6 months studying the various telekung designs to come up with a perfect one which overcame many of the flaws of other designs and started the business using her own savings. Before she started the company, Padzilah was a full-time housewife with six kids, without any business knowledge, which makes the success of SKA remarkable. Padzilah chooses the name 'Siti Khadijah' for the brand, to honour Prophet Muhammad's PBUH beloved wife.

She saw this as an opportunity by creating high-quality and comfortable telekung using innovative facial designs and high-quality materials. Now, the SK range of telekung includes several facial designs in order to fulfil the needs of its different customers. Their patented design focuses on the facial area and is meant to suit different face shapes and sizes. Siti Khadijah® currently offers four unique face designs in its collection of prayer outfits, which are recognizably different from standard designs. Each face design has its range of telekung.

As for the materials, they used cotton with high-quality spun polyesters blended with spandex and sewn together with beautiful crafted laces. They also aim to highlight the heritage values of the telekung by adapting old designs while incorporating new features. Later SKA also introduced other ladies apparel and accessories targeted at Muslim pilgrims going on their Umrah and Hajj. These products include head veils, hand socks, jubah, traditional baju kurung and various accessories.

The company has always focused on premium quality of their brand, and they achieved the ISO9001 certification from SIRIM QAS of Malaysia in 2017.[2] According to their website, the vision of SKA is 'to be the biggest producer of Muslim lifestyle products in the World'. Their mission is to be the best producer of Muslim lifestyle products; to make products which are comfortable, practical and beautiful; to give a sense of confidence and calm to their customers; and, finally, to uphold the Muslim lifestyle and strengthen the economy.[3] Their dedication to quality and branding lead to two awards during the Brand Laureate Award 2017–2018,[4] namely, the 'Brand Leadership Award' for Padzilah Enda Sulaiman and 'Best Brand in Retail-Muslimah Fashion' for the Siti Khadijah brand.

In terms of positioning, the company sees their products as a premium brand and as such commands a higher price than the other telekung brands in the market. In Malaysia, the telekung is often part of the traditional marriage 'hantaran'—gifts from

[1] https://www.sitikhadijah.com/about-us/

[2] https://sitikhadijah.trustpass.alibaba.com/company_profile.html

[3] https://www.sitikhadijah.com/about-us/

[4] http://www.thebrandlaureate.com/page-index-id-535

the bridegroom to the bride, and Siti Khadijah telekung has successfully targeted this market and is often the preferred brand as part of the hantaran.

2 Entry to the UK Market

SKA entered the UK market in 2017. This was their second foreign market after Indonesia.[5] According to Muhamad Munzir, this is in line with their strategy to introduce the telekung to global markets. They decided to enter the UK market as there are an estimated two million Muslims living in the UK from different ethnic groups. Besides the telekung, the company also showcased their other Muslim apparel for women at the 2017 Muslim Lifestyle Expo in Manchester. They also presented eight Telekung concepts for the London Modest Fashion Week 2017 on the 15 and 16 April 2017, at Olympia London.[6] The London Modest Fashion Week 2017 was sponsored by Modanisa, an online shopping website.

SKA soon launched their UK ecommerce site: www.sitikhadijah.co.uk, in Mayfair, London, in October 2017. The event was attended by local media, TV personalities and online influencers. They were also featured in a number of live interviews on major Islamic radio stations in the UK. In these interviews, they went on to tell the story behind the brand, description of the telekung and focusing on the ease of wearing it as well as the comfort. Several Muslimah (Muslim ladies) bloggers were invited to the event. They were given samples of telekung to review, and in their blogs, most felt that the telekung was a great idea. For example, Zahra Rose Alazaibi related her own experiences of how when it was time to pray; she would grab anything available including 'a blanket, your dads jacket, your brothers jubbah, your sisters open abaya'.[7] There are numerous factors that influence fashion, but the role of social media influences cannot be denied. Even in the context of Muslimah (Muslim women) fashion, studies have shown that the style and motivation, the uniqueness and sources of fashion knowledge can positively influence fashion consciousness and indirectly influences consumption of hijab fashion (Hassan & Harun, 2016).

3 Issues Faced by SKA in the UK Market

According to the Centre for the Study of Islam in the UK, Cardiff University, around three-quarters of Britain's Muslim population is from an Asian ethnic background, particularly Pakistani (about 43%), Bangladeshi (about 17%), Indian (about 9%) and other Asians including Southeast Asian (about 6%). A further 6% are of Black African origin. Approximately 4% of Muslims describe themselves as being of white British origin, and a further 7% from another white background—including Arabs,

[5]https://www.pressreader.com/malaysia/new-straits-times/20180117/282462824334790

[6]http://sitikhadijah.co.uk/siti-khadijah-in-london-for-the-muslimah-fashion-show-in-2017/

[7]http://zahrarosea.blogspot.com/2017/10/siti-khadija.html

Turks, etc. This data was based on the 2011 UK Census.[8,9] Also most Muslims in the UK are from the Sunni sect, while an estimated one in ten is Shia. As highlighted above, the UK has a huge Muslim population, but they are quite diverse and made up of different ethnic groups.

As highlighted earlier, the telekung is quite unique to Southeast Asia. Among Muslims, there are several cultural differences between the different ethnic groups, and this extends to religious practices as well. The differences in religious practices may have their roots in the different schools of Islamic thought and sects, followed by majority of Muslims in the different regions. For example, most of the Muslims in Malaysia and Indonesia belong to Shafi'i madhhab, which is one of the four schools of Islamic law in Sunni Islam. It was founded by the Arab scholar Al-Shafi'i. On the other hand, most of the Muslims from the Indian subcontinent belong to the Hanafi school named after the scholar Abū Ḥanīfa an-Nu'man ibn Thābit.[10] Sufism also had a huge influence on Islamic practices. India and Pakistan also has the highest populations of Shia Muslims among various countries in the world.[11] Muslims are certainly not homogeneous.

The representatives of SKA in the UK were trying to highlight the benefits of the telekung as a practical outfit for the daily prayers. The question was whether these Muslim ladies who never had a separate prayer outfit would see the need to own one. As Siti Fazrena Mohamad Fuad, who is the company representative in the UK, pointed out, in the UK, most Muslim women (apart from the Southeast Asians) do not normally have a separate dress for prayers, and it is quite common for them to just wear a long dress and a shawl to cover the upper body, during prayers. According to SK's company profile, Europe accounts for only about 1% of their total revenue. It does not really indicate whether it includes the UK operations. However, there are indications that sales have not really met with their expectations. The management of SKA were not really willing to reveal the revenues from the UK market, but it is still early to decide whether it is a success or failure, but we can make some inferences from looking at their current strategy. Now the top management have decided to focus on the Indonesian market which has a similar culture and where the women are already familiar with the telekung.

4 Conclusions

It should be noted that it is still quite early and it would be wrong to conclude that SKA has failed. It does take time for cultural practices to adapt to new innovations. There are also several factors at play here. As has been seen recently, the 'turban-'style hijab

[8]https://www.bbc.com/news/uk-33715473

[9]http://sites.cardiff.ac.uk/islamukcentre/rera/online-teaching-resources/muslims-in-britain-online-course/module-3-communities/diversities/muslim-ethnicities/

[10]https://veil.unc.edu/religions/islam/law/

[11]http://www.pewforum.org/2009/10/07/mapping-the-global-muslim-population/

which was first seen among hijabistas (the term derived from fashionista and referring to fashionable women who wear hijabs) in the Middle East has gained wide acceptance among hijabi women all around the world (Waninger, 2015).[12,13]

This case also highlights the growing importance of power of social media influencers or opinion leaders on social media, including bloggers, YouTubers and Instagrammers. The growth of consumer-generated advertising represents a very significant step in the evolution of marketing and advertising in particular. Though there is a lack of empirical evidence with regard to the effectiveness of consumer-generated advertising and sponsored content on social media, many companies in Siti Khadijah are now actively engaged with these influencers (Mutum, Ghazali, Mohd-Any, & Nguyen, 2018).

There are now a few studies that are also looking at the fashion choices and motives of the hijabistas who have large followings on social media and specifically on Instagram and YouTube, from a marketing and branding perspectives. For example, Williams and Kamaludeen (2017) examined the different interpretations of what it means to be a hijabista or hijabster. Another interesting study by El-Bassiouny (2018) looking at the hijabista phenomenon in Egypt indicated that the consumption experience of the hijab combined authentic religious meanings with cultural ones. It should also be pointed out that Munzir's numbers might be a bit outdated as the UK's Muslim population was estimated to be around 2.7 million according the 2011 census but has increased to 4.1 million or 6.3% of the total UK population,[14,15] and the Muslim population is still growing. Moreover, research indicates that more and more Muslim women are wearing the Hijab in public. In fact, the term 'contemporary modest wear' has taken off. This refers to clothing targeted at Muslim women as well as others, who prefer a more modest yet fashionable designs.[16] That indicates that there is indeed a huge potential market in the UK, if the telekung does take off and becomes popular.

References

El-Bassiouny, N. (2018). The Hijabi self: Authenticity and transformation in the hijab fashion phenomenon. *Journal of Islamic Marketing, 9*(2), 296–304.

Hassan, S. H., & Harun, H. (2016). Factors influencing fashion consciousness in hijab fashion consumption among hijabistas. *Journal of Islamic Marketing, 7*(4), 476–494.

[12]http://english.alarabiya.net/en/life-style/fashion-and-beauty/2014/10/09/Under-wraps-Style-savvy-Muslim-women-turn-to-turbans.html

[13]https://www.theguardian.com/fashion/2017/jan/11/yuma-malaysian-popstar-hijab-fashion-i-feel-like-the-world-is-catching-up-uniqlo

[14]http://www.pewresearch.org/fact-tank/2017/11/29/5-facts-about-the-muslim-population-in-europe/

[15]https://www.theguardian.com/world/2018/mar/21/muslims-british-national-identity-uk-report

[16]https://www.independent.co.uk/voices/modest-wear-hijab-kanye-west-show-nyfw-debenhams-choice-a7588761.html

Mutum, D. S., Ghazali, E. M., Mohd-Any, A. A., & Nguyen, B. (2018). Avoidance of sponsored posts on consumer-generated content: A study of personal blogs. *The Bottom Line, 31*(1), 76–94.
Waninger, K. (2015). *The veiled identity: Hijabistas, Instagram and branding in the online Islamic fashion industry*. Unpublished thesis, Georgia State University. Retrieved from https://scholarworks.gsu.edu/wsi_theses/48
Williams, J. P., & Kamaludeen, M. N. (2017). Muslim girl culture and social control in Southeast Asia: Exploring the hijabista and hijabster phenomena. *Crime, Media, Culture, 13*(2), 199–216.

Dilip S. Mutum is Associate Professor of Marketing with Nottingham University Business School, University of Nottingham Malaysia. His research interests include digital consumption and sustainable marketing. Dilip has also advised various organisations on strategic marketing issues. His research work has been published within a range of publications—both in print and online.

Ezlika M. Ghazali is affiliated to the Department of Marketing, Faculty of Business and Accountancy, University of Malaya, Kuala Lumpur, Malaysia. She is also currently attached to the Business and Commercialisation Division of the University of Malaya Halal Research Centre. Her research interests include switching barriers, augmented-reality marketing, online retailing, sustainable marketing and social entrepreneurship. Ezlika has widely published in journals including *Information Technology and People, Journal of Retailing and Consumer Services, Internet Research, Electronic Markets* and others.

Halal Advertising on Facebook: A Case Study of Health and Beauty Products in Malaysia

Azmin Azliza Aziz, Nurliana Md Rahin, and Norhazwani Mohamed Asri

Abstract

Nowadays, many businesses utilize social media such as Facebook, Twitter, and Instagram to advertise their products and connect with their customers. This includes the local health and beauty product companies which is one of the fastest-growing businesses in Malaysia. Notably, in order to advertise their products on social media, advertisers are obliged to adhere to the guidelines issued by the government authorities such as the Malaysian Communications and Multimedia Commission (MCMC), Ministry of Health Malaysia, and Jabatan Kemajuan Islam Malaysia (JAKIM). Nevertheless, some advertisers simply ignore the guidelines. Hence, this case study explores five characteristics of *Halal* advertising in the context of the Malaysian health and beauty product industry, by carrying out a content analysis on Facebook advertisements of a local health and beauty product company in Malaysia. The findings show that the advertising practices do not fully fulfil the five characteristics, indicating that despite the product is *Halal* certified, the advertising practices are not 100% *Shariah* compliant. This study is significant and contributes to the body of knowledge as this is the first case study examining the advertising practices of local health and beauty products on Facebook in Malaysia from an Islamic perspective.

A. A. Aziz (✉) · N. Md Rahin
Faculty of Business and Accountancy, University of Malaya, Kuala Lumpur, Malaysia
e-mail: aazliza@um.edu.my

N. Mohamed Asri
International Islamic College, Kuala Lumpur, Malaysia

E. M. Ghazali et al. (eds.), *Management of Shari'ah Compliant Businesses*, Management for Professionals, https://doi.org/10.1007/978-3-030-10907-3_16

1 Introduction

Advertising is a form of communication between the advertiser or marketer and targeted consumers commonly for the purpose of selling products or services. In advertising, consumers are approached through various platforms such as television, radio, newspapers, magazines, and social media. Advertising on social media such as Facebook, Twitter, and Instagram is a prime opportunity for many businesses nowadays, as the campaigns are extremely customizable and can be relatively cost-efficient. According to the Internet Users Survey 2017 (IUS, 2017), Facebook is the most popular social network site in Malaysia (97.3%), followed by Instagram (56.1%).

The local health and beauty products seem to be one of the fastest-growing products in Malaysia. Due to this fact, advertisers of these products utilize Facebook to upload status updates, images, videos, and testimonials in order to market their products, promote brands, connect to current customers, and foster new business. Notably, these advertisers are obliged to follow several of codes of conducts before advertising or posting anything about their product on Facebook. They need to observe and follow the guideline from "the Malaysian Communications and Multimedia Content Code" with regard to the advertisement. Nevertheless, some advertisers simply neglected the guidelines, for example, by exploiting the sensitivity of races or women as well as overclaiming that their health products can cure certain chronic disease. This is prohibited by the "Guideline on Advertising of Medicines and Medicinal Products to General Public" published by Malaysian Pharmacist Department and approved by the Medicine Advertisement Board (MAB) of Ministry of Health (MOH).

Surprisingly, most of these local products especially *jamu*, energy booster, whitening, and slimming products are certified by Jabatan Kemajuan Islam Malaysia (JAKIM) and MOH, yet the advertisements are not truly *Shariah* compliant. In fact, according to the Content Code by the Malaysian Communications and Multimedia Commission, slimming products, whether it is orally or physically taken, are listed as unacceptable. Often, advertisers tend to ignore the issues concerning "*aurah*" of the women, sharing sensitive information as well as posting testimonials especially sexual experiences, as they believe that this approach would attract the consumers' attention. This advertising method seems to be successfully targeting social media users. Even though the objective of the advertisers is only to sell their product in a creative way, yet there is no such "the end justifies the means". The practice is *Halal* because it will be going through the normal sales (*al-bay*) contract between buyer and seller, but it contradicts with the *Shariah* compliance and may contradict with the principles of "*syubhah*." Prevention from harm is still a priority according to the legal maxim, because one of the important things in *maqasid Shariah* is protection of mind or *aql* of the generation.

This case study aims to evaluate the advertising practices of local health and beauty products on Facebook from Islamic perspectives. Therefore, two research questions to be addressed are:

1. What are the characteristics of *Halal* advertising?
2. To what extent is the advertising of local health and beauty products on Facebook *Shariah* compliant?

For this purpose, a case study of a well-known local health and beauty product company in Malaysia was conducted. We first explore the characteristics of *Halal* advertising and, subsequently, analyze the advertising content of the company on Facebook (Anonymized), in order to determine whether they are *Shariah* compliant, based on these characteristics. This study is significant due to the fact that there are very limited studies on *Halal* advertising and to the best of our knowledge, there is no study examining the advertising practices of the local health and beauty products on Facebook yet. Obviously, this study will be beneficial to the researchers and industry, especially the small medium enterprise (SME) and local entrepreneurs, as well as the Muslim consumers. The findings of this study are expected to provide some insights and create awareness on *Halal* advertising.

2 Literature Review

2.1 Advertising on Social Media

Social media can be defined as "a group of internet-based applications that build on the ideological and technological foundations of Web 2.0 and that allow the creation and exchange of user generated content" (Kaplan & Haenlein, 2010). Social media comprises social online networks (e.g., Facebook, Twitter, and LinkedIn) and multimedia sharing sites (e.g., YouTube, Instagram, and Flickr) (Gaber & Wright, 2014). Social media websites are very popular among consumers (Gaber & Wright, 2014) and take up a greater share of consumers' time spent online (Lee, Hosanagar, & Nair, 2018). As such, businesses started to adopt social media widely in their marketing and advertising activities (Gaber & Wright, 2014). Advertising on social media is increasingly become a larger component of business's advertising budgets (Gaber & Wright, 2014; Lee et al., 2018).

According to Kaplan and Haenlein (2010), Facebook is the most popular social media platform. For September 2018, Facebook has 1.49 billion daily active users on average (Facebook, 2018). Facebook is a web-based service that allows users to stay connected with the world, friends, and family by exchanging detailed personal information (Bannister, Kiefer, & Nellums, 2013). With extensive and specific demographic information collection, Facebook is a powerful tool to enable advertisers to reach different segment consumers and target audiences (Bannister et al., 2013) at low cost (Curran, Graham, & Temple, 2011). According to Wolff (2012), Facebook derives 82% of its revenue from advertising. The Facebook advertising effectiveness is measured by cost-per-click or cost-per-thousand ad impression (Celebi, 2015). In other words, it is valuable advertising even by clicking the like button, or surfing on the Facebook pages even without clicking, or sharing a particular type of ad or video ad with friends (Wolff, 2012).

Marketers or advertisers can use different features on Facebook to promote a business. Advertisers can post links, videos, pictures, polls, fan pages, groups, and even ads on Facebook (Curran et al., 2011). There are two forms of advertising on Facebook: the first form is paid advertising, and the second form is free where businesses make a page (Gaber & Wright, 2014). The paid form of advertising is where businesses place advertisements that appear on the sides of the profile page of Facebook users or on their home Facebook page (Gaber & Wright, 2014). The advertisers can customize their advertisement to appear only to their target markets' Facebook page, based on the targeted gender, location, age, and even interests (Gaber & Wright, 2014). The free form of advertising is where businesses can create generic pages just like standard user pages. Once the page is ready, "friends" can be added so that they can gather more friends via "word-of-mouth" promotion (Curran et al., 2011). Businesses can use the page to keep in touch with current customers, gain new customers, promote new products, and share sales/offers and events (Curran et al., 2011).

2.2 Halal Advertising

Facebook also gains popularity as the most used social media and the advertising tool in Muslim countries. Marketers or the advertisers in the Muslim world would benefit by understanding the Muslims and Islamic values (Haque, Ahmed, & Irfath Jahan, 2010). Therefore, it is worth to understand beforehand of *Halal* advertising or Islamic advertising or advertising according to Islamic values and principles.

Halal is an Arabic word that is used to identify an item as lawful and permitted for use by Muslims (Fadahunsi & Kargwell, 2015). Essentially, a product is *Halal* if it is compliant with Islamic *Shariah* law. *Halal* marketing includes product naming, packaging, public relations, promotion, and advertising (Cheng & Low, 2008). According to Anwar and Saeed (1996), *Halal* promotional activities, especially advertising, can contribute to the economic progress and social development of a society. *Halal* advertising tools can be specifically tailored to achieve (1) healthy competition in the market; (2) freedom for consumers to select products which suit functional and social needs; (3) improvement in the quality of products; and (4) enhancement of Islamic moral conduct (Anwar & Saeed, 1996). Abdul Cader (2015) described three Quranic messages that influence *Halal* advertising: (1) *Haram* (impermissible), alcohol, gambling, deceptive advertising, depiction of idols, and non-Islamic portrayal of women; (2) Islamic activities, respecting Islamic duties such as prayer times; and (3) being thankful for blessings of *Allah* (God). Shafiq, Haque, Abdullah, and Jan (2017) defined four general rules of Islamic advertising, which are it should not exploit basic instincts of consumers and should avoid provoking desires that can never be fulfilled; it should be based on truth and complete revealing of all product attributes; the product should not be *haram* neither should it be harmful; and it should advocate consumption as a form of worship and promote moderation in the same.

2.3 Advertising Characteristics in General

A study by Islam and Alam (2013) outlined five dimensions of advertising in Islamic perspective, i.e., precise statement, prohibited elements as a promotional tool, persuasive, transparent, and avoid nudity. Precise statement refers to a specific statement of advertisement objective in terms of what that particular advertisement is intended to accomplish. In other words, advertisers should not exaggerate their offerings in advertisement. The advertisers should not make false promise and convey their messages more than what they actually have in order to attract the consumer's attention (Islam & Alam, 2013). Elements and products such as tobacco, alcohol, and gambling are prohibited in Islam; therefore, it is not appropriate to promote and advertise these prohibited elements (Islam & Alam, 2013). Persuasive advertising is considered effective as it exploits consumers to buy things that they do not need. However, *Quran* (7:31) says "*Eat and drink but waste not by excess*," which warns no excessive and waste. Advertisers should not persuade consumers by playing on their emotions, anxieties, and psychological needs and desires such as status, self-esteem, and attractiveness. In Islam, advertisement should be straightforward and should just provide useful information in making purchase decisions such as price, performance, and other objective criteria (Islam & Alam, 2013). In addition, the advertising should be transparent and honest by providing all accurate information regarding products or services. It is mentioned in *Quran* (36:17): "*And our duty is only to proclaim the clear message*" (Islam & Alam, 2013). Advertising should also avoid nudity especially the portrayal of women in the advertisement. Women are often portrayed as decorative objects or sexually provocative figures. Islam prohibited revealing of women's body in public including advertisement (Islam & Alam, 2013).

Another study by Purnama and Safira (2017) agreed that in the advertisement, women must be covered, except face and hands. Purnama and Safira (2017) provide other Islamic ethical guidelines for advertising, where advertisement does not show inappropriately dressed people, does not use sexual appeal, does not use emotional appeal, does not use fear appeal, does not portray immorality, does not use profane language, does not depict disbelief in Islam, does not encourage extravagance, does not use false testimonies, and does not exaggerate by making claims which are unsupported by evidence. Islamic advertising is also where the advertisement is not deceptive and discloses any faults in the advertised product and features and quality that are advertised are evident in the product (Purnama & Safira, 2017).

Shafiq et al. (2017) described the characteristics of Islamic advertising as ethical, credible, nondeceptive, simple, and humane. Ethical encompasses all the rest characteristics of Islamic advertising. Ethical denotes that it should be based on truth, no deception or exaggeration; the product advertised should be fair, free from all defects and not harmful; even should observed the rights of competitors; etc. Credible represents the truthful, reliability, and honesty in advertisement. Non-deceptive refers to information of the product advertised that should be clear, straightforward, and without any hidden conditions. Simplicity means the advertising should be simple, decent, and humble as Islam dislikes extravagance. Humane implies Islamic advertising should observe the worship to *Allah* and the daily conduct toward human beings (Shafiq et al., 2017). Meanwhile, Kadir and Al-Aidaros (2015) outlined extensive guideline of Islamic advertising. This guideline encompasses various concepts such as truth, content, price allegation, courtesy, faith, puffery, compliance, and globalization.

Many businesses that deal with *Halal* products and services and engage with Muslim markets have set up online presence through their websites and social media, to enhance the relationships they have with their customers (Fadahunsi & Kargwell, 2015). Social media platforms are able to facilitate ongoing two-way communication between a business and a mass audience and can be used to generate brand awareness. With the Muslim market, the advertisers on social media will need to recognize first that central to Islamic consumer behavior is adherence to the *Halal* concept and strategies targeted at Muslim consumers need to be sensitive to *Halal* issues in order not to offend the market they seek to attract through (Fadahunsi & Kargwell, 2015). Communicating with these Muslim segments will likely present both opportunities and challenges for advertisers. At the present time, there are not many businesses using social media platforms to engage with consumers in a manner that revolves around the values and teachings of Islam, and so "early bird" opportunities would seem to exist for businesses that do these to position their brands differently from those that belong to secular advertiser (Fadahunsi & Kargwell, 2015).

2.4 Guidelines by MCMC, JAKIM, and MOH

Other than the guidelines, characteristics, and dimensions of advertising according to Islamic perspective from numerous academic literatures, *Halal* advertising of local health and beauty products should also conform to the guidelines issued by the government authorities such as the Communications and Multimedia Content Forum of Malaysia, Ministry of Health Malaysia, and Jabatan Kemajuan Islam Malaysia.

The Malaysian Communications and Multimedia Commission (MCMC) established the Communications and Multimedia Content Forum of Malaysia (CMCF) to prepare a content code in compliance with Communications and Multimedia Act 1998 (CMA 98). CMCF is responsible to issue the Malaysian Communications and Multimedia Content Code and to govern content by self-regulation in line with the content code. The content code provides general guidelines on content which include indecent content, obscene content, violence, menacing content, bad language, false content, children's content, family values, and persons with special needs (The Communications and Multimedia Content Forum of Malaysia, 1998). With regard to advertisement, the content code lists four principles that shall guide the advertisement content, i.e., all advertisements must conform with advertisement part and to the general guidelines on content; all advertisements should be legal, decent, honest, and truthful; all advertisements should be prepared with a sense of responsibility to consumers and to the society; and all advertisements should respect the principles of fair competition generally accepted in business. The content code also discusses the specific guideline on advertisement that related to legality, decency, honesty and truthfulness, fear and distress, safety, violence/ antisocial behavior, protection of privacy, claims, testimonials and endorsements, prices, free offers, availability of products, guarantees, comparisons, denigration, exploitation of goodwill, imitation, and unacceptable goods and services (The Communications and Multimedia Content Forum of Malaysia, 1998). The advertisement part of the content code also gives special care and attention to the use of people in advertising especially women and children (The Communications and Multimedia Content Forum of Malaysia, 1998). According to the content code, specific advertisements such as on medicines, remedies, appliances, skills, and services relating to the human body are under the authority of the Ministry of Health Malaysia.

All cosmetic and health products must be notified to the National Pharmaceutical Control Bureau (NPCB), Ministry of Health Malaysia. The advertisement of health products should also be approved by the Medicine Advertisements Board who issued the Guideline on Advertising of Medicines and Medicinal Products to General Public, to complement the provisions of the Medicines (Advertisement and Sale) Act 1956 (Revised 1983) and the Medicine Advertisements Board Regulations 1976. The guideline prohibited the advertisement that contains any claims referring to (1) the prevention, treatment, alleviation, cure, or diagnosis of diseases and conditions; (2) practicing contraception among human beings; (3) improving the condition or functioning of the human kidney or heart, or improving the sexual function or sexual performance of human beings; and (4) procuring the miscarriage of women (Ministry of Health Malaysia, 2015). With regard to celebrity endorsement and consumer testimonials, the guideline provides that advertisement must be stated with a statement: "The effect of the product may vary among individuals." Products for weight loss or weight reduction should include the following statement: "This should be taken with a balanced diet and regular exercise." Misleading claims on eating such as "eat as much as you like" should not be advertised (Ministry of Health Malaysia, 2015). The guideline also listed the superlative descriptors, words, or phrases that are not allowed in advertisements such as antiaging, complete cure, excellent, guaranteed, longevity, sexual powers, unique, and wonders (Ministry of Health Malaysia, 2015).

In *Halal* advertising, all health and beauty products should be certified by Jabatan Kemajuan Islam Malaysia (JAKIM) or other body recognized by JAKIM. Advertisers are not allowed to misuse the phrase *Halal* or any statement/pictorial relating to Islamic religion, which includes the use of the verses of the Quran in their advertisement for the purpose of misleading the consumers. JAKIM issued the Manual Procedure for Malaysia *Halal* Certification which contains information about application procedures for *Halal* certification, certification processes, fee charges, and others.

3 Characteristics of *Halal* Advertising

After carefully exploring, reviewing, and categorizing all the characteristics of advertising in the literatures, we propose five *Halal* advertising characteristics, namely, credibility, nondeceptive, simplicity, dignity, and humane. Each of these characteristics is described below.

3.1 Credibility

Credibility is closely related to the trustworthiness, transparency, and reliability of the product or service information perceived by the consumers. According to Scott and Lutz (1989, p. 49), credibility in advertising is described as the "extent to which the consumer perceives claims made about the brand in the ad to be truthful and believable." Similarly, Wathen and Burkell (2002) define credibility as believability. Apparently, this characteristic is very important in online advertising compared to through other channels. This is because information provided online is easily checked for truth or fallacy (Vilčeková, 2016).

Any facts about the product attribute whether it is positive or negative must be informed to the potential customer prior to purchase. For example, the product's guarantee and warranty information must be clearly and sufficiently stated (Kadir & Al-Aidaros, 2015). Also, details such as statistical facts should be obtained from the trusted and reliable sources. Besides that, advertisers frequently use celebrities as endorsers or spokespersons for their products or services as they are seen as credible sources (Goldsmith, Lafferty, & Newell, 2000). This trendy advertising practice has been proven effective in influencing customers' attitude toward the advertisement and consequently increases the purchasing behavior (Ahmed, Seedani, Ahuja, & Paryani, 2015). For health and beauty products, however, issues whether the celebrities really apply the products they are promoting is of concern (Abuznaid, 2012). The credibility of the products is questionable if they themselves are not familiar with the products. Instead of using celebrity's endorsement, advertisers may also let customers experience with their product for themselves over a reasonable period of time in order to prove that their product works.

3.2 Nondeceptive

In Islam, truth and honesty are the base of every action. Hence, advertisement must always uphold the truth without any hidden condition. A *Shariah*-compliant advertisement should reflect true and fair communication to the public and should not resort to any form of deception in promoting their products (Haque et al., 2010). According to the Islamic teachings, a seller is obliged to disclose all facts about the products he is selling (Haque et al., 2010) including the defect (Keller, 1994) or side effect of the product.

Exaggeration, although very common in contemporary advertising, is strictly prohibited in Islam. In one market research study, more than three quarters of respondents responded that most of the claims made in advertisements are exaggerated.[1] Advertisement containing excessive exaggeration of the products description is considered as misleading, lying, and cheating the public. Any content of the advertisement such as the promises and testimonials must be supported with evidence, genuine and presented honestly. The use of subjective opinion and superlatives such as "guaranteed" in promoting products are against the Islamic practice. The saying by Prophet Muhammad "he who cheated is not one of us" clearly shows that one should avoid deceptive advertising. Obviously, this is important to maintain one's integrity.

3.3 Simplicity

Islam portrays a simple, decent, and humble lifestyle. This should be reflected in the advertising practices as well. The advertisers are encouraged to use simple and direct language in conveying messages to consumers to avoid confusion. The delivered information should be relevant and significant. Any statements or visual presentations used in the advertisement must not be offensive to the decency of Islam (Kadir & Al-Aidaros, 2015) and those who are likely to be exposed to them. Advertisement should be non-persuasive as this can prevent wasteful and overspending. Attractive offers such as gifts and discounts, for example, should be avoided as this could indirectly influence consumers to buy the things that they do not actually need it. Similar adjectives to simplicity include fair, straightforward, and clear.

3.4 Dignity

In Islamic teaching, each individual is deserved to be treated in a respectful and dignified manner. Nobody should be looked down or undignified in any ways. The most discussed issue relating to dignity is perhaps associated with the use of women in advertising. Rice and Al-Mossawi (2002) study the gender roles from Islamic perspectives, specifically the role of women in advertising. From the Islamic point of view, the portrayal of women in advertising is allowed in the situation where it is utmost and rightly needed (Shafiq et al., 2017). Even so, the appearance of the women should be properly covered, and the advertisement should not project women as sexual objects or be shown to merely satisfy one's desire. In addition, nudity in advertising is haram and is strictly prohibited under any circumstances. Nevertheless, the issues of dignity are not just about women; rather, it covers anything that offense any specific race, color, or gender. Exploitation of children,

[1]Lab42.com

men, the elderly, as well as the disadvantage people in promoting products must also be avoided as it lowers human dignity.

3.5 Humane

Advertising is permitted in Islam, and indeed, it is used to promote the Islamic faith (Al-Makaty et al., 1996). According to Islamic scholar, Islam is divided into two parts: worship and day-to-day conduct. The former relates to the relationship with the Creator. In this case, it is a great responsibility to ensure that the advertised product is not haram. The health and beauty product, for example, should be made from *Halal* ingredients that can be applied for prayer. On the other hand, the latter emphasizes on the daily conduct toward other human beings, animals, and environment. To be specific, the advertised product should not be harmful to the environment through the use of chemical substance. Besides that, advertisers should not only focus on promoting their product in making sales, but they should also create advertising that can develop community, spread awareness through campaigns, as well as support the moral, economic, and social welfare.

4 Methodology

The objectives of this study are twofold: first is to identify the characteristics of *Halal* advertising, and second is to analyze the advertising content of a local Malaysian company selling health and beauty products on social media, specifically Facebook, whether they are *Shariah* compliant based on these characteristics. The first objective is addressed through an extensive review of literature. Since the term "*Halal* advertising" is relatively new, we search for alternative but similar terms such as "Islam," "advertising," "Islamic advertising," and "Islamic marketing" from various top databases including Emerald, Elsevier, and JSTOR. Based on this search, we manage to collect a number of relevant articles that discuss the characteristics or dimension of *Halal*/Islamic advertising. We scrutinized each paper and assembled those with similarities under one category. For instance, trustworthy, reliability, and celebrity endorsement can be categorized under credibility, while humble, non-persuasive, gifts, and discounts are categorized as ^^simplicity. In summary, we identified five characteristics, namely, credibility, nondeceptive, simplicity, dignity, and humane.

In order to address the second objective which is the case study, we conducted a content analysis on the Facebook page of a local health and beauty product company in Malaysia. Facebook is selected due to the fact that it is the most popular social network site in Malaysia. With more than 2 billion daily active users worldwide, and about 21.9 million social media users in Malaysia in 2016, 97.3% claimed that they owned a Facebook account (IUS, 2017). Furthermore, numerous brands and businesses nowadays have their own Facebook pages as a means of engaging and interacting with their followers, fans, and consumers. For this case study, a well-known local company producing health and beauty products is chosen mainly because of its performance in sales as well as its influence and impact in the society. The founder of this company is a Malay Muslim. This entrepreneur also sponsors many television and radio programs. The company's official Facebook page receives among the highest likes and followers as compared to other local health and beauty product companies. The Facebook page is professionally moderated and appeared to be managed by the company's administrator.

We first recorded the company details such as the number of likes the page has received on Facebook and the types of health and beauty products produced, such as slimming pills and coffee, *jamu*, collagen, and nutritional juice. In order to analyze the advertising practices adopted by this company, a content analysis of the company's official Facebook page was conducted comprehensively. Due to the enormous number of Facebook posts, data was collected over the course of 3 months between 1 March 2018 and 31 May 2018.

The content analysis coding tool was developed for the items under each characteristic described earlier. For example, under credibility, we assessed whether the product information is reliable, the product's guarantee and/or warranty information are clearly and sufficiently stated, and a celebrity is used as endorser. We also imposed coding rules in order to ensure consistencies among the coders. Revisions are consistently done throughout the process to confirm that the coded categories are as exhaustive and mutual exclusive as possible. Altogether, there are 21 items that are proposed: credibility (4), nondeceptive (4), simplicity (4), dignity (5), and humane (4). These items are coded into (1,0) to indicate whether they are present or not, respectively.

5 Findings

5.1 Pilot Study

Prior to actual data analysis, we performed a pilot study based on the 21 coding items developed earlier on another local health and beauty product Facebook page. For this purpose, the advertising practices were analyzed for the duration of a month that is from 1 March to 31 March 2018. The advertising content from the official Facebook page was collected and analyzed by two coders (authors) independently. Krippendorff's alpha was used to test the inter-coder reliability, which yielded the value of 0.8136. Overall, the coding system showed strong inter-coder reliability.

5.2 Data Analysis

In this section, we analyze the advertising practices according to the five characteristics identified above.

5.2.1 Credibility

Browsing through the Facebook page, we found that the most of the product information posted on the page can be trusted. Although no statistical facts or lab results were provided, the advertiser did provide the MOH certificate and code number for some of the products. Also, the products information such as the ingredients used and their benefits were clearly written. This information was also considered transparent although the advertiser did not specifically mention the side effects of the products. It was found from the Facebook postings that the advertiser did warn the public on the usability of the products, for example, the product was not suitable to be consumed by pregnant women or during menstrual as well as the product may have ingredients that could give allergy to sensitive skin.

The use of celebrity as spokesperson or endorser is one of the greatest issues in Islamic advertising. Interestingly, in our case study, the product's founder himself acts as the spokesperson for his products. The appearance of the founder promoting and demonstrating the products could be seen in many Facebook postings and television programs.

5.2.2 Nondeceptive

Advertisement should be free from any deception and do not have any false assertions (Damirchi and Shafai, 2011; Haque et al., 2010). From our observations, most of the advertisements on the products were not overexaggerated. The advertiser made general claims about the products based on the nutritional facts of the ingredients used in making the product. Most of the postings on health and beauty products also did not contain any false promises that seem genuine. Moreover, we found that no superlatives such as "guaranteed" were used in the Facebook postings. Nevertheless, we could not find any proved testimonials on the effectiveness of the products from the existing customers posted on the page.

5.2.3 Simplicity

Based on our analysis, it is agreeable that advertiser used simple and direct language in conveying messages to consumers. However, we found that the advertiser did not deliver relevant and significant product information in promoting the products. In some postings, the photo shown on the packaging does not reflect the product to be sold. For instance, we identified few products such as soap, lipstick, and feminine wash displayed the founder's photo on the product's packaging instead of using relevant photo to the product itself.

Besides that, the product information used in the advertisement are found to be offensive to the decency of Islam and society. In Islam, men are not allowed to imitate women and vice versa. However, from our analysis, it was found that there exist advertisements displaying man wearing woman's products such as makeups and henna. An eminent Muslim scholar, Sheikh Yusuf Al-Qaradawi, issued a fatwa on this issue:

> Muslim scholars ruled on the use of henna by both men and women. They regarded it desirable and recommendable for women to use henna on their hands and legs, as this was a pre-Islamic practice that Islam accepted.... As for dyeing the hands and legs with henna for men, Imam ash-Shafi'i views that this is forbidden unless there is a medical necessity for using it, as Islam forbids men from copying women. The Prophet (peace be upon him) said, 'Allah has cursed men who copy women as well as women who copy men.'

Obviously, Islam forbids the dyeing of the hands and legs of men with henna unless it is for medication.

Halal advertising should be non-persuasive. However, this was not the case for the company under study. Most postings showed normal price and promotion price to attract customers, while some products were sold in set with cheaper price. Advertiser also offered discounts and gifts such as free perfume when buying a product. In some postings, the advertiser offered huge discounts if the payment was made by certain day. This indirectly forcing the customers to decide and buy the product quickly although they may not really need it.

5.2.4 Dignity

In terms of dignity, all the advertisements did not contain nudity and did not offense any specific race, color, or gender. Nonetheless, through our analysis, we found that the appearance of women in the advertisement was not properly covered. For example, the advertiser portrays a woman with beautiful hair to promote hair products such as shampoo. The advertiser also exploited children in promoting their products by using famous animation characters on the packaging of the children's products such as nutritional drink, shampoo, and bath wash. This advertising practice is intolerable in Islam as it creates unhealthy character of children.

5.2.5 Humane

Apparently, the advertising practices of this case study fulfilled the humane characteristics. It was found that all the advertised products are *Halal* and the products are not harmful to the environment. For example, it was clearly stated that no chemicals such as paraben, triclosan, and steroid were used in the cleanser and face cream products.

As mentioned earlier, advertising is allowed in Islam, and it should be used to promote the Islamic faith (Al-Makaty et al., 1996). Besides promoting products, we could also identify several postings that act as reminder toward submission to the Almighty. For example, the advertiser would normally post some Islamic quotes or prayers that remind the followers to seek forgiveness and grace from Allah. In addition, advertising in Islamic context should also be able to develop community, spread awareness through campaigns, as well as support the moral, economic, and social welfare. This practice could be seen in many postings where the advertiser posted self-reminder from time to time, shared the benefits of Ramadhan during the fasting month as well as created awareness campaign on election.

Based on the analysis on the company's Facebook content, it was observed that only humane characteristics were fully fulfilled while others not. To conclude, the findings showed that although the product is *Halal*, the advertising practices were not 100% *Shariah* compliant.

6 Conclusion

Halal advertising is an emerging field that has attracted both the academics and practitioner. This study explores into details the five characteristics of *Halal* advertising and conducts a case study of a well-known local health and beauty product company in Malaysia. To be specific, the advertising practices of this company on Facebook were evaluated based on these characteristics in order to determine whether they are *Shariah* compliant. The findings of this study are useful to the advertisers or marketers, especially the local entrepreneurs, in formulating their strategies to ensure that not only the product itself is *Halal*, but the advertising practices used in promoting the product are according to *Shariah* as well. In addition, the findings will also provide insight and create awareness among the Muslim consumers, in general, on *Halal* advertising.

To the best of the authors' knowledge, this study is the first study of its kind in Malaysia to examine the advertising practices of the local health and beauty products on Facebook. Looking at the wider perspectives while considering the five characteristics, we believe that similar findings would be obtained from other health and beauty product companies in Malaysia. Nevertheless, future research may consider replicating this study to other companies to confirm the findings. It would also be interesting to conduct such research using different methodologies such as text mining to evaluate the content of the advertisements. Moreover, analysis of advertising content from other social media platforms such as Twitter and Instagram can be undertaken.

References

Abdul Cader, A. (2015). Islamic challenges to advertising: A Saudi Arabian perspective. *Journal of Islamic Marketing, 6*(2), 166–187.

Abuznaid, S. (2012). Islamic marketing: Addressing the Muslim market. *An-Najah University Journal of Research (Humanities), 26*(6), 1473–1503.

Ahmed, R., Seedani, S., Ahuja, M., & Paryani, S. (2015). Impact of celebrity endorsement on consumer buying behavior. *Journal of Marketing and Consumer Research, 16*, 12–20.

Anwar, M., & Saeed, M. (1996). Promotional tools of marketing: An Islamic perspective. *Intellectual Discourse, 4*(1–2), 15–30.

Al-Makaty, S. S., van Tubergen, G. N., Whitlow, S. S., & Boyd, D. A. (1996). Attitudes toward advertising in Islam. *Journal of Advertising Research, 36*(3), 16–26.

Bannister, A., Kiefer, J., & Nellums, J. (2013). College students' perceptions of and behaviors regarding Facebook© advertising: An exploratory study. *The Catalyst, 3*(1), 2.

Celebi, S. I. (2015). How do motives affect attitudes and behaviors toward internet advertising and Facebook advertising? *Computers in Human Behavior, 51*, 312–324.

Cheng, P. L. K., & Low, K. (2008). The brand marketing of halal products: The way forward. *The ICFAI University Journal of Brand Management, 5*(4), 37–50.

Curran, K., Graham, S., & Temple, C. (2011). Advertising on Facebook. *International Journal of E-business development, 1*(1), 26–33.

Damirchi, G. V., & Shafai, J. (2011). A guideline to Islamic marketing mix. *Interdisciplinary Journal of Contemporary Research in Business, 3*(3), 1339–1347.

Facebook. (2018). *Company Info*. Retrieved from https://newsroom.fb.com/company-info/

Fadahunsi, A., & Kargwell, S. (2015). Social media, consumer behavior and marketing strategy: Implications of "Halal" on Islamic marketing operations. *Journal of Small Business and Entrepreneurship Development, 3*(1), 36–43.

Gaber, H. R., & Wright, L. T. (2014). Fast-food advertising in social media. A case study on Facebook in Egypt. *Journal of Business and Retail Management Research, 9*(1), 52–63.

Goldsmith, R., Lafferty, B. A., & Newell, S. J. (2000). The impact of corporate credibility and celebrity credibility on consumer reaction to advertisements and brands. *Journal of Advertising, 29*(3), 43–54. Retrieved from http://www.jstor.org/stable/4189151

Haque, A., Ahmed, K., & Irfath Jahan, S. (2010). Shariah observation: Advertising practices of Bank Muamalat in Malaysia. *Journal of Islamic Marketing, 1*(1), 70–77.

Islam, M. E., & Alam, M. Z. (2013). Advertising: An Islamic perspective. *International Journal of Ethics in Social Sciences, 1*(1), 105–116.

IUS. (2017). Retrieved from. https://www.mcmc.gov.my/skmmgovmy/.../MCMC-Internet-Users-Survey-2017.pdf

Kadir, A. Y. A., & Al-Aidaros, A.-H. (2015). Factors influencing advertising in Malaysia from an Islamic perspective: Case of Kedah State. *International Review of Management and Business Research, 4*(1), 189.

Kaplan, A. M., & Haenlein, M. (2010). Users of the world, unite! The challenges and opportunities of Social Media. *Business Horizons, 53*(1), 59–68.

Keller, N. H. M. (1994). *Reliance of the Traveler a Classic Manual of Islamic Sacred Law* by Ibn Naqib Misri. Evanston, IL: Sunna Books (translated).

Lee, D., Hosanagar, K., & Nair, H. S. (2018). Advertising content and consumer engagement on social media: Evidence from Facebook. *Management Science.* https://doi.org/10.1287/mnsc.2017.2902.

Ministry of Health Malaysia. (2015). *Guideline on advertising of medicines and medicinal products to general public.* Kuala Lumpur: Pharmaceutical Services, Ministry of Health Malaysia. Retrieved from https://www.pharmacy.gov.my/v2/sites/default/files/document-upload/latest-guideline-advertising-medicines-and-medicinal-products-general-public-1-sept-2015-amended-16.pdf

Purnama, F. A., & Safira, A. (2017). Investigating Islamic advertising ethics: Perceptions of Indonesian Muslims. *Journal of Emerging Economies & Islamic Research, 5*(2), 43–57.

Rice, G., & Al-Mossawi, M. (2002). The implication of Islam for advertising messages: The Middle Eastern context. *Journal of Euromarketing, 11*(3), 71–96.

Scott, B. M., & Lutz, R. J. (1989). An empirical examination of attitude toward the ad in an advertising pretest context. *Journal of Marketing, 53*, 48–65.

Shafiq, A., Haque, A., Abdullah, K., & Jan, M. (2017). Beliefs about Islamic advertising: An exploratory study in Malaysia. *Journal of Islamic Marketing, 8*(3), 409–429.

The Communications and Multimedia Content Forum of Malaysia. (1998). *The Malaysian communications and multimedia content code.* Off Jalan Damansara: The Communications and Multimedia Content Forum of Malaysia.

Vilčeková, L. (2016). Advertising credibility across different media channels. *International E-Journal of Advances in Social Sciences, 2*(4), 126–129.

Wathen, C. N., & Burkell, J. (2002). Believe it or not: Factors influencing credibility on the Web. *Journal of the American Society for Information Science and Technology, 53*(2), 131–145.

Wolff, M. (2012). The Facebook fallacy. *Technology Review, 115*(4), 70–72.

Azmin Azliza Aziz received her PhD in Operations Research from the University of Warwick, UK, and is currently a senior lecturer at the Faculty of Business and Accountancy, University of Malaya, Kuala Lumpur, Malaysia. Her research interest is in the area of transportation optimisation, logistics and halal-related studies. Dr. Azmin Azliza Aziz can be contacted at aazliza@um.edu.my.

Nurliana Md Rahin is currently a senior lecturer in accounting at the Faculty of Business and Accountancy, University of Malaya, Kuala Lumpur, Malaysia. She holds a PhD in Accounting from Flinders University, Australia. Her research interests include corporate social reporting, corporate governance, financial accounting and Islamic accounting.

Norhazwani Mohamed Asri received her MBA specialised in Islamic banking and finance from International Islamic University Malaysia (IIUM), Malaysia, and is currently a lecturer at the School of Management, International Islamic College, IIUM, Kuala Lumpur, Malaysia. Her teaching areas include Islamic banking and finance and also other business administration subjects. At the moment, she is involved with research in the area of Islamic banking and Halal-related studies.

MIX
Papier aus verantwortungsvollen Quellen
Paper from responsible sources
FSC® C105338

If you have any concerns about our products,
you can contact us on
ProductSafety@springernature.com

In case Publisher is established outside the EU,
the EU authorized representative is:
Springer Nature Customer Service Center GmbH
Europaplatz 3, 69115 Heidelberg, Germany

Printed by Libri Plureos GmbH
in Hamburg, Germany